Those Who Work, Those Who Don't

Those Who Work, Those Who Don't

Poverty, Morality, and
Family in Rural America

Jennifer Sherman

University of Minnesota Press
Minneapolis
London

Part of chapter 2 was previously published as "Coping with Rural Poverty: Economic Survival and Moral Capital in Rural America," *Social Forces* 85, no. 2 (December 2006): 891–913. Copyright 2006 by the University of North Carolina Press. Reprinted by permission of the publisher.

Published by the University of Minnesota Press
111 Third Avenue South, Suite 290
Minneapolis, MN 55401-2520
http://www.upress.umn.edu

Library of Congress Cataloging-in-Publication Data

Sherman, Jennifer.
    Those who work, those who don't : poverty, morality, and family in rural America / Jennifer Sherman.
        p.   cm.
    Includes bibliographical references and index.
    ISBN 978-0-8166-5904-3 (hc : alk. paper) — ISBN 978-0-8166-5905-0 (pb : alk. paper)
    1. Rural poor—United States.   2. United States—Rural conditions.
I. Title.
    HC110.P6S473   2009
    362.50973'091734—dc22   2009018656

20 19 18 17   10 9 8 7 6 5

Contents

Preface
Preserving Anonymity

Those Who Work, Those Who Don't tells the story of the people and community of Golden Valley, California. Golden Valley is not its real name, and all of the names mentioned in this book are pseudonyms, including the names of all people, places, and businesses. With qualitative and ethnographic research, it is not uncommon to use pseudonyms to protect the anonymity of subjects. Because they are often sharing personal or controversial information, it is necessary to offer subjects some protection from either embarrassment or the negative reactions of those who might disagree with their perspectives. Respecting and maintaining the subjects' privacy is vital to the completion of a project of this nature. In the case of Golden Valley, I have taken this practice as far as I can. The stories presented here are personal ones, and for many people they were difficult tales to tell. All interview subjects signed consent forms that acknowledged their willingness to participate in interviews and be quoted from them. The forms explained that recordings and transcripts of their interviews would be identified by numbers rather than names and would be kept locked and available only to me. Consent forms also pledged that subjects would remain anonymous and that all identifying details would be changed in any writing about this research to ensure their anonymity. Thus, not only are names changed, but in several cases small details have also been altered to make it more difficult for Golden Valley residents to recognize one another in the pages of this book. These details were generally minor, such as people's specific injuries, places of work (also pseudonyms), or the number of children in their families. I hope that such small deviations from their truths will help to keep their identities concealed.

To further protect the privacy of Golden Valley residents, the sources of information have been omitted in some sections of the book. Much of the background information about the community presented here comes from local sources or those that mention the community or county by name. This includes newspaper articles, county statistical reports, and information from the Web sites of local organizations. When such sources are used, no citation is given so as to ensure that Golden Valley remain anonymous even to those whose curiosity might compel them to take the extra step of tracking down an original source and through it discover the community's identity. Particularly, much of the information in chapter 1 bears no citation. I hope that the reader will trust in the accuracy of the data and understand that keeping my promise to the people of Golden Valley to prioritize their privacy must take precedence over full disclosure of all data sources.

Acknowledgments

Many people thought I was crazy to move to such a remote, isolated place as Golden Valley. I often agreed with them through the long, dark days of winter, the rainstorms that flooded the creek banks, the snowstorms that stranded me miles from town, and the frequent blackouts that deprived me of both electricity and running water. But those who visited in the spring and summer were able to see the other side: the amazing views of mountains and the evening alpine glow, the wildlife of all kinds, the apples in the orchard and the asparagus in the garden. Golden Valley was a place of extremes, with a climate that varied from hot, sunny, parched summers to oppressive, damp, cold winters that caused widespread seasonal depression for many of its residents, including me. It was not an easy place to live in, nor was it an easy place to conduct research in. I have many people to thank for my survival there and the completion of this project.

First, I express my deepest gratitude to the people of Golden Valley. They exhibited incredible strength and beauty in the face of overwhelming struggle and hardship and were amazingly generous with both their time and their limited resources. I could not have managed there without their selfless gifts, from fixing broken cars to helping stack wood, to lending their pets, to keeping me company at strange hours and simply befriending this lonely outsider. I cannot thank them enough for all the kindnesses they showed me, in particular their willingness to open their homes and share their stories with me. More than anything, they wanted the assets of their community to be recognized alongside its harshness. I hope I managed to portray it at least somewhat accurately, although I know I can never fully do it justice.

I thank individually Raelyn, Amy, Ben, Bianca, Pat, Rachel, Dave, Annette, and Wes for their combination of friendship, help, and support. Your kindness and companionship meant so much to me. A year in Golden Valley would have been much more difficult, if not impossible, without you.

This project would never have begun without the support of my incredible mentors and friends back at the University of California– Berkeley. Raka Ray deserves much of the credit for all I have accomplished. From my first days at Berkeley she supported and believed in me, providing invaluable advice and wisdom as well as incisive critiques of my work. Neither of us can count the number of times I have cried in front of her or the number of times her strength and the sheer force of her will compelled me to believe in myself and keep persevering. While her urban soul was appalled by the idea of moving to a place like Golden Valley, she never wavered in her confidence in this work and in her ability to see its sociological merit regardless of its "exotic" setting. Because of her I have learned to be a sociologist first and to apply sociological inquiry and analysis to any setting or subject matter. This gift is priceless, as is her encouragement, criticism, and friendship. She demanded from my work higher standards than I would have imagined possible, and I am still surprised at what is achievable with the right mentorship. I am blessed to know you and to have worked with you. Thanks for putting up with me for all these years.

I also benefited greatly from the support and assistance of several brilliant professors at UC–Berkeley, whose comments and insights made sure that this work fulfilled its potential. Mike Hout, Laura Enriquez, Louise Fortmann, and Sandra Smith helped me so much over the years, making sure that I understood the sociological concepts and literatures with which I engaged and pushing me to always create something better. They have been more supportive than I deserved at times, but they never allowed me to produce less than my best. I have been extraordinarily privileged to work with such talented individuals.

Louise Fortmann deserves special thanks for getting me started in the field. Without her contacts and familiarity with the northern forest region, I never would have been able to locate, let alone conduct research in, Golden Valley. Though I regret she was not able to pay me a visit while I lived there, her own experience in the community opened doors for me that I could not have budged on my own.

A number of exceptional colleagues contributed substantially to the final product. Gretchen Purser provided feedback and insight on many chapters, for which I am extremely thankful. She helped me to question my findings in new ways, to see all the treasures that my data provided, and to fully explore and flesh out unfamiliar concepts. Her knowledge of sociological literature and creative thinking about it were invaluable. Kerry Woodward, Ofer Sharone, and Jessica Vasquez also offered critical feedback and support on drafts of chapters, which was greatly appreciated. They helped me throughout this process, providing fresh eyes for my words and sounding boards for my ideas. Extra thanks to Kerry and Jessica for making the long trek to visit me in Golden Valley.

This project received generous financial support from a number of institutions. The early years of research and development were funded by a fellowship from the National Science Foundation. Subsequent years of fieldwork and writing were funded in part by the University of California–Berkeley; the sociology department of the University of California–Berkeley; the RUPRI Rural Poverty Research Center; the University of California Labor and Employment Research Fund; the National Institutes for Health; and the Family Research Laboratory at the University of New Hampshire. I am grateful for all of this assistance.

Finally, I thank my family and friends who supported me through this project and throughout my career: my parents, Joel and Judy Sherman, as well as Sami Kitmitto, who remains one of my closest and dearest friends. I also recognize Michael Sullivan, who spent many a long weekend with me in Deer Run and beyond. Thank you for your love and support. I am deeply appreciative.

Introduction

Poverty, Morality, and Family in Rural America

In October 2003, on a bright, windy morning in the tiny mountain town of Golden Valley, California, I met Greg Smith[1] for an interview in the public park. Greg was a 42-year-old man, neatly dressed in a plaid shirt and jeans. Before I turned on the tape recorder and started the formal interview, Greg began to discuss the recent gubernatorial elections, in which California had voted to oust incumbent Democratic governor Gray Davis and replace him with Republican Arnold Schwarzenegger. Greg complained that politics were all about advertisement and selling oneself, but he commented in particular on the sexual harassment allegations that had plagued Schwarzenegger during his campaign. Greg seemed interested and yet indifferent to the issue and explained that he would rather have a governor who grabs women's asses than one who grabs men's. He said he was glad we haven't gone that far yet, that we haven't yet elected a gay governor. He felt that would be a terrible day for the state.

While Greg Smith had a clear set of moral beliefs about the acceptability of homosexuality, his stance on other moral issues was perplexing and seemed to depend on the particular behavior being considered. He proudly described his life to me as one filled with high-profit illegal activities, from drug dealing to fraud. Yet throughout his interview, he

1

repeatedly espoused the virtue of honesty, offering numerous anecdotes about how his father was an honest man and how he himself taught this value to his children. He told me that he brought his family to church regularly, yet he also encouraged his children to drink and "party"[2] with him, as had his father before him. He complained bitterly about the current welfare system that pays good taxpayer money as public aid to lazy people, yet he himself was receiving Supplemental Security Income (SSI) for a disability and had been living primarily off of this income for more than two years. He struck me as amoral in certain ways, and yet clearly he considered himself to be a moral person. In particular, he felt morally superior to those who received need-based forms of public aid. His social status in the community was marginal, it was true, yet still higher than those who received welfare. My interview with Greg begged several questions: How does a criminal on SSI come to see himself as morally superior to a welfare mother trying to scrape by? What forces are at play that allow this sense of morality to exist and flourish in a conservative rural community like Golden Valley? What exactly is the meaning of morality, and what is its role in this particular subset of American society? How do poverty and unemployment—both enormous problems in the community—contribute to the evolution of specific understandings and roles of morality, tradition, and family values there? What are the consequences of these moral conceptions and discourses, both for this community and for rural America more generally?

This book addresses these questions, which were raised repeatedly over a year of conducting research in and around this struggling timber town. Golden Valley, like all of the names of people and places in this book, is a pseudonym. But its story and the stories of its people are real. The name and exact location of the community are obscured to protect the privacy of its residents, who shared so many intimate details of their lives and their personal histories with me as part of this research project. But in many ways, the name and location of the town are unimportant. Golden Valley, despite its uniqueness, shares much in common with declining communities throughout rural America. A multitude of rural places all over the United States have weathered forces similar to those that ravaged Golden Valley in recent years, including rapid industrial decline, severe job loss, and persistent poverty. From Golden Valley's experiences we can learn much about the experience of rural America in the late twentieth and early twenty-first centuries, a time of widespread change and loss for many of the nation's forgotten small places. In the history of Golden Valley and the narratives of its people there is much that may resonate for those familiar with other rural American communities, whether their economies have been tied to timber, mining, manufacturing, or farming. Their struggles and adaptations are similar in many ways, despite differences in landscapes, cultures, and industrial histories.

Using Golden Valley as a window through which to view a particular experience of rural America, this book investigates a number of issues related to morality, including its various meanings and its ability to structure social, economic, political, and family life in small, poor, rural communities. It explores the importance of moral values and norms to people living on the margins of U.S. society who experience extreme labor market and economic stress, yet choose to see themselves as inheritors of some version of the American dream. Their lives entail a series of contradictions, which their cultural, moral, and gender discourses help them to navigate in ways that allow them to feel integrated and consistent with their pasts. They rely heavily on moral concepts and moral discourses to make sense of their lives, to create and sustain a sense of success, and to configure their social worlds. In this setting and in many like it, moral norms and moral discourses influence multiple aspects of social and personal life. They dictate the proper behaviors and coping strategies for people experiencing labor market stress. They influence how families form and how meaning is ascribed to the family as a concept. Moral norms create social pressure to marry and stay married; they also create social consequences for failing to do so, particularly for those couples with children. Morality informs gender norms and gender roles, affecting both the daily activities people undertake and the ways in which men and women treat one another. Moral concepts even influence the amount of power people hold within their families and households.

This book explores various outcomes of Golden Valley's focus on morality, which exerts its power in multifarious ways throughout people's lives. A man with a family to support chooses part-time, seasonal, and informal work over the economically more reliable option of government aid because of his belief in the moral value of hard work and the immorality of accepting "handouts." A teenager gets pregnant while still in high school and chooses to marry her child's young father rather than raise the baby on her own, influenced by pressure from her relatives, her church, and her school. A poor family keeps a woman out of the workforce to allow her low-wage-earner husband to be the sole provider because their values dictate the importance of male breadwinning. A married woman drives sixty miles in an unreliable vehicle to use her food stamps in a town where no one recognizes her, afraid of her entire family being deemed lazy and immoral by people who know them locally. The community as a whole votes for conservative politicians who appear to share its moral stance, regardless of the economic policies they pursue. Each of these scenarios occurs frequently and repeatedly in Golden Valley. Without fully understanding morality's roots, its forms, and its consequences, we cannot hope to understand the choices and actions of the people of Golden Valley or of rural America more generally.

Morality as a Social Force

The reasons for morality's power are, at first glance, somewhat obscure and often mistakenly attributed to single influences like religion or politics. Particularly for those whose worldviews and social settings are not so clearly dominated by moral discourses and norms, it is often easy to dismiss communities like Golden Valley as backward, uneducated, and "redneck." The residents of rural America are often well acquainted with these stereotypes, which serve to further reinforce the separation between those people who do and those who do not base the bulk of their social understandings, actions, and decisions in moral norms. More than anything, morality's power lies in its ability to create and sustain these types of social divisions. It is for this reason that morality is often the most potent and visible in situations where few other types of social distinctions exist. Above all else, in social settings like Golden Valley, morality aids in the creation of symbolic boundaries between groups of people for whom there are few other forms of distinction available. This is its strength, regardless of which specific form it takes or which particular aspects of morality are highlighted.

For Greg Smith, as well as for many Golden Valley residents, morality is more than a set of values based on culturally shared beliefs; it is a force that actively structures social life and the social hierarchy of the community. Greg's sense of himself as morally upright allows him to separate himself from other people, both in the community and outside of it. Morality works as a symbolic boundary marker for Greg, placing him above those of lesser moral status, regardless of their economic standing relative to his. His belief in his moral superiority gives him a sense of success compared to other, perhaps equally poor and unemployed individuals. For many in Golden Valley, morality allows them to create these types of invisible barriers between themselves and others. Such symbolic boundaries exist in many forms throughout different U.S. societies and communities, allowing individuals to organize themselves into groups and groups to distinguish themselves from each other.

According to Lamont and Fournier, human beings are constantly engaged in this process of differentiation.[3] We create groups among ourselves and distinguish between these groups through observable differences in resources, behaviors, and beliefs. It is through this process of distinction that we create our social order, as well as an understanding of where each of us fits within this order. Social boundaries are generally based on discernible traits such as economic status or other social status markers and are explained and justified by the cultural norms of the societies in which we live.[4] Knowing one's place relative to others is part of what defines the experience of being human and what gives success and failure their subjective meanings. The need to create and sustain a sense of self relative to others is a fundamental human requirement, which exists alongside many other more basic needs that are now more difficult to fulfill than ever in Golden Valley's ruined economy.

Modern American life, with its complex communities and subcultures and its frenetic pace, generally provides access to many types of social boundaries. We can differentiate ourselves by income and class, by race and ethnicity, by culture and tastes, by family structure, by religious beliefs, and by political stances. These and many other sources of social distinction may be available to differing degrees, depending on the size and diversity of a community. As individuals, our senses of self are crafted around the concerns that are most salient to us. We tend to feel the most allegiance with those whose sources of distinction are similar to our own, whether the basis of our similarity is wealth, education, religion, or ethnic backgrounds. According to Arlene Stein, although the need to consolidate a sense of self through the creation of social boundaries is universal, "symbolic boundaries become more important during periods of rapid social change."[5] In Golden Valley, where the last decade has seen rapid restructuring of the labor market and a

precipitous decline in fortunes and life chances, it is thus not surprising
to uncover an abundance of discourses that are focused heavily around
sources of symbolic boundaries.

Golden Valley, a once bustling logging and mill town, is a community on the decline, characterized by unemployment, job instability,
and poverty. Its denizens are caught in a struggle to define themselves
as successful despite their economic and labor market failures. Their
community is isolated and experiencing only limited in-migration. It
has little diversity along economic, ethnic, or cultural lines. In this
context economic distinctions are fading in importance, as so few people have access to jobs that pay well or have any real security. Ethnic or
racial distinctions are also scarce; being white, in and of itself, goes
only so far as a form of distinction in Golden Valley, since most everyone
there is white. Similarly, given its cultural homogeneity and almost complete lack of access to high culture markers, culture also provides little
by way of social distinction between community members and serves
rather as a source of cohesion. As poor rural whites in a community of
poor rural whites, they are limited in their sources of distinction. But
like people in all societies, they still desire to organize themselves into
social groups and some sort of hierarchy. Morality is one of the few remaining axes upon which to base this hierarchy. When jobs, incomes,
and other sources of identity are stripped away, it is still possible to find
ways to define themselves and their entire community as morally upstanding. Thus, morality often becomes a dominant social force and
social boundary marker precisely in places like Golden Valley, which
are relatively homogeneous and lacking in sufficient other sources upon
which to base social distinctions.

The rise in importance of moral discourses and moral politics in rural America has been noticed by scholars and political analysts,[6] yet it
is often treated as a type of false consciousness that needs to be neither
respected nor addressed seriously.[7] As a nation, we seldom acknowledge
the degree to which our culture is built upon an extremely moralistic
set of doctrines, particularly the belief in the moral value of hard work
and the doctrine of individual achievement.[8] Such ideas as the individual's personal and moral responsibility for his or her own success or failure permeate our culture and our worldview. These moral ideas frequently
become most important when other status markers are unattainable or
unusable. As Golden Valley and its residents will illustrate, a focus on

moral discourses is far from irrational or out of step with that of the nation. These discourses may arise in significance due to particular sets of circumstances, in this case the loss of other forms of distinction and avenues of access to the American dream. But as others have shown, poverty and downward mobility are not the only factors that can create an environment where morality flourishes.[9] Homogeneity of any kind, combined with other cultural norms or social needs that encourage it, can cause morality to develop a crucial role in the social life of many different types of American communities.

The consequences of a focus on morality are varied and can affect communities in both positive and negative ways. Moral discourses have numerous roles in Golden Valley, many of which have developed or changed since the recent economic collapse. Moral discourses there now have protective functions, such as providing women with justifications to avoid abuse and empower themselves relative to men. They also can provide men with the emotional tools necessary to adapt to the changing labor market and resulting threats to their masculine identities. However, moral discourses can also hurt those who are most in need of the community's help, often depicting them as personally deficient and responsible for their own misfortunes and thus unworthy of support or aid. Moral discourses in Golden Valley also contribute to voting patterns and preferences that result in increasing difficulties for the poor and the local economy, from welfare reform to the destruction of natural resources, to a protracted war whose casualties are drawn disproportionately from poor rural places.[10] This book will explore several of morality's functions and key discourses in Golden Valley to understand both why they arise and how they affect the lives of the rural poor.

Sources and Forms of Moral Ideas

For Greg Smith, morality did not follow a single, clear-cut set of rules established by a church or other institutional source of moral authority, although undoubtedly some of his moral understandings were influenced by his church life and religious beliefs. Overall, his concept of morality was based in his own experiences and seemed flexible enough to suit his preferences and personal contradictions. Moral discourses in Golden Valley, as in the United States as a whole, do not form a single, coherent ideology but rather a conglomeration of ideas drawn from social, cultural, religious, and psychological sources. According to Sayer, with regard to social boundary creation, morality "figures not as formal norms or teachings based on religion or on ethical theories tenuously linked to our sentiments, but as grounded in the social psychology of emotional responses as evaluative judgements."[11] Morality is thus a constantly moving target, dependent on setting and social relations for its specificity. As with Greg Smith himself, morality in Golden Valley has numerous forms that are at times obviously incongruent with one another, many of which are not based in any formalized doctrine of religious or similar origin. The most dominant forms of morality there are drawn mostly from cultural rather than religious sources and images. While religious doctrines are important as well, they inform only a small portion of the moral pronouncements, judgments, and decisions that make up much of the day-to-day fabric of social life in Golden Valley.

The purpose of this book is not to uncover or explicate a single, precise definition of morality. Instead, it will explore the variety of ways in which morality as a concept and as a discourse is defined and used by Americans living on the margins, and it will look in depth at the different outcomes of its use. Moral discourses can encompass a number of separate ideas and worldviews, and often an individual's understanding of moral norms is based in an amalgam of sources. As Golden Valley's residents will illustrate, morality does not necessarily follow a single, consistent set of rules. For some, like Greg Smith, it is malleable and used to rationalize one's own behaviors while vilifying others'. For others, moral understandings are more clearly focused on specific sets of ideas, such as the value of hard work or the importance of caring for children and sustaining healthy families. Like its forms, morality's roles are also varied. Morality creates symbolic boundaries based on beliefs and actions, but it can also create social rules and act normatively. It can provide justification for choices, but it can also influence the choices people make. Moral value can even become a type of symbolic capital,[12] a symbolic boundary marker that can be traded for other real and symbolic forms of capital, such as economic rewards or social ties.

In Golden Valley different conceptions and functions of morality exist side by side and combine to create a unique culture based on a shared set of understandings and values. Yet, as this book will illustrate, not all definitions and types of morality have equal weight or importance in Golden Valley. Moral discourses focused around work ethics are generally the most powerful there and have the most influence over social life and behavior in the community. These discourses are normative in nature, and failure to adhere to their prescriptions can have concrete consequences. Moral discourses around the family, although extremely important in Golden Valley, are not policed as stringently and are neither rewarded nor punished to the same degree. While they can take on normative functions, they more frequently provide essential justifications for people's choices, as well as sources of self-esteem. Although there are fewer consequences for violating family-based moral norms, they still act as vital sources of social boundaries and personal self-worth. Each type of morality in Golden Valley places an individual, and by proxy his or her entire family, at a different position in the community's social hierarchy.

As with any source of symbolic boundaries, the degree to which individuals call upon one or another source of morality differs according to the social meanings granted to each type, but also according to their abilities to access them, depending on their own behaviors, life histories, and personal preferences. Thus the poor may focus on the moral value of hard work, but perhaps see it as divorced somewhat from economic rewards.[13] For the wealthy, on the other hand, affluence and personal success may be signs of moral strength, the apparent result of a much different type of work activity and work ethic that relies more on skill, knowledge, and intellectual achievement than on physical strength and stamina.[14] As Purser illustrates with regard to immigrant day laborers, groups of individuals who are almost identical in their cultural backgrounds, ethnic origins, and economic status can nonetheless create and draw upon opposing moral discourses to explain their specific behavioral and survival strategies.[15] In this case each group relied on particular moral discourses that justified its approach as moral and branded the opposing group's strategies as both immoral and emasculating. The association of morality with masculinity is found both in Golden Valley and throughout the United States, as the characteristics of dominant groups are often reified by their cultures. In Golden Valley moral understandings are often entwined with ideas and images of masculinity; divorcing the two can be difficult, particularly for men. Even so, morality can be called upon to justify and define vastly different types of masculine identities. Each type of moral understanding and source of moral belief makes up a part of the cultural tool kit[16] that people have at their disposal for making sense of their lives.

The multiple shapes that morality can take in Golden Valley create and sustain its power, making it accessible to different degrees to people with disparate personal histories, abilities, and religious beliefs. It thus presents a potent force by which to maintain social order, particularly as other sources of differentiation disappear. Morality is at least somewhat accessible to most people, yet capable of creating discernible boundaries between those who make claims to its ownership. Morality is of utmost importance to Greg Smith because it is his source of self-worth and his justification for believing himself superior to others. Yet at the same time, the community's understanding of moral norms allows it to easily place Greg in a hierarchy, below those with jobs and with more clearly demonstrated "family values" but above those whose moral bankruptcy manifests through such evidently immoral pursuits as welfare receipt or homosexuality. Its universality, combined with a specific set of cultural norms that creates a tacit understanding of the hierarchy of its forms, makes morality an easy choice as a stand-in for other social boundary markers that are no longer accessible to the bulk of Golden Valley's population.

The sources of moral discourses in Golden Valley are as diverse and unrelated as its forms. Moral understandings in Golden Valley are based in mainstream American culture to some degree and its cult of the individual.[17] They also draw heavily upon a more localized frontier culture, which has long valued individualism, self-sufficiency, and work in the form of manual labor as both moral and masculine.[18] Moral understandings in Golden Valley have also borrowed heavily from the family-values discourses popularized by political conservatives, which glorify "tradition" and a past culture and family formation pattern that never really existed and certainly was never dominant in places like Golden Valley.[19] Such family-values discourses were crafted specifically to resonate with people for whom life holds few attainable rewards outside of the family context.[20] In the case of Golden Valley, they have successfully reached and resonated with this target audience.

Moral ideologies have their roots in religious sources as well, although these are, interestingly, less significant in Golden Valley than are many of the more secular and culturally based ideas.[21] As suggested by Greg Smith, church life plays an important role for many people in the community. However, it is neither the sole nor even the dominant source of moral discourses for most of the residents. Most people who considered the church to be an important part of their lives nonetheless drew heavily from other sources of morality in their everyday assessments of themselves and others. The two-thousand-person community has six established churches within its boundaries, representing Assemblies of God, Catholic, Mormon, Community, Jehovah's Witness, and Seventh-Day Adventist faiths. These churches exert varying amounts of influence over the lives and minds of their congregants, ranging from small but extremely tight-knit and insular religious communities to congregations that are fully integrated into the community's mainstream social networks. By most accounts the sizes of the church congregations have fallen in the decade following the recent economic collapse, and several residents complained that only a small minority of members still attend their churches regularly. For a small group of adherents to the stricter and more all-encompassing religious communities, the churches do, in fact, profoundly influence their moral discourses and beliefs. But the bulk of Golden Valley residents look to their churches for a combination of social support and spiritual guidance that can be called upon or ignored according to their own time constraints, personal needs, life cycles, and seasonal rhythms. Moreover, the churches' spiritual influences are often surprisingly absent from the residents' day-to-day moral judgments and declarations, particularly with regard to the ways in which they separate and distinguish themselves from others.

Take, for example, Andy and Carol Newton, a married couple in their early 60s who describe family as the main focus of their life together. When their children were younger they were extremely active in their church, where Andy took on leadership roles and was involved with the youth group. When asked specifically about the religious values they taught to their children, they discussed their church activities and the importance of imparting such values as "respect for their neighbors, respect for property, and consideration for other people." Yet throughout their interviews, Andy and Carol both repeatedly referenced and espoused moral ideas that were more secular in nature and consistent with those of the community at large. For Andy, men who have "a good moral standing within their own homes" are those who illustrate "not only their work ethics, [but] they was more or less disciplinarians." Carol talked at length about the importance of teaching her children the value of hard work and making sure that they did their part for the household: "We taught them that it wasn't one person's responsibility to run everything." Andy similarly criticized other young people in the community "that have no interest in working":

> Just everything they ever wanted was handed to them. They didn't know what discipline, self-discipline, family discipline, or anything like that was. . . . If you give 'em everything, it's like when they come out of school—they think somebody owes 'em something. And they really don't have that work ethic or values or drive. Now there's a lot of families that do, don't get me wrong, but there is an area—these are the ones I was talking about—that they wouldn't work if they had an opportunity to work.

Although Carol and Andy were quite active in their church in the past, and still attend services regularly, the moral values on which they daily judge themselves and others tend to be based more in notions of self-discipline and masculine work ethics than in church doctrines such as loving one's neighbor.

The same pattern holds true for Brian and Nicole Goodman, a married couple in their mid-20s with two young children. They are both active in a nondenominational church to which they referred repeatedly with regard to the social community it provides for them. Brian, who was raised in a Christian household and even attended a Christian college, feels particularly tied to the church as a form of social support. He enthusiastically described the social networks the church provides for them and also mentioned feeling more comfortable with coworkers and friends who are Christians. With regard to moral values, however, his only mention of the church was with reference to his children and his hopes that they will not make bad lifestyle choices, such as being homosexual. Nicole quickly countered that they would never disown their children for anything less than murder, however, explaining that, with regard to their religious beliefs, "the biggest thing of those beliefs is love." Brian further explained, "I don't plan on shoving religion or my spiritual beliefs down their throat." Religious doctrines inform their worldview to a large degree, yet their moral values also focus heavily on the importance of hard work and self-sufficiency—ideas that they do not attribute to religious teachings or church sources. Although they feel they should not judge their children even for non-Christian lifestyles,

Brian had a harder time remaining nonjudgmental regarding people he saw as the community's undeserving poor:

A lot of people's problems is they're not willing to do the lesser work. They don't wanna clean, they don't wanna work in [the grocery store], or do that kind of stuff. That's just what you have to do sometimes.

Nicole confessed to being angered by those with poor work ethics: "I've even gotten mad at Brian's brother for bein' unemployed." For Brian and Nicole, the Christian doctrine of love appears to coexist alongside a moral judgment of those whom they perceive to be lacking proper work ethics.

As these examples show, morality is not synonymous with religious belief in Golden Valley, nor do religious sources provide the dominant moral understandings there. In a cohesive place like Golden Valley, with its strong sense of isolation and independence from the outside world, morality has its deepest roots in shared cultural norms and belief systems based in the community's unique history and customs. Yet people also draw moral understandings from multiple sources, including their affiliations with churches and support groups as well as schools, family, politics, and popular culture. Their messy, malleable set of moral ideas and moral discourses nonetheless has enough coherence within the community to wield a significant influence over the lives of most of its residents. The outcomes of this influence, as discussed earlier, are witnessed daily in Golden Valley. In their everyday struggles to survive and to make sense of their lives, morality has increasingly become one of their most crucial tools. Based on a year I spent living in and conducting research in Golden Valley, and witnessing its residents' struggles and joys firsthand, this book will illustrate in depth both why and how morality has come to play such a significant role in their world.

Research Methods

Small, isolated places like Golden Valley are difficult to study for many reasons, most notably that locals tend to be wary of outside observers and often are guarded around them. As Burawoy argues, the resistance that field researchers often encounter frequently "discloses much about the core values and interests of [the group's] members as well as its capacity to ward off danger."[22] Chapter 1 will begin to explore and explain some of the multiple factors that contribute to the community's suspiciousness of outsiders, particularly those with any kind of journalistic intent. Although I eventually received trust and acceptance, at least in part due to my own background and experiences growing up and working in rural places, I nonetheless had to work hard to gain initial access to Golden Valley's close-knit community. Because of the pervasive distrust of newcomers, I knew that to be successful in understanding Golden Valley and its inhabitants, I would need to immerse myself in the community as much as it would allow me. Thus, although my original research design relied heavily on semistructured interviews, I ultimately decided to conduct ethnographic fieldwork as well as the interviews.

My approach toward field research was heavily influenced by Burawoy's "extended case method," which "applies reflexive science to ethnography in order to extract the general from the unique, to move from the 'micro' to the 'macro.'"[23] It positions the researcher not as a detached observer, but as a participant who maintains a dialogue with the subjects themselves, filtering that dialogue through an understanding of the macro-level forces at play, simultaneously sustaining a constantly evolving dialogue with the theoretical ideas through which experiences are being interpreted. Thus, although I did base much of my research on more formal interviews, I also participated in the community as part of it, learning continuously from its inhabitants and modifying my understandings of their beliefs and experiences through constant interaction and discussion with them. Not only were their reactions to my interpretations helpful for gauging the accuracy of my understanding, but their attempts to influence and color my observations spoke volumes about their concerns, boundaries, and fears.

The combination of the complementary methodologies allowed me to learn about Golden Valley in ways that neither could have facilitated on its own. The interviews allowed me to go into greater depth with individuals and broach subjects that they might not have been willing to discuss in more informal and less controlled settings. It gave the subjects the opportunity to be consciously self-reflective and assign their own meanings to the experiences they discussed.[24] On the other hand, the ethnographic methods were vital to learning about people who were less comfortable with the formality of a tape-recorded interview (often those with lower social standing in the community) and were also extremely useful in discovering the inconsistencies between people's on-tape declarations and their daily lives, feelings, actions, and behaviors. My ethnographic informants included professional relationships, informal acquaintances with whom I interacted frequently, closer friends, and sometimes even strangers who happened across my path. Almost all of my ethnographic subjects were aware of my research agenda. Although like most ethnographers I was in danger at times of blurring the lines between key informant and friend, it was often these informant/friends who provided the sounding boards against which to test my understanding and measure the limits of my comprehension.

I moved to Golden Valley in the summer, one of the busier times of the year. It is in the spring and summer that men's employment is at its peak, as the bulk of the remaining jobs there are seasonal. I began my work with a list of names provided to me by an employee of a local nonprofit organization who had grown up in a nearby community and lived in or near Golden Valley her entire life. I told her that I was looking for people who had been affected by the mill closure; thus, many of my original subjects were former mill employees. From the initial list of about twenty names I began the interviews and built a snowball sample. At first my subjects tended to be mostly retired mill workers, as they had the most time on their hands during the busy work season. As they referred me to family, friends, acquaintances, and former coworkers, my sample grew. My volunteer and ethnographic work exposed me to new networks from which I also recruited interview subjects and built new snowball sample networks. It was my aim to interview people from as many different social networks and diverse histories as possible. I focused in particular on men (and their families) who had experienced labor market struggles, although I also made a concerted effort to interview several men and women with more stable work and financial situations.

In general, I contacted prospective subjects by phone to set up interviews. In situations where they had no phones, I generally contacted them through their places of work or other public spaces they frequented. In many instances setting up a single interview required a series of phone calls, for various reasons. Often women were reluctant to schedule interviews without first consulting their husbands. Men tended more often to assume their wives' participation, even when their presence was not specifically requested or discussed. I came to realize that married men often included their wives in the interviews because it was considered unseemly for them to meet a young woman alone in their homes, particularly to discuss intimate subjects. When married men chose to meet me alone, they seldom did so in their own homes, but preferred public spaces or their places of employment—neutral territories that were observable by others, even if the conversations were still private. At first I was frustrated by the experience of arriving at an interview only to discover a second participant whom I had not expected. I feared that a spouse's presence would cause both subjects to edit themselves. Undoubtedly this type of self-editing did occur to some degree, as people were likely to avoid discussing or admitting to things that might upset their spouses. However, with a spouse present it was often more difficult for a subject to be dishonest, as one spouse would often interrupt to reproach the other for recounting something inaccurately, insisting that he or she tell me the full truth. I found it was actually much easier for people to be dishonest and attempt to manage their on-tape images when they spoke to me alone. In these cases, it was often my ethnographic knowledge of subjects that alerted me to their interview inaccuracies. On the other hand, alone they were often willing to delve into subjects they might have avoided had a spouse been present. Thus, I simply agreed to interview whoever was present and interested in taking part in the project, aware of the benefits and pitfalls of each scenario.

Although men were more likely to directly decline the interview than were women, for the most part people were willing to take part, and it was unusual for a prospective respondent to outright refuse to be interviewed. Much more common were different forms of passive resistance to the interview. These included screening phone calls and not returning messages; making appointments and then canceling; and making appointments and not showing up for them. Usually, I made several phone attempts before giving up on a potential subject. Similarly, I was generally willing to reschedule at least a couple of times with subjects who canceled or "forgot" their appointments, particularly in this community in which people were unaccustomed to keeping calendars and scheduling their days. In many cases, a second or third appointment did eventually yield an interview. Nonetheless, after an individual canceled or failed to keep an appointment more than three times, I typically took it as a sign of passive resistance and gave up the chase. On the flip side, interview opportunities occasionally arose out of casual interactions in other settings. Particularly as I became better known in the community, I was approached by several residents who had heard about me and the project from friends and relatives and were interested in participating. In a few cases a subject who had initially resisted the interview later contacted me to set one up after learning more about me from someone else whom he or she trusted.

For those subjects who agreed to be interviewed (about three-quarters of those approached), the majority of interviews took place in their homes at their convenience. Thus I visited a number of Golden Valley's "nicer" homes, mostly consisting of small houses (often built by the occupants), some double-wide trailers, and a few small rental cabins. Most subjects who lived in quarters worse than this chose to do their interviews elsewhere, such as the public park, places of work, and other secluded public spaces that I was able to arrange (such as classrooms at the public library). While for the most part the subjects' houses were in town and close to other dwellings, occasionally I agreed to meet someone in a more isolated location in the woods or farther from the center of town. Only once did I cancel such an interview out of fear for my safety after the potential respondent seemed hostile and expressed significant distrust and animosity toward the "environmentalists and communists" that he believed made up the bulk of the University of California–Berkeley community.

Over the year that I lived in Golden Valley, I completed fifty-five tape-recorded, semistructured, open-ended, in-depth interviews with native and longtime members of the community, as well as a full year of ethnographic fieldwork done there and in its surrounding communities. I interviewed about equal numbers of men and women (twenty-five women and thirty men), singly and in couples, depending on the subjects' preferences. The average interview lasted between one-and-a-half and two hours, with the possibility of a second follow-up interview. The subjects ranged in age from 23 to 60 years old. The average age of the sample was about 39. The majority (92 percent) of subjects were white, reflecting the racial composition of Golden Valley. The remaining 8 percent reported some Native American heritage, which is about the same percentage of Golden Valley residents who reported this race on the 2000 U.S. Census. Nearly 78 percent of the subjects were married, remarried, or cohabitating, and the remaining 22 percent were single, including those who were widowed or divorced without remarriage. Most (88 percent) had children. About 30 percent were not in the workforce, although this does not include those subjects whose jobs were seasonal or unstable, but who were employed at the time of the interview. With only a few exceptions, most subjects had low incomes that placed them below or close to the poverty line, which also reflects the class makeup of the community itself, in which two-thirds of households have annual incomes under $30,000.[25]

The interview questions covered several subject areas, but mostly focused on the individual's history in Golden Valley, family life, work life, relationship issues, and feelings about the changes the community had undergone.[26] Throughout the interviews, the bulk of the questions were open-ended, as my aim was to give the subjects the space to narrate and interpret their life stories for themselves.[27] There was also unstructured time at the end of the interview for them to bring up anything else that they felt was important and that I should know about them or their community. Interviews were later transcribed and coded for themes that emerged through analysis. While I entered the field with a number of specific questions I hoped to answer, the interviews were open enough to allow subjects to take them in their own desired directions. This fluidity permitted unexpected sets of ideas to arise and take shape over the course of the research. The community's focus on morality, for example, permeated the interviews in ways that I neither expected nor specifically sought.

For my ethnographic data, I tried to experience life in as many different settings and social circles as possible. Thus, I regularly frequented social spaces such as the local bars and restaurants and attended the few social events held in Golden Valley, from the county fair and rare adult dances to community meetings and several festivals that occurred during my stay. At times I also discovered that much could be learned from chance encounters while walking along back roads or hiking in the woods, where I often met people I never would have been able to reach or perhaps even have known about otherwise. Frequently those people with whom I interacted on a nonprofessional basis imparted unique information and perspectives on the community. All of this information helped me to gain a fuller understanding of Golden Valley and its particular set of norms, customs, and concerns.

I also volunteered consistently with several local businesses and charitable organizations and taught an adult education yoga class twice a week. My volunteer work was an important component of my ethnography in several ways. While doing small projects for local businesses, I learned much about important events and changes in the community's daily life, and I witnessed such things as the process by which job seekers were filtered and chosen by those who had jobs to offer. The richest single source of ethnographic data for me was the Family Empowerment Alliance (FEA), a support center for parents of young children. I volunteered my time at FEA in as many ways as they would have me. For FEA I helped set up and monitor different events at the grade school, including dances and a science fair; standardized-testing days for which we provided snacks; and the culturally fascinating "etiquette dinner," for which we turned the fairgrounds dining hall into a mock four-star restaurant so that junior high school children and their families could learn the basics of how to eat an upscale, multicourse meal. I also did charity work for FEA, including sorting clothing donations and finding clothes for children who came to school inadequately dressed. For the Christmas holidays, another FEA employee and I made several trips over the mountains to the "big city" of Hillview to shop cheaply for clothing that FEA donated to children whose families were unable to provide gifts for them. I even volunteered my services for certain distasteful jobs such as periodic head lice checks for the grade school children. In return, the FEA staff graciously allowed me to take part in a number of their daily activities, including play groups and a parents' support group, through which I learned volumes about young mothers' experiences and struggles in the community.

While my gender presented challenges in interviewing men and interacting with them informally, it was an asset with regard to women and the FEA, allowing me an amount of access to women's worlds that a man would not have easily gained. I was different from them, and an outsider in many ways, particularly since I was both unmarried and childless in a setting whose purpose was to support young parents. Nonetheless, being of childbearing age and female made me relatively unobtrusive and thus privy to the women's daily conversations, complaints, and gossip sessions. Several of the women I met through FEA became close friends of mine; others became key informants and interview subjects. Through this work I witnessed much about family life in the community and got to know some of its most needy families. This work, together with the rest of my interview and ethnographic data, assisted in my understanding of multiple aspects of Golden Valley life.

It should be recognized that my ethnographic experiences with FEA allowed me to understand women's perspectives and daily lives in much more depth than men's. It is for this reason that my interview sample is slightly skewed toward men, to address this imbalance to some degree. While FEA provided access to women, I found men to be more accessible through their workplaces, and thus I made sure to take advantage of any opportunities that arose for conversation with men in the other settings in which I worked and lived. I often learned about men through brief conversations when they provided small services to me, from chatting with the employees of the hardware store to engaging in long conversations with men who delivered the wood to heat my house. Men were also more likely than women to both frequent and talk openly with me at the local bars. These briefer encounters could not, of course, yield the same depth and richness as the data I collected on women through my ethnographic work with FEA. As a researcher, one's own identity will always provide a barrier to some populations and an entrée to others. While it was more difficult to achieve the same level of daily intimacy with men that I did with some of the community's women, they were often more open on tape than I would have expected, taking advantage of this rare outlet for voicing emotional and personal information. I became good friends with several local men as well, who provided their unique insights and opinions on Golden Valley and helped me to understand men's perspectives and concerns in ever greater depth. As a researcher, I did my best to be aware of the limitations and challenges that my identity presented and tried to compensate for them in as many ways as I could.

Overview of the Book

This book begins its investigation through several chapters that explore in detail the community of Golden Valley and its distinct but interwoven forms and roles of moral discourses. Chapter 1 sets the stage for the following chapters by providing an introduction to the community and its recent history. It explains the challenges of living there and doing qualitative research there. It gives accounts of Golden Valley's past and the economic and political forces that produced its present situation, including a brief history of the spotted owl ruling, which was significant in changing the community's labor market opportunities and remains, a decade later, a fresh wound in the minds of many locals. Chapter 1 also compares and draws parallels between Golden Valley's situation and those of other rural American communities. It further provides an introduction to the people of Golden Valley, using both demographic data and their own testimonies. Census data illustrate both the changes the community has undergone and its current struggles as well as its impoverishment compared to the rest of California. Ethnographic and interview data are used to explain why people have chosen to stay in this economically ravaged community. Testimonies demonstrate the unique challenges and rewards of life there according to Golden Valley residents, including the importance of culture, community, and outdoor environments versus the lack of sufficient work, business, and educational opportunities. Thus chapter 1 provides an introduction to Golden Valley both with regard to its history and makeup as well as with regard to why its residents have chosen to remain despite the immense hardships that life there entails.

Subsequent chapters explore the meanings and roles of morality in this setting through investigating different discourses that structure daily life in Golden Valley. Chapter 2 begins with an exploration of discourses around survival strategies, drug use, and work ethics. It illustrates the ways in which such outward signals as the state of one's home are taken as indication of one's moral status and the belief that the community's problems are due to increases in welfare acceptance and poor work ethics versus poverty itself. The chapter then introduces the concept of moral capital and its relation to economic survival in Golden Valley. It goes on to explore coping activities in depth and to present them along a moral hierarchy from most to least moral capital, illustrating these distinctions with examples. Chapter 2 argues that morally acceptable coping strategies, particularly low-wage and subsistence work, are ultimately the most profitable in terms of both social and economic capital. Those who best manifest their work ethics through work activities are the first to be hired for the few remaining jobs and the most likely to receive social and economic support from others in the community. Certain forms of state aid, such as unemployment insurance and disability assistance, bring fewer rewards but are still more highly valued than means-tested welfare receipt because of their perceived (and actual) link to previous work activities.

Public aid in the form of welfare and food stamps, on the other hand, is perceived as having no connection to work ethic and work-based morality and is thus highly stigmatized. Its receipt actually removes moral capital from the recipient and is both socially and economically penalized within the community. With regard to welfare receipt, chapter 2 also explores the real and perceived connections between welfare and drug and alcohol abuse in the community and the ways in which the implications and interpretations of alcoholism in particular have changed over the years. While it was once an accepted workingman's problem, it is now almost universally recognized there as a sign of weak moral character and poor work ethics, which similarly sap one's moral capital. Finally, the chapter ends by summing up the importance of moral capital to economic survival in Golden Valley, particularly with regard to job opportunities and community charity. It argues that moral capital is necessary to have access to either of these other forms of economic capital.

The next two chapters move from work and economic survival to moral discourses around the home and family. Chapter 3 focuses on family-values discourses and the connection between morality and "traditional" family life. It argues that while discourses around family and tradition are not the basis of tradable forms of capital, they do structure community life in several ways. The morality embedded within discourses around the family is the basis of several key social divisions between the deserving and undeserving poor both within Golden Valley and between it and the outside world. Discourses around family values and tradition prescribe the prioritization of family stability over individual needs and pursuits, with outcomes that include nuclear families as well as extended families with multiple unrelated children. These family discourses also dictate clearly marked boundaries between healthy and unhealthy behaviors, marking such things as domestic violence and substance abuse as not just destructive, but morally reprehensible. And finally, discourses around family values and safety justify the choice of Golden Valley as a home for its residents, allowing them to create and sustain a belief in the righteousness of their decisions to remain there despite its economic devastation and social isolation. Particularly with regard to this community-level discourse, the moral valuation of family conceals both race and class biases and prejudices, reconstituting them instead as moral virtues.

Family-centered moral discourses thus have both normative and symbolic value in Golden Valley, dictating the proper behavior for parents and adults in the community and distinguishing the deserving from the undeserving poor. The meaning of "traditional" is relatively fluid in this context and often unconnected to individuals' pasts. Nonetheless, its different definitions allow several types of families to claim ownership of the moral stance that it represents, thereby distinguishing themselves from those families—both within and outside of the community—who are believed to fail to embody it.

Chapter 4 builds on the discussion begun in chapter 3, extending outward from family values to gender roles and identities, particularly within the family. It first contextualizes the issues by exploring the rise in single-parent families in Golden Valley and arguing that the forces responsible for this increase are unique from those commonly found to be most significant in the urban setting. It suggests that nonmarriage is not the most common route to single parenting in this community in which moral discourses around family life hold so much importance and where shotgun weddings are still common for pregnant teenagers. Thus, the chapter focuses on exploring factors that contribute to the instability and breakup of existing family units. It looks in particular at the gender discourses of both men and women and argues that flexibility with regard to gender identities and roles is one of the most important factors that affect family stability. While women are shown to be generally flexible and willing to take on new roles, men often have more difficulty adapting to the current situation, in which they are seldom able to be the main breadwinners. The degree to which a man is willing to refocus his aspirations away from breadwinning to more attainable goals such as active fathering has major consequences for the happiness of his spouse and ultimately his family's long-term stability.

Those families with flexible gender ideologies appear to have less tension and better likelihoods of long-term stability compared to those who remain rigid with regard to gender. The "rigid" families are more likely to be characterized by power struggles between spouses and lowered male self-esteem, as well as greater tendencies toward substance abuse and marital breakup. The chapter gives examples from both "rigid" and "flexible" men and illustrates that discourses around family values and the moral worth of fatherhood play a pivotal role in enabling "flexible" men to remake their image of masculinity around active parenting rather than breadwinning. Overall, the chapter demonstrates the importance of discourse to facilitating adaptation to changing structural conditions, and once again highlights the importance of moral discourse in providing access to self-esteem under difficult circumstances.

Finally, the conclusion draws out the major implications of the book and suggests policy implications of the research. It argues that moral values influence behaviors from family life to coping strategies to the voting booth. It suggests that the failure to recognize the importance of moral values to rural poor populations can stymie both political success and the success of poverty alleviation policies. Politicians who ignore the influence of morality over voting behaviors will be unable to reach such populations. Additionally, the policies they enact will often fall short of the mark when they do not anticipate the ways in which moral and cultural understandings affect geographic mobility, poverty survival strategies, and gender roles. In particular, welfare reform was created with the belief that the poor lack proper work ethics and must be coerced into the labor force. Such a policy was inappropriate for a population like Golden Valley's, where work ethics and the desire to work are strong but the labor market has collapsed. Similarly, welfare reform attempted to push marriage as a solution, once again ignoring places like Golden Valley, in which marriage is highly prioritized but nonetheless does not protect families from poverty. Finally, the conclusion urges policymakers to think more broadly about the effects of seemingly unrelated policies, which may have unintended consequences for local populations. While morality has become an increasingly important force in rural America, it does not trump more concrete concerns. It is up to us to understand and address these concerns in ways that will allow all people access to the full vision of the American dream.

1

The Place I Found:
An Introduction to Golden Valley

The logging was way down before the mill left. There's a lot of different
views on that and everything, but the bottom line of it is, in Jefferson
County, logging was the economic base. And that base just isn't there
no more. Made it really tough, especially on a town like Golden Valley.
Miner's Gulch, you know, may be more of a tourist [town]; I mean, they
do have a tourist trade. I don't even understand how you found this
place. You know, I mean, because Golden Valley just ain't well known.
(Jake Robbins, 55-year-old small-scale mill worker and married father
of two)

After an initial visit in the fall of 2002 to make contacts and gather
background information on the community, I moved to Golden Valley
in June 2003. Its location six hours away from the San Francisco Bay
Area made commuting an impossibility, and regardless, I wanted to live
full-time in my field site to fully immerse myself in its unique set of customs, cultural norms, and daily rhythms. Thus, the first challenge of my
fieldwork was finding a place to live in Golden Valley—not an easy task.
The town has little in-migration and limited rental housing. People
warned me early on to avoid the notorious trailer parks, supposedly
home to the community's most transient populations, including the
welfare recipients and drug dealers who were communally feared and
scorned. I instead began my year of fieldwork in a temporary situation,

renting a small room in the house of a recent in-migrant retiree from the Bay Area. The ranch was five miles from the center of town on an arid hillside and thus not served by the town's water supply. Its private well did not produce sufficient amounts of water during the two dry summer months that I stayed there, making it a tense and untenable situation. Soon after settling in, I began to look for alternate living situations in Golden Valley. After a few weeks of frustrations with the substandard housing on the open rental market, I found my ideal situation through informal channels. It was a two-story, three-bedroom, two-bathroom house on ten acres of land in the tiny neighboring community of Deer Run for $300 a month.

The house belonged to a couple who had built it themselves, living in a tent for several years with their young daughter while they worked on it. The remains of their original homestead, including the raised wooden tent platform and a small cooking shack, still stood on the property, which also included a barn, apple orchard, fenced-in garden, and workshop still stocked with tools. The owners had lived there for twenty years, but after the mill closed had relocated to San Jose to find work. They still hoped to retire in Deer Run, however, and had a caretaker living in the house who was responsible for the basic maintenance. He had been there for nearly a decade and considered it his home but needed to leave for a year to receive medical treatments elsewhere. His misfortune was my good luck, and I inherited the beautiful, mostly furnished house for the year. Its ten acres included forests, gardens, and meadows, as well as access to Deer Creek, and abutted hundreds of acres of U.S. Forest Service land on a mountain that rose sharply to the west. Maintenance included watering the gardens and landscaping in the summer and making sure the pipes didn't freeze in the winter. The only source of heat was a wood stove, which miraculously kept the large house comfortably warm even on the coldest nights. Water came from a private well only ten feet deep that tapped into an underground portion of the creek. Although the previous caretaker warned that the well sometimes ran dry in the fall, I managed to make it through the dry season without running out. But the water smelled of sulfur and I didn't drink it; I bought bottled water for the ten months that I lived there.

My house in Deer Run was beautiful both inside and out, but it was a solitary, isolated existence, a far cry from the urban life I'd left behind. There is no mail delivery in Golden Valley, which houses the nearest post office. I had to pick up my mail there, more than ten miles away. My house didn't have an address and was located on a private dirt road, which made things like getting the phone turned on extremely complicated. It also made getting in and out difficult in the winter; my four-wheel-drive station wagon could pass over the muddy ruts in the rain, but it was useless against heavy snowfalls. With no one to plow my half-mile stretch of dirt road, there were several winter weeks during which I had to leave my car at the other end and drag my supplies in and out on an old inner tube with a tin bowl stuck in the middle to cover the hole. I was at least half a mile away from the nearest neighbor, and if I didn't go into town it was generally guaranteed that I would not run into another human that day. Instead, my only visitors (besides the occasional Jehovah's Witnesses) were birds, deer, rabbits, stray cats, and a black bear, which luckily was nocturnal and thus rarely seen despite abundant evidence of its nightly rambles. There was no 911 service in Deer Run, and occasionally I had nightmares of being trapped in the house when danger arrived, with no one to call and no one to hear me scream. These are the realities of life in Golden Valley; the better housing situations are difficult to find and still lack most of the amenities that urban and suburban Americans take for granted.

My friends back in Berkeley and many of the people I met in Golden Valley tended to ask me the same question with regard to my field site: "How did you find this place?" It was a fair question. Although I had lived in and visited numerous rural places all over the United States, I had never been anywhere as physically and socially isolated as this community. Golden Valley is a town of slightly less than two thousand people. It is surrounded by several small unincorporated places such as Riverbend, twenty miles to the west, and Deer Run, ten miles to the south, which add about another five hundred people to the 2000 U.S. Census population figures. Golden Valley is located in Jefferson County, which, with fewer than fifteen thousand residents, is one of the state's least populated counties.[1] It is in the northern part of the state, straddling several mountain ranges. Golden Valley itself is nearly two hours from the closest interstate freeway, and most of this drive is over steep mountain roads. Although it lies only about seventy miles from the nearest city of Hillview (population less than one hundred thousand), the drive can take up to two hours due to the relentless hairpin curves that force all but the most experienced mountain drivers into slow speeds and constant braking. In the winter the roads can become impassable due to snow on the high passes and eroding hillsides at the lower elevations.

The truth is that few people find Golden Valley who aren't looking for it. Unlike many other rural California towns, it is far too isolated to sustain any real tourist economy. It is not on the way to any place that cannot be reached more easily by another route. Thus, Golden Valley lacks the sorts of cutesy tourist amenities that might give it some sense of charm. It is a mill town built on top of a sparsely populated ranching community, and little more. Its main "business district" is located along Highway 7, the two-lane road that connects the community to the world outside, heading west from the county seat of Miner's Gulch into Golden Valley and then south through town until it joins Route 42 just past Deer Run, which winds east/west for several hours until it hits either the Central Valley or the coast. The town's few stores mostly cluster along Highway 7, including its one gas station, two grocery stores, video store, health food store, convenience store, diner, small department store, and a few other businesses such as a gift shop, florist, and two hair salons. There are a few other businesses in town, including a hardware store, a feed store, and a satellite television dealer, which are set back from the main road. But there is little else to the town besides the grade school and high school, a public library, a senior center, and a small community center. The old mill site takes up much of the land adjacent to Route 7, where it looms empty as a ghost town, its rusting structures slowly decaying.

Moving to Golden Valley from an urban area felt a bit like going back in time at least a decade. In 2003 there was no cell phone coverage in the valley, no beepers, and no high-speed Internet service except via satellite. Similarly, there was no television reception except with small satellite dishes, whose giant and now defunct ancestors littered yards throughout the area. The nearest hospital was forty-five minutes away in Miner's Gulch and had limited services and an uncertain future. In emergencies people were often flown by helicopter to the hospital in Hillview, and many residents purchased special insurance to cover this expense. There was no curbside garbage pickup (there were few actual curbs), thus garbage had to be hauled to the dump and paid for by the bag. Since most residents felt that this was an unnecessary expense, household garbage was typically hoarded all year and then burned in the winter once the fire danger had decreased, with toxic and nontoxic items alike going up in smoke that hung over the valley during the winter's heavy atmospheric inversions.[2] Golden Valley had no chain stores or restaurants. Eating out was limited to one diner, a pizza place open at irregular hours, and a gas station and convenience store that both had delis. The selection of products available in the town's few stores was extremely limited and pricey, causing many families to buy the bulk of their necessities in Hillview, entailing periodic four-hour round-trips over the mountains.

How did I find such a place? It was a question I asked myself multiple times over my year there as I struggled to endure the lack of urban conveniences to which I had become accustomed, as well as the isolation of my lonely house in Deer Run. I found Golden Valley because I was looking for it, or a place very much like it. My original research design had in mind a community like Golden Valley, whose profile, although extreme, is nonetheless common throughout rural America. Although the industrial histories, ethnic and racial makeup, and local cultures may be distinct in each region, throughout much of rural America the latter half of the twentieth century was characterized by a trend toward rapid deindustrialization and catastrophic job loss. The trends include the loss of manufacturing jobs in the rural Northeast and Midwest;[3] declines of farm ownership and employment in the Midwest, West, and South;[4] declines of extractive industries throughout Appalachia and the Midwest;[5] and declines in fishing[6] and forestry[7] along the nation's coastlines. These changes have been accompanied by a shift toward what Nelson and Smith[8] refer to as "bad jobs," meaning the replacement of full-time, well-paid work by part-time, low-wage, and often feminized work. Industrial restructuring throughout rural America has resulted in poverty, underemployment, and changing workforce demographics as well as changing social, family, and gender relations.[9]

It was my intent to study the micro effects of these macro changes on a community in rural California. I was thus looking for an isolated rural community with a long-standing tie to a specific industry that had rapidly and recently abandoned the area due to industrial and economic forces beyond the community's control. In California this meant mostly formerly logging-dependent communities, and I began the project with several similar small communities in mind. I eventually narrowed my choices to three communities in three northern forested counties. Background research into each of their demographic histories and current realities revealed Golden Valley to be the clearest example of all the above trends: it was small, extremely isolated, and almost completely forest dependent, and it had experienced a severe loss of jobs and income over the previous decade. This profile—combined with a reasonably good set of contacts through the local nonprofit Forest Resource Development Center (FRDC), which had at different times employed academic researchers—made Golden Valley my first choice. I believed it to be the best environment in California in which to study the effects of poverty, industrial restructuring, and rapid job loss on a mostly white rural U.S. community. It would prove to be an ideal location for observing the ways in which declining life chances can lead to the evolution of specific cultural and moral discourses that help people adjust to their changing circumstances and compensate for their inabilities to achieve success through more traditional avenues.

Historical Background: Changing Times in Golden Valley

We have lost our way of staying who we are. That's your heritage. We cannot regenerate our heritage anymore. We are gonna become a town that not only changed, but continues to change. (Ted Dorsey, 42-year-old small business owner and married father of two)

Golden Valley's economy has always been mostly land based. Its original settlers were Native Americans of several interrelated tribal groups whose descendants still make up a significant proportion of Golden Valley residents. Elements of their subsistence lifestyle endure there, as the local culture still highly values hunting, fishing, and gardening for food, building one's own housing, and gathering one's own wood for heat. The region did not see significant European American settlement until the gold mining boom of the nineteenth century. By the mid-1800s Golden Valley became an agricultural and ranching center to sustain the region's mining operations, mostly concentrated near Miner's Gulch, about thirty miles away over the mountains. By the turn of the next century, ranching was slowly replaced by timber production as the community's main industry. At this time most logging operations were small and family owned, many begun by dust bowl refugees. By the 1930s there were fourteen sawmills in the immediate vicinity of Golden Valley. After World War II these smaller operations were slowly made obsolete by new technology, and Northwest Timber Industries established its large-scale mill in Golden Valley, which by the early 1990s employed about 150 people year round.

Golden Valley hit the peak of its relative prosperity in the late 1980s, as both the logging industry and local businesses were booming. Unemployment rates in Jefferson County fell to less than 11 percent in 1987 as local timber harvests reached record highs. But fortunes would soon change. Although many locals believe that the forest industry had peaked and would likely have begun to decline anyway, its gradual progression was interrupted by an abrupt and momentous change in environmental regulations. The 1990 listing of the northern spotted owl as threatened under the Endangered Species Act would alter the economic landscape of Golden Valley irrevocably. The spotted owl decision, explained in more detail in the following section, resulted in federally enforced bans on timber harvesting through much of the Pacific Northwest to preserve the owl's habitat. This decision affected all of the local public forests, which made up nearly 80 percent of the land area in Jefferson County. Timber harvests in the region dropped by 80 percent between 1989 and 1994 as a result.[10]

The spotted owl ruling was destructive to virtually all aspects of Golden Valley's economy. The first jobs to evaporate were those in the forests, including logging and reforestation. Thirty jobs were lost in the local U.S. Forest Service office alone. Next, the remaining sawmills closed one by one. In 1996 Northwest Timber, which was the last and largest remaining mill, closed permanently. With it went 150 jobs and the foundation of the community's economy. Although Northwest Timber outlasted several smaller mills in the area, in the end it was simply not profitable to bring in timber from outside the region to fuel it, considering Golden Valley's physical isolation and remoteness. Forty percent of the community's payroll disappeared during the decade of the 1990s. This loss was mostly in the manufacturing industry, whose employment fell precipitously, from 27 percent in 1990 to just 6 percent by 2000.[11] According to county figures, salaries in this industry also plummeted; unadjusted average annual earnings in manufacturing dropped from $16,322 in 1990 (or $21,510 in 2000 dollars) to $11,994 in 2000. It was the only local sector to experience a drop in unadjusted earnings over time. Most residents who were there at the time remember the 1990s as a period of community-level depression, from which they are still struggling to emerge. The job loss in the forest industry had ripple

effects throughout Golden Valley, including the closing of almost half
of its businesses during the 1990s. Thus, by the time I moved there in
2003, Route 7 was littered with shells of former businesses, including
grocery stores, a video arcade, a hardware store, and a movie theater
that had not survived the economic collapse.

The effects on the community have been noticeable as well. Golden
Valley experienced population loss throughout the 1990s, as many laid-
off workers relocated to other towns and counties to find work, sometimes taking their families with them. Those who remained experienced
significant hardships. One measurement often quoted to illustrate the
change is the percentage of schoolchildren receiving free and reduced
lunches: it climbed from 54 percent in 1990 to nearly 80 percent by the
end of the decade. Interestingly, according to the U.S. Census, individual poverty rates decreased slightly over the decade, dropping from 27
percent in 1990 to 24 percent in 2000. This is not actually due to large
numbers of people moving out of poverty, but rather to the out-migration
of residents who could not find work, as well as women's increased workforce participation and some in-migration by wealthier retirees. The percent of households receiving public assistance[12] also dropped in half over
the decade, from 19 percent to 9.5 percent,[13] although this significant
decrease is likely due more to welfare reform and growing stigma (which
will be discussed in more detail in chapter 2) than to a lack of need.

Unemployment in Golden Valley, on the other hand, rose over the
ten-year period, from 11 percent in 1990 to 21 percent in 2000. This
increase was mostly in men's unemployment, which more than doubled,
from 10 percent to 25.5 percent, while women's unemployment rose only
slightly, from 11 percent to 15 percent. For women, both workforce participation (actively seeking work) and employment have risen slightly
over the decade,[14] suggesting that women's rising unemployment is related to an increased proportion of the female population looking for
work compared to the past. For men, the opposite is true: both their
workforce participation and employment rates dropped substantially
over the decade, suggesting that more men are dropping out of the
workforce entirely when they are unable to find work. That either group
experienced a rise in employment during this period is surprising, as the
local economy was in a severe decline. Women and men of working age
are now employed in about equal proportions in Golden Valley, which
is a significant change from 1990. Even in 1990 the effects of the forest

industry's decline were becoming visible. In 2000, however, the collapse was complete, as is clear in the men's employment trends.[15]

These employment figures reflect not just the loss of jobs in the area's forest industry, but also a skew in the nature of the jobs that remain. It is not an accident that women's employment is on the rise while men's has declined. The bulk of remaining jobs in Golden Valley are in the service and sales sectors,[16] feminized sectors characterized by low wages and part-time employment. Women are to be found working behind the cash registers at most local businesses, as well as in administrative positions in the local government and schools. They also make up the bulk of local schoolteachers of all grade levels and find employment caring for the very young and the elderly in both formal and informal settings. These jobs make up the majority of employment in Golden Valley now and are generally unappealing to its men. While men are willing to take retail positions in a few instances, such as clearly masculine settings like the hardware and feed stores, they by and large refuse to consider employment in other types of service and administrative settings and rarely do care work for either young children or the elderly. However, while women now have an easier time finding employment than do men, their wages and working hours are not equal to the men's jobs that were lost. Mill jobs were generally full-time and paid more than minimum wage, but most women's jobs are neither full-time nor well paid. In 1999 only 11 percent of working-age women were employed full-time and year round, compared to 28 percent of men. While women earned on average slightly more than men for full-time, year-round work ($29,306 versus $23,594), overall they earned an average of just $13,000 per year, compared to $21,000 for men when part-time work was included.[17] These average earnings are low no matter how they are figured and make it extremely difficult for either men or women to comfortably be the sole supporters of their families. In 1999, the official poverty line for a family of four in the United States was $17,029.[18]

Golden Valley, although following a pattern not uncommon across rural America, looks very different from the average California community.[19] It is not unusual for residents of the northern part of California to conceive of themselves as mostly separate from the larger state and to talk at least semiseriously about seceding from the rest of California. The differences between Golden Valley and the state as a whole are evident, both in lifestyle and demographics. In 2000 Golden Valley had much higher poverty rates for individuals than all of California (24 percent versus 14 percent), and median household income was just $22,824—less than half the state median of $47,493. Golden Valley also had three times the state's unemployment rate (21 percent versus 7 percent) and a considerably lower labor force participation rate (45 percent versus 62 percent). Sixteen percent of Golden Valley households lacked telephones, compared to just 2 percent across the state—an indication of the kinds of amenities the rural poor sometimes go without. Another amenity Golden Valley households generally lack is central heating. Natural gas, which heats more than 70 percent of California households, is not available in the community. Instead the majority of its households are heated with wood (67 percent), which is plentiful and relatively cheap compared to other options, while the rest mostly rely on bottled/tank gas (12 percent), electricity (6 percent), and kerosene (14 percent).[20] Over my time there I also came across a number of homes that had various alternative forms of heat and electricity, including many that were not on the local power grid. These homes often relied on solar, wind, and hydro power for electricity and ran such appliances as propane refrigerators and wood-based water heaters.

As these figures suggest, Golden Valley lags far behind the state in most commonly quantified quality-of-life measures. Even before the collapse of the local forest industry, Golden Valley was not a prosperous town.[21] But its overreliance on this industry set it up for even greater economic distress, as is the case with rural communities throughout the United States that are dependent on single industries. Golden Valley has yet to recover in any real way from the devastation wrought by the spotted owl ruling and forest industry restructuring. Multiple factors prevent its recovery, including its physical isolation, small population, and lack of "skilled" or educated workers. While 72 percent of Golden Valley adults (age 25 and older) have finished high school, just slightly lower than the state average of 77 percent, only 11 percent have a bachelor's degree or higher, compared to 27 percent in California as a whole.[22] To date very little business or industry has come in to replace the forest jobs that were lost, and the limited job retraining that has been received has been largely unhelpful, as the jobs themselves never materialized.

Golden Valley provides an example of some of the worst economic hardships faced by rural communities whose lives and livelihoods are tied to a single industry, be it natural resource, farming, or manufacturing. As in communities throughout rural America,[23] in Golden Valley the decline of the forest industry resulted not only in severe job loss and unemployment, but also the loss of a "way of life" that its residents held dear. They now find themselves mired in a daily struggle to survive. At the same time, they are fighting to make sense of their lives and to reinvent themselves and their community in ways that stay true to their past, but create hope for the future. Considering all they have lost, it is not an easy task.

"Save a Logger, Shoot an Owl": The Spotted Owl Controversy

The spotted owl ruling resulted from an unprecedented convergence of the interests of wildlife biologists, environmentalists, and even, to some extent, big forestry business. What began as a campaign to save a rare species of bird ended with a rapid and massive change in Pacific Northwest forest regulations. Although Pacific Northwest timber employment had peaked by the mid-1980s,[24] and it is likely that the forest industry would have continued to decline in Golden Valley even without the spotted owl ruling,[25] residents were not exaggerating when they blamed it for the sudden and devastating deterioration of their town and the local labor market. I repeatedly heard locals complain that the decision was never really about saving an owl. Instead, they saw it as a deliberate and direct attack on their economy and way of life.

For most people outside of the Pacific Northwest, the spotted owl controversy was just slightly higher profile than the usual battle between environmentalists and extractive industries, with slightly higher stakes. Although in reality it was fought in wildlife biology departments, environmentalists' offices, government agencies, and courtrooms, the spotted owl battle was mostly visible to the general public through media sound bites and bumper sticker slogans. Many of these bumper stickers are still visible on vehicles traveling the back roads in the forested regions of California, Oregon, and Washington, although they are becoming increasingly rare. Among common slogans from the time were "Save a Logger, Shoot an Owl"; "Save a Logger, Eat an Owl"; "Save the Spotted Owl: They Taste Just Like Chicken"; and "Don't Like Logging? Try Wiping with a Spotted Owl." Although humorous, these slogans represented serious concerns and passionate belief systems that were set on a collision course in the late 1980s and early 1990s.

However, they also portrayed the controversy, as did the press and media more generally, as a fight between two main interest groups: owls and loggers.[26] The irony of this portrayal is not only that there were several other major players in the drama, but that, more important, both owls and loggers were affected populations that had little to no agency in the decisions.[27] While loggers had major stakes in the outcome, ultimately they were just workers within the forest industry; they were neither organized nor well funded enough to have any real impact of their own in the fight. Ultimately, they were unable to influence the outcome in any area except the public's imagination. And unfortunately, for the most part, the public stood firm against the interests of loggers, who were repeatedly portrayed in the press and media as uneducated, dirty, and ignorant enemies of trees and all things natural.[28] Loggers were bloodthirsty animals whose only desire was to clear-cut old-growth trees.[29] This portrayal, however inaccurate, has had grave emotional impacts on the residents of logging communities. In Golden Valley, it helped to widen an already wide gulf in perception between the rural logging community and the rest of the hostile urban and suburban world.

If it wasn't really about an owl, as so many Golden Valley residents assert, then what exactly was behind the ruling that dismantled an entire region's way of life? In the beginning, it was in fact about an owl, but that owl came to be a symbol and surrogate for the entire forest ecosystem.[30] Its cause had a juggernaut quality as it progressed, taking on larger and larger significance—and larger and larger tracts of forest land—as its fame grew.

The spotted owl is a rarely seen and oddly tame bird, which comes when called and doesn't fly away when approached.[31] It first flew out of obscurity in 1968, when Eric Forsman, a wildlife biology student at Oregon State University, encountered the uncommon raptor while on summer fire patrol in the Willamette National Forest. Forsman subsequently began to study the bird and went on as a graduate student to team up with several other wildlife biologists to expand and continue his research on spotted owls.[32] Among his most critical findings was the owl's preference for old-growth forests.[33] This discovery led Forsman and his colleagues to begin a campaign to preserve the last stands of old-growth timber in the Pacific Northwest, which at that point were rapidly falling victim to clear-cutting.[34]

It was here that the interests of the scientific community converged with those of the burgeoning environmental movement. For environmentalists, the owl became the perfect stand-in for old-growth forests. The owl emerged as an "indicator species" for both the scientific and the environmental communities:[35]

> If the owl disappeared, it meant that the forest system itself was collapsing. . . . The owl came to symbolize first an entire kind of forest, and then a worldview: a way of seeing nature, and man's role in it, different from anything the general public had accepted before.[36]

Although scientists' calls for protection of the owl's habitats began in the 1970s, the demands grew louder once environmentalists began to recognize the bird's significance and potential. At first the victories were small concessions, the protection of small tracts of Bureau of Land Management and U.S. Forest Service land. These small preservations infuriated the timber industry,[37] while leaving scientists and environmentalists unsatisfied.[38] By the early 1980s, environmental groups were paying increasing attention to the issue but were unable to agree on a strategy.[39] They dragged their heels on working to have the owl listed as endangered, fearful that they lacked the momentum necessary to take on the timber industry.[40] Large mainstream groups like the Sierra Club actually resisted battling the industry over land that had little recreational value. Eventually, in 1989 a small environmental group from New England broke rank and successfully petitioned for the owl's listing as threatened under the Endangered Species Act.[41] It was officially listed on June 26, 1990.[42]

In the years that followed, the opposing interest groups became increasingly polarized in their demands, despite the early waffling on both sides. In the mid-1980s, battles between the U.S. Forest Service and environmental interest groups resulted in the preservation of some land for the owl but not a significant amount of its habitat.[43] Before the listing, big timber interests actually tolerated some amount of woods closures in the hopes that it might weed out competition by smaller scale sawmills. Overcutting and falling timber prices, along with foreign competition, were beginning to plague the industry.[44] But once the owl was listed, environmental groups began filing lawsuits to shut down and protect vast tracts of forest land. The industry fought back, both in the courtroom and through organizing and funding pro-timber demonstrations, mobilizing loggers to put a human face to the issue. Playing on and exacerbating the loggers' fears of job loss, the timber industry encouraged workers to blame owls and environmentalists, in part to hide its own complicity in logging's decline.[45]

In the end, this effort succeeded in polarizing the issue further and permanently separating the perceived interests of forest workers from those of environmentalists. While both the forests and the timber workers were ultimately victims of the same corporate greed and exploitation, in the end the workers sided with the industry that provided their livelihood—a livelihood that was on the verge of extinction so that an owl could be saved from it. For loggers, the controversy was widely perceived "as fundamentally a clash of urban versus traditional rural cultures, with the latter being overwhelmed and devalued by the former."[46] This antagonism between perceived interests persisted through the decade of the 1990s and was still strongly evident in Golden Valley in 2003.

The final blow to logging came in the form of a lawsuit filed on behalf of the Sierra Club and National Audubon Society. In 1991, Judge William Dwyer ruled in favor of the environmental groups and argued that the U.S. Forest Service and U.S. Fish and Wildlife Service had failed to secure sufficient amounts of land to save the owl.[47] He placed an injunction on all timber sales in the owl's range. This effectively shut down 80 percent of timber sales west of the Cascade Mountain range.[48] Timber towns throughout the Northwest were devastated by job loss and economic collapse.

Some hope returned briefly in 1994, when the injunctions were partially lifted following the acceptance of the Clinton administration's Northwest Forest Plan. The new plan permitted the harvest of one billion board feet of timber on federal forest land in Washington, Oregon, and California, but this amounted to less than one-quarter of the level of the 1980s.[49] The new plan was flawed in many ways and failed to bring large-scale logging back to the region. The lost jobs were never replaced. In a bitterly ironic twist, the lost spotted owls were never replaced either; their numbers continue to drop due to unforeseen dangers such as forest fires, West Nile virus, and the in-migration of the barred owl, a natural predator from the Midwest.[50] Meanwhile, thinning and clearing have become extremely difficult due to the Northwest Forest Plan's restrictions, thus increasing the vulnerability and likelihood of significant loss due to forest fires.[51]

In Golden Valley, the owl's legacy includes not only fire-scarred hillsides, but also job loss, out-migration, and a passionate hatred of environmentalists, liberals, and the Clinton administration. The fact that the community exists at all is somewhat remarkable, considering the dire predictions of the time that timber-dependent towns like Golden Valley were "going to dry up and blow away." To the extent that environmental interests considered the impact of the spotted owl ruling on these communities, they assumed that they would either transition to more tourism-based economies or simply diminish and fade away. Although Golden Valley's isolation prohibited it from engaging in any significant amount of tourism, it has astonishingly failed to disappear. Despite considerable population loss, Golden Valley persists. Its residents stubbornly refuse to give up their community and what is left of their way of life. Their love of the place and its people outweighs, for many, the serious hardships that life there now entails.

Why They Stay: The Rewards and Struggles of Remaining in Golden Valley

Reasons to Stay

> Work's hard to find. It's tough to make a living here, but I find we're happier here with [more] time and little money, as compared to the city life, which we've tried. We love it here. . . . Having venison to eat, having organic beef that we raised—the stress level here is just so easy to deal with compared to [the city]. And you know, on average here I'll probably make half of that, that I made in Hillview. . . . And it's amazing how sixty miles away, in this little rural community here, you seem so much wealthier with half the income. (Keith Bartlett, 32-year-old married, unemployed former logger)

One of the biggest challenges to gathering comprehensive and accurate information about Golden Valley from its residents was their strong desire to depict their community in only the most positive light. Golden

Valley had been spotlighted in newspaper stories a few times before, mostly during the forest industry collapse immediately following the spotted owl decision. These previous media treatments had generally been unfavorable to Golden Valley, often portraying the community as down-and-out and its residents as uneducated, angry rednecks who hated trees and the environment. Several people who had provided interviews for these stories felt they had been misquoted or their quotes had been taken out of context and were still angry about it. Thus, a number of potential subjects asked multiple questions about the nature of my research before agreeing to take part and required repeated assurances that I was not affiliated with any newspaper and was not an environmentalist. For many it was important that I understood how much they loved their community and that I saw its strengths, not its weaknesses. Sometimes their pride stymied my research; for example, many respondents refused to give me names of people whom they did not feel appropriately represented their community, telling me that these individuals wouldn't agree to talk to me. Their attempts to limit my exposure to the most troubling aspects of life there meant that I had to make extra efforts to reach certain groups of people. On the other hand, I learned much about what residents believed the community's strengths to be and the multiple reasons that most had chosen to remain in Golden Valley despite all the struggles they endured.

There are many ways in which Golden Valley is unique for its residents and not interchangeable with another California community that might have better economic prospects. Golden Valley's population demographics are very different from those of California as a whole. The town's population is about 85 percent white compared to less than 60 percent in California. While the state has significant African American (7 percent), Asian (11 percent), and Hispanic (32 percent) populations, in 2000 Golden Valley had only three African American residents and four Asians and less than 5 percent of its population was Hispanic. On the other hand, while only 1 percent of Californians reported Native American race, 8.3 percent of Golden Valley did.[52] Because of their long ties to the region, most families of Native American descent are considered to be among the pillars of Golden Valley's population, and there are several large local families who trace their roots there to Native ancestors. Most of the local Native Americans are members of unrecognized tribes without reservation land and have thus lived as integrated members of the Golden Valley community for generations. Respondents who self-identified as white often told me proudly of their Native American roots in the region. Nonetheless, negative stereotypes of the "drunken Indian" variety were common there as well, among both those who did and those who did not have Native ancestors.

The treatment that Native Americans receive is different from that received by the rare Latinos, African Americans, or Asian Americans who mostly have settled in Golden Valley more recently. While occasionally a particular Latino family will be grudgingly accepted into the community, for the most part all nonwhite newcomers are viewed suspiciously as interlopers to this tight-knit community. As will be explored in greater detail in chapter 3, the unique identity of Golden Valley is constructed around the experience of rural whiteness. It is fluid enough to encompass Native Americans of local origins and integrates much of their cultural history into its own. However, this identity is constructed in stark contrast to the nonwhite experience of Latinos, Asians, and African Americans who occupy the rest of California. In many ways, Golden Valley is fiercely protective of itself as an oasis for working-class white rural families, isolated in time and space from the rapidly diversifying, mostly urban state in which it lies.

The people of Golden Valley are for the most part a proud group, with a powerful sense of community and strong ties to the region. Few people end up in the town by accident, and most who remain have made a conscious choice to be there, particularly as the labor market and economy crumble. Although many of its employees relocated for work when the mill closed, over the years a number have returned, choosing to retire early or take their chances with retraining and scrambling to find other types of work in order to stay in the community. For the most part they cite family and lifestyle concerns as their central reasons for returning, although the main focus issues tend to differ by gender. Since remaining in Golden Valley requires making compromises with regard to income as well as availability and price of retail products, most residents have deeply held reasons for living there rather than someplace with more conveniences and healthier economic prospects. As Fitchen[53] found in rural New York, in Golden Valley home is much more than just a place on a map. The rural environment, community, and lifestyle are extremely important to its loyal residents, most of whom can't conceive of life anywhere else. Linda Cole, a 34-year-old woman of Native American descent, explained the difficult and deliberate choice to stay in Golden Valley:

> The people that are left here are survivors, not only from a traditional cultural standpoint. They're survivors for the lives that they've tried to build here and that they're still trying to hold onto. And those connections and those roots run really, really deep in rural communities. And I think that's real important.

For Golden Valley's men, it is often the outdoors that holds them there. Most of the community's men are strongly tied to the mountain, forest, and river environments for their leisure activities, which generally include hunting, fishing, and camping. This leisure interest combines with vehemently pro-rural attitudes shared by women and men alike in Golden Valley, who tend to eschew the crowdedness of cities and dislike the flat, mountainless landscape of California's Central Valley. I was constantly asked by my subjects, friends, and acquaintances in Golden Valley how I could possibly survive in the awful urban environment of Berkeley. For many, the pluses of the rural lifestyle outweigh the minuses of the local labor market. As Eric McCloud, a 48-year-old married father of two put it:

> You have to be somewhat of a loner, I think, to do this kind of life. . . . These people up here are very into the trees and the fresh air and the lack of city noise. . . . But we just like being up in the hills. I can put up with a bad job or whatever here, but I couldn't put up with a foul job in Hillview.

Keith Bartlett, a 32-year-old married former logger, focused more clearly on the value of Golden Valley's outdoor amenities when describing his reasons for staying there despite chronic unemployment:

> It's, for me, just all this country, bein' able to explore it. I love to hunt, fish, backpack, camp, and just all those mountain things. I wouldn't trade it, unless I could find steeper, more beautiful mountains.

Eli Jordan, a 42-year-old married father of three and disabled former logger, put a similar sentiment more succinctly: "I don't want to live anyplace where I can't pee in my own backyard."

For many male residents of Golden Valley, there is a sharp contrast between the freedom and space of the rural environment and what they perceive as a suffocating density, restriction, and surveillance in urban areas. Many hold onto a frontiersman identity that prizes self-sufficiency, solitude, and independence as inherently masculine and moral values.[54] This identity makes it difficult for most of Golden Valley's men to conceive of life outside of the region, and many who tried to live elsewhere eventually returned for quality-of-life reasons related specifically to the rural setting. For most, their reasons for staying in Golden Valley were expressed explicitly in contrast to the alternative of urban life, which they described as frightening, limiting, cacophonous, and claustrophobic. Sam Acton, a 33-year-old disabled former logger and mill worker, described the fear and hemmed-in feeling he experienced in cities in comparison with the freedom and quiet of Golden Valley:

> I went through L.A. this year for the first time in ten years, and it scared me. I mean, they got razor wire wrapped around the signposts and the city never ends—you can't get away from it. Up here, in three minutes I can be where I may not see anybody for the rest of the day. That's tough to beat. I mean, you know, everybody has their different standard for what life is, but to me it's livin' in peaceful—you know, there's nothin' wrong with this kind of community, if you can afford to live here.

Cody Wilson, a 30-year-old single father and maintenance supervisor, expressed a similar sense of freedom that he felt in rural versus urban areas. He told me, "I gotta be next to the mountains or I'll go nuts." Cody further explained:

> I'm not a city person. The city and I—I would be dead or in jail. I don't do the city very well. I gotta go out and hunt. I gotta be able to, you know, if I get mad, I gotta be able to jump in my pickup, drive out on some four-wheel-drive hill, stop, look down at everything, and think about it. You know, in the city, you're always running into people no matter where you go. You can't get away. And I have to be able to get away. I have to take my shotgun out and shoot, or, you know, somethin'.

For Golden Valley's men, the community is much more than a place to live. It is a place in which they can practice a particular lifestyle, which in their minds is not available in most other parts of California or the United States. The few men who had any real interest in leaving Golden Valley generally wanted to move someplace similarly or even more rural, such as Oregon or Idaho, where they thought the hunting and fishing might be even better and the regulations looser.

Women, on the other hand, tended more often to bring up the importance of community and family when discussing their reasons for staying in Golden Valley rather than the need for space, freedom, or outdoor activities. They contrasted the rural community with the city, where, as many complained, you could live "for twenty years and not know your neighbors." Many respondents who were parents or who had been teenagers in Golden Valley had anecdotes to tell of parents being informed about their child's wrongdoings by friends, family, or neighbors before the child even returned home from the event.[55] Jeanie Mayer, a 45-year-old single parent of two, was one of many mothers who reported this phenomenon, here with regard to her teenage son:

> I mean, Matt tries to do something wrong, I hear about it usually within a few hours. You know, somebody's seen them—kind of a neighborhood-watch-type thing. They don't have that in the big cities. They don't have that, where the neighbors look out for each other and call each other, tell them what's happening, you know.

Stories also abound of the community raising money for its sick and needy members, most frequently to help the uninsured with hospital bills. As 38-year-old married mother and administrator Angelica Finch explained, "You know, the whole town will stand behind you in a time of need. They've always done that. It's just the way it is." The strong sense of community ranks high among the many benefits female respondents cite as reasons to stay in Golden Valley despite its economic struggles. Grace Prader, a 45-year-old married mother and secretary, similarly expressed this sentiment:

> What it all comes down to is the fact that in a small community everybody is there for everybody else. I might not like you today and I might not like you tomorrow, but if your house catches on fire, I will be there.

In addition to valuing the sense of community, women commonly discussed family ties and obligations, particularly to ill or aging parents, as among their top reasons for staying in Golden Valley. While women did refer to the beauty and peacefulness of the area as important, their main reasons nonetheless tended to cluster around family and community as the most essential aspects of Golden Valley's unique lifestyle for them. For example, 52-year-old Barbara Robbins, when asked what she liked about the town, talked at first about the rural environment and community:

Not too many people, not too much traffic. And it's beautiful. It's
green, we get all seasons. It's nice and peaceful. People know you.

But when asked why she chose to stay in Golden Valley after her husband lost his mill job, her answer focused more on the importance of
being close to her ailing mother:

> We own our home, and we like it here. The family—most of my family's
> here, my mom. Yeah, Mom wasn't doing well, and my dad had passed
> away. She wasn't doing well. And the girls are all gone, so somebody
> needed to be here for her.

While the men commonly felt they couldn't survive somewhere urban
or away from the mountains, women tended to be more open to the
idea of living elsewhere but committed to staying in the area because of
their strong social and kinship ties. Their specific discourses to describe
the choice to stay in Golden Valley are very much tied to their gender
roles and identities, in which women still conceive of themselves as
homemakers and the pivots of family life. Men, on the other hand, are
more likely to portray themselves as centered outside the home, where
the forest environment allows them to provide for their families either
through paid work or subsistence activities. These discourses are rooted
in traditional gender roles in Golden Valley, where women were historically centered in and around the home and focused on the maintenance of family and community. Most of the work that women did traditionally focused on raising children and running a household. For men,
the traditional gender roles focused on providing for a family through
work that occurred primarily outside of the home. Before Golden Valley's economic collapse, men's work mostly consisted of manual labor,
often either out in the woods or at least using materials that had been
harvested from the forests. Although these roles are changing out of
necessity, most people's conceptions of the community are still an-
chored in romanticizations of these traditional gender norms and their
rapidly fading way of life. Regardless of the new roles they must undertake, men are still emotionally tied to their identities as loggers, hunters,
and outdoorsmen and women to their identities as mothers, daughters,
and pivots of social and community life. These gender roles and identities also inform their conceptions of morality, as will be explored in the
chapters that follow.

The Price They Pay

What's been the hardest thing about staying here?

LAURA: Nothin' to do.

ELI: And nothin' for the kids, and no way of makin' it.

LAURA: And I don't mean nothin' like every day you have to go out and do something. It's just two hours to go the movies, it's two hours to go shopping. You know, you can't go to Hillview without it taking you five hours at least. It's just impossible. (Laura and Eli Jordan, 38 and 42 years old, married parents of three)

Although there is a specific set of socially constructed discourses around appropriate reasons for staying in Golden Valley, they nonetheless correspond to real and intense desires to remain there. Staying in a community with so few opportunities is a struggle, even for those with deeply felt ties to the region. And while most people remain there because they love the community and the area, they are consciously aware of the sacrifices they are making and the ways in which their beloved town has been deteriorating since the loss of timber industry jobs. Even those who were the most staunchly dedicated to remaining in Golden Valley often complained about the ways in which the community had declined over their lifetimes. Most did not expect or hope that their children would remain in the community, despite their desires to keep their families centered there and tied to their land and heritage. A sense of loss and frustration permeated most interviews, particularly when I asked people how the community had changed since the spotted owl decision.

For most, the ramifications of the spotted owl ruling were immediately apparent. Many people reacted to the initial decision with feelings of fear and despair, as they understood what it would mean for their community. Although the results were quickly evident across the entire forest sector, for most it was the mill closure that had the most critical and personal effects. Andy Newton, who worked in the mill at the time, described the experience as "kinda like getting hit in the face with a wet blanket." Local business owner Ted Dorsey recalled his reactions to learning of the mill closure:

When the mill went out, it was the other shoe dropping. I mean, it was devastating, I remember it being devastating. I seriously went home and was just like, "Oh my God." We all thought that within a few years our schools would be on the verge of closing. I thought my job may not be in existence. Everybody just sucked in, pulled back, and held on, and thought, "What's gonna happen?"

What happened, according to most residents, was a noticeable shift in the makeup of the local population and the town itself. Almost everyone talked about what they believed to be major demographic transformations caused by the job loss and mill closure. Fred Graham, a 50-year-old Forest Service employee, described the changes he had noticed:

> The local kids are leaving and we're getting a lot of welfare families who have replaced the younger generation in the school, so you got a lot more lower socioeconomic group in here, which makes for a larger free-lunch program and problems in the schools. On the other hand, we're getting a lot of retirees that have more free time, and some of them are getting involved in community activities, but it's not so much youth-oriented, so that's different. And I think it's really raised the property values.

Many people expressed similar perceptions of the demographic shift and seemed convinced that the community had received a significant influx of poor and welfare-dependent families from outside the community, while the majority of local "hardworking" families had left. Most also believed that there was a concurrent influx of retirees and telecommuters. In general, it appeared that the amount of in-migration by both the poor and the middle class was exaggerated in the local perception and that the community was experiencing only minimal in-migration by outsiders, be they wealthy or poor. As mentioned earlier, public assistance receipt has actually fallen by 50 percent since the mill closed. Yet the belief persists, at least in part because few locals want to admit that it was common for Golden Valley's long-term residents to be on welfare before the mill closure as well.[56] Kenny Blake, a 25-year-old clerk at the gas station, described the two major demographic changes as he saw them:

> [There was] a major loss in actual work income when the mill left, and then a giant influx in state-aided families moving in, and then that's been dropping off. And there's another influx of money from out of the area coming in, people who made a bunch of money on the Internet and just dropped out and came up here, and they're buyin' property and puttin' their money in.

These two groups were perceived very differently by most residents, but neither was completely welcomed. While families who received welfare were almost universally disdained, urban in-migrants were accepted with less clear contempt but nonetheless a great deal of ambivalence. Some people welcomed them as new blood while others believed, like Fred Graham, that they were responsible for a lack of interest in the local community and a rise in local housing values. Many bemoaned a general loss of community action and social responsibility in the wake of the spotted owl decision and believed that overall the demographic shifts had resulted in the community having fewer people who were truly invested in its well-being. Kate Burton, a 30-year-old hairdresser, described what she thought was a general trend toward decreased civic participation among those who remained in Golden Valley:

> I would say that there's a less percentage helping, and part of that would be because the mill closed and a lot of the families that really cared, that worked hard, they're gone. So the majority, I would say, of the ones that are here now are lower economic situation. But still, to me that's no reason not to come to open house [at the elementary school] or whatever. So yeah, we lost a lot of our families that are really interested in participating and helping when the mill closed, and that's a bummer.

Although people may have had different opinions on whether retirees or telecommuters were positive or negative additions to the community, most agreed that they did not participate in its social upkeep to the same degree as the mill worker families who had left.

But the decline in civic participation was only one of the major ways in which most residents felt that the community had degenerated. The loss of population and disposable income had destructive effects on most of the local businesses, particularly those that provided social and leisure activities for adults and children. While a handful of local businesses were flourishing due to the lack of competition, other business owners complained that there were fewer people with enough money to buy goods and that the post-mill-closure years had produced dramatic drops in sales. One of the other most common complaints among Golden Valley residents was the lack of leisure opportunities there beyond outdoor activities. Several respondents shared their memories of lost businesses and their frustrations with the current dearth of social spaces and activities:

You know, we had a lot of small fringe businesses that were making it, and when a hundred families moved out, boom, that was it. You know, we had four grocery stores and we have two now. A lot of restaurants, a lot of gas stations . . . aren't here anymore. (Ted Dorsey, 42)

After the mill closed, Golden Valley went downhill. I mean, there was never a lot to do here, but you could at least go downtown and see cars cruisin' around or, you know, go have a hamburger that you could actually afford, and, you know, hang out. They used to have arcades at a certain time. This is all when I was a teenager. It was fun. (Laura Jordan, 38)

We need a bowling alley around here or something that you do with a family. Then your kids can be older or they can be younger. But you could still go out and eat pizza and bowl or whatever. But there's not even that. There's nothin' now. I mean, before at least you had a community, and now it's nothin'. We barely even have a store. The only thing that seems to survive is the bar. It'll be here when nobody else is here. (Eli Jordan, 42)

Well, when I was *young* young, earlier than ten, Golden Valley was just booming. Three or four restaurants, three or four gas stations and a movie theater, three or four bars, a couple of different laundromats, a bunch of different stores—and lots of things to do, lots of activities for people, and just big community get-togethers and stuff like that. Since the mill closed, a lot of families have been forced to move because there just aren't jobs. And when families move, kids move with 'em. So your friend groups get smaller and smaller and smaller until there's only ten kids your age in the area, and you have to drive up to thirty miles away to see half of 'em because Golden Valley encompasses almost half of Jefferson County in its school district. (Kenny Blake, 25)

Overall, most people described a shift in town life away from the public sphere and increasingly into the home. While many of the businesses that had once provided entertainment and social spaces had closed, others remained but had been slowly abandoned due to decreased disposable incomes and changing cultural norms. The community's bars, once full of working men stopping by for a drink after their shifts, were now mostly deserted, frequented regularly only by the most serious of drinkers. The few remaining restaurants were similarly empty much of the time. Parents and teachers also complained about the lack of parental support for the local schools and the decreasing attendance for extracurricular events, dances, and sports matches. Bud and Emily Richards, a married couple in their early 40s, both complained about the lack of parents at school assemblies and sporting events:

> BUD: I coached T-ball all the way up to senior league, and I coached baseball, and Emily, we coached together, and we saw it all there too. I mean, there's these big stands, and you got fourteen kids in the dugout and there's three parents out there. And it's, like, it's the same three parents every time. It's sad for the kids.

Most people blamed the decline in public life on a combination of out-migration of the "better" families, in-migration of the poor, and the problems that they associated with poverty, such as substance abuse. High poverty rates, combined with changing social norms and the paucity of operating businesses, mean that there are now few venues in Golden Valley in which adults regularly interact socially. People's shame around unemployment and poverty further dissuades many from appearing in public even when the opportunities arise.

Together, all of these changes lead to bleak outlooks for the people who remain in Golden Valley, and there are few reasons for young adults to stay. In a community that fears change, one of the hardest things for many people is watching their children move away and turn their backs on the only lifestyle they have ever known. But there are few options; the only higher education available locally consists of a limited offering of distance-learning courses through Hillview Community College. Between the lack of educational opportunities and the scarcity of decent work, those who want to invest in human capital tend to leave. Given the perceived decline of the community, only a handful ever return once they have completed their educations. School-teacher Cathy Graham explained the conundrum of the brain-drain phenomenon, which is a widespread problem throughout rural America:[57]

> You're sending off all your good treasures, but truly there's no employment here. So you can't ask your son or daughter to stay, because there's nothing for them to do. You know, there's no jobs. I don't know what they would do if they did stay here. And I would think that a lot of them—the kids that are college-bound, obviously—they all want to experience the city before they decide. I mean, this is a decision you have to make.

While on the one hand, receiving a college education is of little use in a community with so few job opportunities, prospects are not much better for those who choose not to go to college. While the previous generation was able to find stable employment in the woods or sawmills without college degrees, now there are very few such "unskilled" jobs. Ted Dorsey articulated the anger and frustration felt by many of the community's parents over such issues:

> There's some folks that are still here that, you know, found another way to make a living. Most of 'em are gone. But the big thing is that we're not getting any new ones. You know, from the time that mill closed in '96, virtually every graduate of every class since then has had to leave. So we're not gettin' 'em anymore. They have to go. Not that I would have wanted my kid to stay and work in the mill. I probably wouldn't have wanted him to—it's a tough life—but if that's what he wanted to do. . . . And there's a lot of people that aren't college material, you know. There's a lot of people that are never gonna be a rocket scientist.

Many Golden Valley residents blamed the community's decline explicitly on the spotted owl ruling and in particular on the urban environmentalists who were behind it. They believed that it did much more than save an owl's habitat; it simultaneously exterminated a human population's way of life. The spotted owl decision was in most people's minds single-handedly responsible for all of the negative trends discussed in the previous passages. Although after knowing them, one could easily argue that Golden Valley residents love the local forests on a much more personal level than do the urban environmentalists who fought so hard to preserve them, almost everyone there agreed that some amount of timber harvesting should be allowed. Many were also quick to point out that environmentalists did not take into account the vulnerability of California's forests to uncontrollable wildfires if they are not cut and thinned with some regularity. The decade following the spotted owl ruling saw a number of devastating forest fires in Jefferson County, the remains of which were almost indistinguishable from the scars of abandoned clear-cuts.

Nonetheless, many people expressed concern and ambivalence over the clear-cutting practices of the pre-closure days, and not everyone wanted to see large-scale logging return or at least to be practiced in the same way as in the past. Many felt that the logging companies had taken advantage of them, destroying their beloved woods without proper respect for the environment and the forest ecosystems. Andrew Harper, a 26-year-old unemployed man whose father had worked in the mill, declared:

I'm personally glad that there's not this, like, big profit motive to log all
around here anymore. I mean, like, today we went through two major
clear-cut areas. And you know, they were clear-cut when I was a little
kid, and there's still, like, ugly, scraggly pines there. It's not—that way
of doing it wasn't the way to do it.

Most people who openly admitted that they opposed the practice of
clear-cutting also immediately added caveats to explain that they'd like
to see some amount of sustainable logging and thinning occur. Statements like the following, from public employee Derek Lord, illustrate
the tension between Golden Valley residents' conflicting desires to
conserve their local resources and to make their livings from its forests:

> I think [that] some of the policies that were in place needed to go down
> in flames. But I think resource extraction in rural communities just has
> to happen. It has to happen. . . . I am [an environmentalist], and I'll tell
> 'em. I said it at public hearings—I thought people were gonna shoot
> me—I said, "I'm an environmentalist. I think the environment should
> be taken care of." But I think that there could be harvesting practices
> that can do that.

While not everyone was willing to call him or herself an environmentalist, several Golden Valley residents—including many who had worked
in the logging industry—felt that large-scale clear-cutting was neither
desirable nor sustainable. At the same time, most believed that at least
some timber harvesting was necessary, both for the local economy and
to keep the woods from burning. But they repeatedly asserted that they
had a better sense of how to sustainably harvest and manage their own
resources than did outsiders, whether environmental or corporate interests. Many expressed substantial resentment over the government restrictions that currently prevented them from doing so.

Often at the end of interviews, when I asked subjects if there was
anything else they would like to discuss, they spontaneously launched
into long rants against environmentalists and the spotted owl ruling.
Ted Dorsey was perhaps the most articulate and eloquent in his dia-
tribe, only a portion of which is presented below:

> The part that I'm afraid for is our schools, though, because we're not
> rejuvenating, we're not keeping young—there's not a lot of opportunities
> for young families. That's the part that bothers me. And that's the part
> that really offends me about what happened here. Even though I think
> that things are going to be OK, I really do, I am still angry over the lie

that was perpetrated. I never have believed that it was about an owl. It never was. . . . It was about something much, much greater than that. . . . It makes me angry because this is our heritage. This was our opportunity to keep our community, to keep people . . . and I feel that they took that from us, they took that over a lie. And we have—there's no question about it, that there need to be some changes in the forest and the timber harvesting. But we know how to do it. They have the technology—they know, they have the science, they know how to do it right. And it'll never come back to Golden Valley. We'll never have another mill. And it'll never have that kind of economic impact. So it's gone, you know, forever, and that's why I'm angry over that.

Despite acknowledging the problems with the timber harvesting practices of the past, many people in Golden Valley, particularly its men, felt that the loss of forest jobs was devastating in more than economic terms and represented a loss of their culture and heritage. Eli Jordan, who had worked for more than twenty years as a logger, expressed the sense of loss and grief that many men felt over not having the chance to pass on their skills and lifestyle to their children:

I can't show 'em what I did. And they can't say, "Well, I can do that." Even now, if I could teach 'em how to cut a tree, in another ten years if they knew how to cut a tree, they could probably make a good living just in the city. 'Cause there's not gonna be very many people that know how to do that, you know, so—it's not gonna happen though.

For those who remain, Golden Valley has become a bittersweet place. Life there is punctuated by the daily struggle to survive from one season to the next and the constant feeling that something vital was stolen from them. Despite all the benefits of the place—forests, mountains, peace and quiet, family, and community—there is also a pervasive sense of defeat and decline, which for many is expressed as anger and hatred toward outsiders. Many feel, quite reasonably, that their lives were sacrificed for that of an owl. And although most of Golden Valley's current residents are dedicated to remaining there, for most it is a hardship on many levels. They must be willing to forgo both economic and cultural capital, to live without movies and ballet lessons and fast food and many of the other amenities and opportunities available in most of the United States. They do so with pride as well as stubbornness, anger, resentment, and resignation. But no matter how much they love their community, few are entirely happy with its current condition or the

forces that created the situation. Theirs is a story of survival and adaptation in a place that was written off as unimportant, an acceptable
casualty in a war between environmental interests and extractive industries. They rely heavily on cultural and moral discourses to help
them survive its aftermath. As the following chapters will demonstrate,
their beliefs in their own moral superiority allow them to defend their
decisions to stay there and to make sense of their lives in their new
context, bereft of many of the benefits that originally drew their families to Golden Valley.

2

Workers and Welfare: Poverty, Coping Strategies, and Substance Abuse

Living with Poverty, Past and Present

As you drive south into Golden Valley on the narrow and winding Highway 7, the landscape unfolds majestically as you glide down off of Gold Mountain. The sharp, bare mountaintops give way to forests that frame the road, which then recede into the open fields and flat land of Golden Valley. The highway gradually straightens for the brief respite that Golden Valley provides from its otherwise nonstop hairpin turns. As you approach the valley floor, houses and homesteads appear. Some are lavish ranches, with large houses set back from the road amid acres of meadows. Others are dilapidated shacks surrounded by their own private garbage dumps. It is the gorgeous thousand-acre ranches that catch the attention, with cattle or deer grazing in wide pastures at dawn and dusk. The small, poorly kept-up houses often go unnoticed, somehow invisible and easy to ignore despite their closer proximity to the road. The eye has a hard time taking in their abstractionist array of tar paper roofs, boarded-up windows, broken appliances, old vehicles whose useful parts have long ago been scavenged, and garbage spilling out of bags into the yards.

It is easier for a newcomer to focus on Golden Valley's beauty than its chaos. Its residents, however, are well aware of the more run-down homes. Comments such as "I wish people took a little more care of their places" often expressed one of the ways in which they felt the community had deteriorated in recent years. When asked to pinpoint when exactly these changes had occurred, however, most people admitted that junker cars and refrigerators in the front yard had always been ubiquitous parts of the landscape in Golden Valley, as they are throughout much of rural America.[1] The following exchange occurred between Bud and Emily Richards, a married couple in their 40s, as they discussed the way the community had changed over their lifetimes:

> BUD: You see a lot of stuff running down. Just—there's not that much money coming into this town, you know. It's hard to . . .
> EMILY: Not a lot of pride in their places and things . . .
> BUD: That's bad, yeah. . . . But most of those that are real bad have been here forever and they would'a been here if the mill would'a closed or not.

The closing of the woods and sawmills certainly have exacerbated unemployment and its effects in Golden Valley. However, poverty is not new to the valley, which has always had its share of people who lived marginally. A young woman named Christy declined to do an interview with me because she thought that I was interested only in hearing about how the mill closing had had an impact on people. She explained to me that her family hadn't been affected by it at all, because her parents had never worked. She had grown up in a remote cabin on an unpaved road that was inaccessible to vehicles at certain times of year and had lived without running water or electricity for most of her childhood. She said that she had grown up in an intergenerational welfare family and that she had broken the cycle by being the first one to get a job. It appeared from her description that there had always been two kinds of people in Golden Valley: those who worked and those who did not. It was also clear that she felt shame because her father was one who did not.

Yet Christy's story was not anomalous in Golden Valley. Many of my subjects grew up with fathers who were only marginally attached to the paid workforce, often because they had either chosen a subsistence lifestyle or had sustained debilitating injuries while working. Whether or not their fathers had worked, none of my respondents could recall a time before poverty was commonplace in Golden Valley. The main thing that has changed since the closing of the woods and mill is the proportion of the population who do not work, particularly the proportion of men who are not working. The shacks with the poorly maintained yards have always existed, but now there appear to be more of them. As 48-year-old Eric McCloud explained:

> In the '70s, it was a booming town, but welfare hit it. But both sawmills were running and everything was cool. The sawmill kind of kept that all mellowed out. And you had two factions, three factions: You had a few retirees, you had the workers, you had the welfare. So then when the mill left, it became, I feel, retirement and welfare, but more welfare than retirement. So yeah, I'd say we went through big changes here.

Jeanie Mayer, a 45-year-old woman who spent most of her life in Golden Valley, was one of many residents who made observations similar to Eric's:

> I know that there's families here that haven't worked in three or four generations. They brag about the fact that, you know, they've never worked a day in their lives. Welfare.
>
> *So there are people here on welfare who have been here for a long time?*
>
> Yeah, yeah. There's cyclic, generation after generation of welfare people that don't want to work. Or they just work a little bit here or a little bit there, but for the most part they don't contribute. . . . So that's to me the biggest change that we've had that I don't like.
>
> *Because there's more of that than there used to be?*
>
> I think so.

Eric and Jeanie's comments, like Christy's refusal, suggest a strong social disgrace around unemployment and welfare receipt. Unemployed poverty has long been unacceptable in Golden Valley and is commonly blamed for most of the obvious problems in the community. Although as shown in chapter 1 welfare receipt has not actually increased, the perception of welfare as a problem and the stigma around its receipt has.

Working poverty, however, has historically had a different social interpretation. Like welfare receipt and unemployed poverty, working poverty has been a fact of life in Golden Valley for generations. A job alone has never been a guarantee of wealth here. Whether they were from working families or not, few of my subjects grew up in any kind of affluence and most recalled poverty being a part of their daily struggle to

some degree. Many subjects grew up with a working father whose salary
barely kept the family afloat, and lacking electricity and telephones
was as common for them as it was for those whose fathers didn't work.
Women in the workforce were less common then than they are now and
were particularly uncommon among the more stably married families.
Without a second earner, even a mill salary afforded only the barest of
middle-class lifestyles, as average annual earnings in the manufacturing
sector were less than $17,000 in 1990, just about $3,000 over the poverty
line for a family of four at the time.[2] A mill salary was considered a respectable one since it generally paid enough for a man to support his
family and eventually own a home, even if it took years to reach this
kind of comfort level. This did not mean that the family had any
money to spare, though, and most residents recalled clothes, toys, and
store-bought food being in short supply. As Eric McCloud recalled it,
"When I was growing up, this was a community of poor working people.
They were poor, and some of them stayed poor, and some of them saved
every penny they made and ended up with a fairly nice retirement."

The key to respectability was thus not necessarily wealth, but rather
having a male earner who provided as much as he could through hard
work. As long as someone in the family was working for the money,
there was little shame in living on meager wages then or now, and subsistence activities were highly valued as part of the culture of Golden
Valley. Almost everyone I met who grew up there remembered subsistence activities being a part of everyday life to some degree, whether it
was hunting and fishing to help supply the family's dietary needs or cutting and chopping their own wood for heat in the winter. Many people
believed then (and now) that it spoils children to give them too many
things for free and that boys in particular should work for their luxury
items from a young age. Often the local environment supplied what
salaries could not for the enterprising man and his family. Most men,
as well as a lot of women, grew up helping provide for the family in
nonmonetary ways from a young age. Forty-five-year-old Grace Prader
remembers her childhood as being filled with subsistence work and tries to
raise her sons to emulate the demanding work ethic of her own youth:

> Growing up I always had goats, and we had fair animals and stuff like
> that. We had a huge garden. There was five kids. And on a school-
> teacher and a custodian salary we had to have the garden and the
> animals for freezer and table. And I can remember other kids going,

"I don't know what I'm gonna do after school today, I'm so bored." I was like, "Shit, I wish I had time to get bored," you know? And so as a result, there's a lot of kids who are still that way, but my boys, I try to keep them pretty busy.

Thirty-year-old Rod Mitchell recalled a similarly tough childhood, although with a bit more anger than Grace. His family moved from the San Francisco Bay Area to Riverbend when he was 9 years old. His stepfather, whom he described as "old school," sold firewood for a living and expected his sons to pitch in whenever they weren't at school. As Rod recollected,

> It was an interestin' life growing up here because, I mean, we had to work for it. It's hard to make a living in this place. So basically I've been working since I was 9 years old. I kinda liked it when I was a kid. But I do have my resentments. Just the upbringing, the hard life.
>
> *Because you had to work?*
>
> Yeah, the work. A normal kid of 8 shouldn't have to go out and bust his tail after school and be working weekends. I just feel I grew up way too early. But you know, it helped me out, 'cause my work ethics are excellent. I mean, I think I've only drawn unemployment once in seventeen years. I mean, I've never gone more than a week without a job.

Like Grace, Rod found a feeling of respectability in the hard work demanded by poverty despite the sacrifices it required of him. I discovered the same sentiment among most respondents, for whom chores and responsibilities were simply part of the Golden Valley lifestyle during their childhoods and were vital in the purveyance of strong work ethics. The culture of Golden Valley was built around the value of hard labor for its own sake, with survival and masculine pride often being its only rewards. Poverty per se was not looked down upon, but rather poverty in the absence of work. It is this kind of poverty, the poverty of those deemed lazy and unproductive, that is symbolized for many by houses and yards that are in poor repair.[3] A man with a decent work ethic, whether or not he is poor, is expected to keep up the appearance of respectability.

Thus, the difference between the past and the present is not simply the existence of poverty. The main distinction between then and now appears to be the gendered nature of work and breadwinning. In my sample, 41 percent of all respondents had grown up with a mother who worked at least part-time. However, of the women in my sample who were either married or parents, 83 percent were working. The ability of the male breadwinner to support the family, rather than the average standard of living, is in many ways what separates the present from the past. During the forest industry's heyday, a solid lower-middle-class lifestyle was more commonly achievable without a working wife, particularly if the couple had hardworking children to help with the family's survival.

Today, it is much harder for families in Golden Valley to achieve this same lifestyle without the addition of a working woman, and as discussed in chapter 1, women's workforce participation is on the rise. Meanwhile, unemployment and lack of workforce participation have become much more common for men over the decade. Given the cultural context, this presents a difficult challenge for the men of Golden Valley. Not only must they fight for material survival, but they must also fight harder than before just to retain respectability within the community. It is not easy for men to manifest their work ethics in the absence of work, and for many it is becoming increasingly difficult to distinguish themselves from the ranks of the intergenerational welfare families whom they were taught to scorn. It is thus not surprising that poverty has become more visible to those who live in Golden Valley. Among its most commonly cited personifications are the people waiting impatiently at the post office on the first day of the month for their welfare checks to appear in their mailboxes. Another is the state of disrepair and disregard of many of the valley's homes. While neither of these phenomena were unknown to previous generations in Golden Valley, they have apparently become harder for its current population to ignore. Thus the run-down houses that visitors can easily overlook have become for residents the most salient symbols of their beloved community's decline.

This decline is not simply material in nature for most of them, however; it also is a decline in what they perceive as the moral value of hard work. Just as it is harder for the unemployed to manifest their own work ethics, they are also assumed to be unable to pass these values onto their children. A telling example comes from Dawn Bartlett, a 30-year-old teacher at Golden Valley Elementary School, who expressed what she saw as the major difference between her childhood and the experience of the children who are her students:

I think about those things that were instilled in us very young, that made us—you know, strong work ethics—those things that I look around now and I'm like, whoa, I don't think they have it. Or they're not being modeled to work. Or unfortunately some teachers and I will talk about these kids that'll look at you and be like, "I don't need to work. I'm just gonna collect a check when I get out of school." And they are dead serious. That is their goal, and that is what they'll do. And that is so sad, but those are the models that they have. I had highly motivated working parents that were like, gung ho, you know, were always doing something, always.

Dawn herself had grown up in poverty, miles from town in a house without either electricity or running water. Her parents were "highly motivated" to work in unpaid subsistence activities that nonetheless ensured the family's survival and provided their most basic needs. When she remembered this past, she did not recall feelings of shame or guilt; instead she remembered learning strong work ethics and survival skills that strengthened her as a person and would sustain her regardless of what life threw into her path. This provided for her a sharp contrast with what she saw as today's growing problem of poverty in the absence of a proper work ethic. Dawn, like most of my respondents, felt that the community's biggest problem was not so much an increase in poverty as it was the increase in malaise and hopelessness that seemed to have accompanied the loss of the male jobs. Whether this increase in negative values is real or perceived is difficult to quantify, but its importance to social life translates into pressure on the poor to prove that they are not deadbeats, particularly if they hope to find work in Golden Valley. As this chapter will explore in detail, Golden Valley's small size and tight-knit community structure mean that no one is anonymous, and reputations and collective opinions can have a serious impact on people's social lives and labor market experiences.

Coping with Rural Poverty

All the things I do for recreation either gain you money or help you not spend money. Hunting and fishing is meat coming in; gold mining and gemstone mining are money coming in. And money's pretty bad, but it's just part of living here. You have to understand that it swings in seasons. Winter is really, really bad, and you kind of go hungry sometimes. And then summer you put in a garden, which is essential, virtually. And things go better in the summer and fall, and then in winter it goes back. (Kenny Blake, 25-year-old gas station clerk and cohabitating father of one)

Moral Capital and Survival

There are a number of ways in which the experience of rural poverty is distinctly different from that of urban, inner-city poverty. Most notably, several of the options available for surviving poverty are unique to the rural setting. While on the one hand certain types of paid informal-sector work may be harder to find in a rural area than an urban one, on the other hand there are many more options for unpaid subsistence work to help sustain people in lieu of cash. The urban setting, with its ever-expanding underground economy, includes not only illegal work such as drug dealing and prostitution, but also a growing sector of work that is "basically licit but takes place outside the regulatory apparatus covering zoning, taxes, health and safety, minimum wage laws, and other types of standards."[4] This semilegal work includes everything from magazine vending to larger scale informal-sector work such as sweatshops, which may be permanent and full-time, albeit also unregulated and poorly paid. Dohan describes this type of informal work as "otherwise legal economic activities that took place outside the purview of government regulation," versus illicit work, "which produced and distributed goods and services that were themselves illegal."[5] His research looks in depth at two urban Latino communities in which the bulk of income comes from illegal work, illicit work, and welfare.

While the possibility of "under the table" paid work exists in rural areas as well, in Golden Valley it is on a much smaller scale and generally consists of short-term and/or part-time jobs such as child care, yard maintenance, fuel gathering, and temporary construction work. Consistent informal work opportunities like day labor are virtually unknown in Golden Valley, although a limited number of informal construction and maintenance jobs do emerge there from time to time. Similarly, the opportunities for informal vending such as flea markets[6] are scarce in Golden Valley, which lacks a permanent informal market of this kind. Occasionally individuals attempt to sell odd junk in a vacant lot in town, but this does not occur regularly and thus does not approach anything like a steady income or livelihood. The illegal economy is also underdeveloped in Golden Valley as compared to large urban settings.

There is little petty theft there, and I may have been one of the only people in the entire valley who regularly locked the doors to my house and car. While some illegal drug production and dealing (particularly marijuana and methamphetamines) does exist there, it is on a much smaller scale, and in 2003 it was mainly the realm of outsiders and social pariahs.

On the other hand, many people engage in significant amounts of subsistence work in Golden Valley, most of which is unheard of in urban settings. The bulk of this type of work is unpaid and heavily focused on self-provisioning in the forms of hunting, fishing, fuel gathering, growing gardens, and raising livestock. For many people these activities are simultaneously hobbies that they enjoy and serious work that is vital for their family's survival. Growing up in poverty or near-poverty conditions in Golden Valley helped prepare most of my respondents for the possibility of surviving it as adults. While few had hoped to be poor adults, most were grateful for the kinds of survival skills and abilities that their hard upbringings had provided them. Although most would happily become less reliant on these skills if they were to become unnecessary, they were appreciative of the security they felt in knowing they could survive on very low incomes.

Scholars of poverty in both the urban and rural setting have described the various ways in which the poor make do.[7] In urban settings these coping strategies range from those that are consistent with mainstream cultural norms to those that explicitly resist the mainstream.[8] Researchers who study urban drug dealers find that their behaviors and coping strategies are often based within a "backlash" culture that disdains white mainstream values in favor of street toughness and focuses on the perceived financial rewards of illegal activities such as the drug trade.[9] Economically, these strategies may be sensible, promising potentially higher earnings than most low-skill jobs in the legal workforce. The existence of the resistance culture allows individuals to preserve self-esteem and social standing while pursuing economic gain through ethically and legally questionable means.

In urban communities, heterogeneity in cultures, values, and activities allows for competing options for surviving poverty while retaining dignity. Social microclimates can influence which strategies are chosen and which are seen as inaccessible or irrational.[10] For some, the frequency and proximity of illegal activities allows them to be viewed as morally

appropriate.[11] For others, morality continues to be constructed in opposition to illegal pursuits. As Lamont argues, adherence to mainstream
moral standards often allows individuals to maintain self-worth when
they are unable to achieve success in economic terms.[12] Thus, despite
the lure of illegal opportunities, many individuals in the urban setting
prioritize mainstream morality over economic maximization. Edin and
Lein[13] and Newman[14] found that poor single mothers and low-wage
workers tended to choose the most legal and morally accepted coping
strategies over more economically lucrative but illegal ones because
these activities provided them with greater "self-respect." Gowan[15] and
Duneier[16] found that, even among homeless populations, some individuals chose less profitable informal work activities over either drug dealing or panhandling because they provided greater self-esteem through
the connection to mainstream American morality and work ethic.

As these diverse studies suggest, in the urban setting poor individuals are often able to choose between economic maximization and cultural optimization.[17] The same does not necessarily hold true in rural
areas, in which mainstream American culture is often more pervasive
and hegemonic[18] and alternative lifestyles such as illegal activities are
less plentiful.[19] In rural communities, survival strategies tend to be heavily influenced by local cultural and gender norms,[20] which often dictate
a preference for informal work and self-provisioning.[21] Such culturally
appropriate provisioning activities as gardening, woodcutting, hunting,
and fishing are often supplemented by barter and trade in rural communities.[22] Furthermore, struggling families will often choose only those
coping activities that are consistent with local cultural ideals such as
self-sufficiency, even when this means cutting back on what they con-
sume.[23] Additionally, it is generally found that public assistance use is less
common among the rural poor than the urban poor[24] and often carries
with it a powerful stigma.[25]

Within the literature that looks at informal work activities and poverty
survival, rural subsistence activities are relatively understudied,[26] as are
the ways in which these culturally appropriate adaptations are encouraged and enforced through social support and sanction.[27] Wilson suggests that small rural communities are more cohesive than many urban
communities.[28] As discussed in the introduction and chapter 1, Golden
Valley is also much less diverse than most urban areas, both ethnically
and economically. But as previous researchers have noted, even in the

absence of clear class differences, social distinctions may arise based on noneconomic factors such as behavioral and moral norms.[29]

According to Lamont, morality can allow those of low social and economic status to locate themselves above others of similar or even higher status.[30] Sayer similarly argues that moral criteria are used by social groups to distinguish between themselves and that moral considerations often constrain economic activities.[31] In Golden Valley, moral worth has evolved into a form of symbolic capital. This "moral capital" allows the poor to create distinctions among themselves in the absence of significant economic capital.[32] Perceptions of individuals' moral worth are often based on their coping behaviors, including how much they do or do not work and their involvement in illegal activities. A person's moral status contributes to more than just his or her reputation, however. Those who are perceived as having lower moral worth are often denied access to the community's increasingly rare jobs, as well as to many forms of community-level charity. Thus, moral capital can be traded for economic capital in the form of job opportunities and charity or social capital in the form of community ties and social support.[33]

Although non-work-related behaviors such as drug and alcohol abuse also contribute heavily, a large component of moral capital comes from individual and family-level coping strategies. Such strategies carry with them varying degrees of social acceptance. As Wilson hypothesizes, unlike in the urban ghetto, in more cohesive and stable communities like Golden Valley, residents "may be able to exercise a range of illegal or unacceptable solutions to their problems, but the widely held mores of their community, reinforced by economic and social resources that keep the community stable, strongly pressure them to refrain from such activity."[34] Sayer suggests that values and the shame they can engender among those who do not adhere to them are common controlling factors in tight-knit communities. He explains that "the stronger the commonality of values, the greater the possibilities for shaming."[35] In Golden Valley the cohesion of the community results in the establishment of clear definitions of appropriate and inappropriate behaviors, which translate into judgments of deserving versus undeserving poor. Consequences of being deemed "undeserving" range from shame and self-loathing to exclusion from many parts of social and economic life there.

My findings from Golden Valley suggest that the small size, cultural homogeneity, and lack of anonymity in a small rural community together can create greater social pressure on the poor to be culturally acceptable according to the existing standards. For those whose coping strategies are not morally adequate according to local norms, the result is often community-level censure that further affects their quality of life and chances for eventually escaping poverty. On the other hand, as discussed above, those who have higher moral capital generally have more access to both social and economic capital. In this way the rural setting differs substantially from the urban, which allows for a greater range of survival strategies that are acceptable within separate subcultural spheres.[36] This constriction of acceptable possibilities with regard to economic survival has numerous consequences for Golden Valley's poor, including that many choose to exclude themselves from most of the nation's formal poverty-alleviation programs.

Coping Strategies

Those who either lack jobs or whose incomes are inadequate must choose between several available survival options in Golden Valley. By far the most popular and respected of strategies are those related to subsistence food provision. These include hunting and fishing as well as growing sizable gardens and raising livestock. The first two options are almost universally practiced as cherished pastimes by Golden Valley's men, whether or not they rely on them for sustenance. Hunting and fishing are important and pervasive parts of Golden Valley's culture and cited by almost every one of the male respondents as their favorite hobbies and main reasons for remaining there. They represent a man's first line of defense against economic problems as well as his tie to the land and to historic forms of the male provider role. Being the most highly valued of the local subsistence options, they are also the best way for a poor man to contribute nonmonetarily to his family's basic needs with little loss of respectability. They are practiced legally as well as illegally by people who cannot afford the proper licensing or who cannot limit themselves to the short designated hunting seasons. As the son of a game warden explained, enforcement sometimes ignores those infractions committed by people in need:

> Wintertime's hard for everybody, and things can be overlooked that make children's lives better.... When people don't have money for food, there's lots and lots of food just runnin' around the woods. And when you're truly broke, it's something that has to be done.

For the truly poor, however, hunting and fishing are nonetheless in-sufficient to meet all of their daily needs. Thus, among those who are struggling financially, subsistence activities are generally combined with several other possible coping strategies, whose social interpretations cover the spectrum from acceptability to contempt (see Figure 1). Having women enter the workforce, either in addition to or in lieu of men, has always been one option among Golden Valley's poor, and it is becom-ing more and more commonplace and socially acceptable since the mill closure. In addition, particularly for younger couples, family support also plays an important role in keeping struggling individuals and fami-lies afloat. Although few people's parents have significant amounts of money to lend, a number of struggling young couples mentioned rely-ing on family support with some frequency when their own resources were stretched too tight. Poor families in Golden Valley often create networks of support similar to those found in urban communities,[37] rely-ing on one another for money, child care, and temporary housing. While receiving help from family members is not the same as working oneself, it does nonetheless keep one tied to the community's work ethic. Family help implies that someone in the family or extended family is a worker, and thus social capital in the form of family ties can also contribute to moral capital.

Also generally accepted and often used are the opportunities that Golden Valley offers for living rent-free or for very low rent. This strat-egy is generally available only to those with long histories and/or social ties in the valley, although occasionally newcomers like me manage to find such situations through networking. Many people have inherited their parents' or grandparents' properties and occupy them. For other financially strapped families, there is the curious but common custom of "caretaking." Caretaking generally implies little to no rent on a property that the tenants are allowed to inhabit in return for providing basic maintenance on it. My own living situation was considered a caretak-ing position, as the rent was well below market rates. The custom of allowing struggling families to caretake properties is one of the less openly acknowledged ways in which Golden Valley's more prosperous community members take care of its less fortunate. It is becoming in-creasingly more common since the mill closure as men who want to stay securely employed and make higher salaries generally have needed to move elsewhere to find better jobs. While many mill workers originally

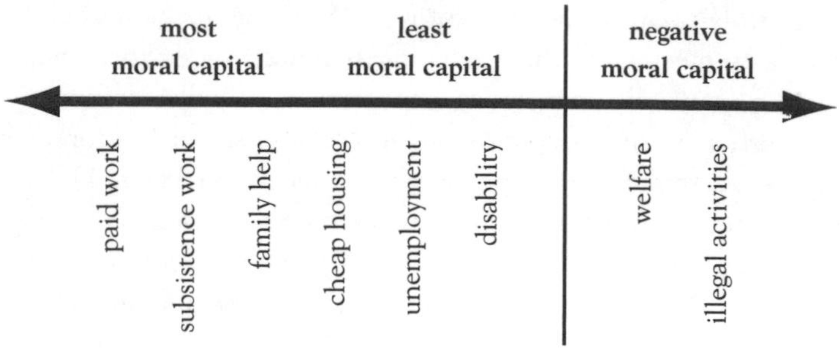

	most moral capital			least moral capital			negative moral capital	
paid work	subsistence work	family help	cheap housing	unemployment	disability		welfare	illegal activities

Figure 1. Moral value of coping strategies.

left their families behind in Golden Valley when they moved to follow the work, over time whole families ended up moving out semipermanently as well. Like my landlords, their plans were often to return to Golden Valley for their retirement and thus they chose to hold onto their homes and properties there. As those who could afford to move have left the valley, many of those who remain have benefited by having their cost of living greatly reduced through the discounted or nonexistent rents. While most of these caretaking properties are nowhere near as nice as the one I rented, they at least provide shelter to families who might otherwise be without it. Cheap housing does not necessarily contribute to a person's social capital, but is generally available only to those who already have significant amounts of social capital in Golden Valley.

For those who still cannot manage to make ends meet or who are unable to take advantage of other coping strategies, government assistance is the last resort. Not all forms of assistance are equal in the minds of Golden Valley residents, however, and there is a clear hierarchy of social acceptability imposed on the various income maintenance programs. The most acceptable of these is unemployment insurance, which a large proportion of local men receive at some point during the year. The few men's jobs that remain in Golden Valley are mostly seasonal. The U.S. Forest Service lays off most of its local employees in the winter. The rare logging and field and brush jobs in the area are similarly seasonal in nature. Even many of the jobs that do not have seasonality built into them are nonetheless unstable. The few small-scale sawmilling operations that remain have trouble retaining all of their employees and are constantly laying off those with the least seniority. For men who

are either seasonally unemployed or temporarily laid off, unemployment insurance is an acceptable way to survive until work reappears. It
is rarely conceived of as government assistance as such, but rather is
viewed as income that a person deserves and has basically worked for.

After unemployment insurance the most socially acceptable form of
government aid is disability assistance. This benefit is provided by Social
Security, mostly in the form of Supplemental Security Income (SSI) as
well as some Disability Insurance (DI). The two programs have the
same eligibility rules but differ in that SSI is means-tested, while DI is
available only to workers who have previously paid into it, regardless of
income.[38] Together, they are known locally as simply "disability" and
their receipt is exceptionally common in Golden Valley. Logging and
sawmill jobs are exceedingly dangerous in nature, and almost all of the
men I met who had ever worked in either had been seriously injured at
some point. One 30-year-old former logger described it this way: "I don't
know if you've ever even seen logging operations, but everything out
there is tryin' to kill you. Everything." Many of the tasks required by both
logging and mill work require the use of dangerous equipment, from
heavy machinery to chain saws. Much of the work also includes heavy
lifting and exposes employees to the risk of being struck by large, sharp,
and heavy objects. Along with injuries to the hands and feet, severe
back and neck injuries were common among my sample. Between the
employees' typical lack of health care and the companies' resistance to
paying for work-related medical concerns, injuries often did not receive
proper treatment, causing them to progress into chronic and eventually
debilitating conditions. Nearly 40 percent of Golden Valley's men between ages 21 and 64 are disabled, and 76 percent of the disabled are
not employed. This compares to 21 percent disabled and 40 percent of
the disabled being unemployed in the state of California as a whole.[39]

Although startlingly high, Golden Valley's disability rates have risen
only slightly since 1990, and the percent of the disabled who are without work has fallen marginally over this time period.[40] Yet the belief
locally is that the receipt of disability is on the rise and directly related
to both welfare reform and the community's economic collapse. It is
difficult to discern how many of the disabled might be able to work;
while some "disabled" subjects admitted they could work but chose instead to receive disability assistance, others made many attempts to continue working despite serious injuries. While most recipients of disability

do have some sort of valid claim, it is likely that many of them would still work if there were more jobs available. Fifty-year-old Susan Elders, frustrated by her difficulties in finding reliable workers to do maintenance on her rental properties, explained, "[Since] they can only stay on welfare a couple of years, what I'm seeing now is all of a sudden there's an increase in disability. People are trying to find whatever excuses to get on disability."

Despite insinuations of its abuse, disability receipt is still much more socially valued than the receipt of welfare because disability carries with it the assumption of a dangerous, hardworking past. Because it is socially constructed as a "deserved" form of aid, disability allows a person to receive government assistance while still manifesting some degree of symbolic work ethic. But as Susan suggests, in many families it does seem as if disability assistance has evolved into a new form of welfare, suited to the conditions of Golden Valley's current economy. While women's workforce participation is becoming widespread and necessary, men are increasingly falling out of the workforce and remaining unattached to it. For many of these men disability assistance has become their main tactic for contributing monetarily to the household without holding a job. Women tend to be accepting of this scenario, and even those whose patience with out-of-work husbands was clearly beginning to wear thin made such comments as, "It's not his fault. He can't help it that he's injured." There is a growing incidence and acceptance in Golden Valley of stay-at-home fathers on disability, while the mothers go off to work and contribute substantially to the family budgets.

Means-tested welfare options are considered by most to be the last resort. While about a quarter of respondents admitted to having received some form of welfare (including cash assistance and/or food stamps) at some point, most considered the experience to be humiliating, particularly given Golden Valley's small size and insularity, which make it difficult to receive welfare anonymously.[41] Receiving welfare was so shameful and stigmatizing that many people in Golden Valley confessed to having traveled an hour or more to spend their food stamps in other communities just to avoid being seen by people they knew. The following exchange between employed couple Bud and Emily Richards provides an example of the community's typical stance toward means-tested assistance programs and of the distinction made between unemployment due to "laziness" and that due to physical disability. They discuss the one time they accepted food stamps for two months while Emily was pregnant and Bud had been laid off from work:

EMILY: It was totally embarrassing, and we'd drive to Miner's Gulch to use our food stamps. We couldn't bear to use them in Golden Valley! Everybody knows everybody. So there's no way. I think we drove to Miner's Gulch and went to Hillview or something. It was only for a couple of months, but it was bad.

Why was it so bad if so many people use them here?

BUD: That's a good question...
EMILY: I don't know. I think it's because I don't want to be considered lazy or a freeloader or something like that. You just don't want that stigma.
BUD: I don't want to be one of them.
EMILY: You want people to think you're a hard worker—and, you know, we pride ourselves on that. There's no reason why we shouldn't work. We have not really any physical problems.

Welfare is viewed as qualitatively different from either unemployment or disability assistance, mostly because it does not carry with it the requirement of past work experience. As argued by Fraser, means-tested welfare programs position the recipient as "dependent clients" versus the "rights bearing beneficiaries" who receive unemployment or disability assistance.[42] In Golden Valley, while these latter forms of government assistance are deemed acceptable, welfare is almost always discussed with either disdain or shame, and welfare recipients are often characterized not just as deadbeats, but as alcoholics and drug addicts as well.[43]

In Golden Valley welfare is associated with run-down houses, children whose basic needs are not being met, and parents who are lazy and unproductive. The receipt of welfare is absolutely incongruent with the work ethics of Golden Valley, and thus those who consider themselves hardworking try desperately to avoid it or at least keep their tenure on it brief. Those who receive welfare for any length of time are quickly labeled and shunned, deepening their marginalization well beyond that caused by poverty itself in Golden Valley. People who dare to use their food stamps at the local grocery stores are often ridiculed by the checkout clerks within moments of exiting the store—a practice I witnessed multiple times over my year there. In the minds of most Golden Valley residents, living off of welfare is only slightly less detestable than selling drugs, and most believe that the two go hand in hand to some degree.

Drug dealing is the most socially reprehensible of coping strategies in Golden Valley, particularly if the drug being pedaled is crystal meth (methamphetamines), the most commonly produced and abused local substance. Marijuana growing and selling was common for a time in the 1980s, but the federal crackdown during this period caused many local growers to seriously scale back their operations, if not quit the business entirely. Several people complained bitterly, without a hint of irony, that marijuana production in Northern California has been taken over by Mexican cartels that bring in their own illegal workers.[44] Those who still sell drugs on a large scale are generally isolated from the community, both as a form of self-protection as well as a result of social censure around their lifestyle choice. While the local marijuana industry has constricted[45] and become dominated by outside interests, methamphetamine production and selling in the area has been on the rise, and numerous subjects made reference to specific trailer parks that they believed housed crystal meth producers and dealers.

While many long-standing community members are believed to be users of crystal meth, the purveyors are generally believed to be mostly transient outsiders who moved there from urban areas. My ethnographic research, as well as the drug busts that occurred in Golden Valley and the surrounding region over my year there, substantiated this belief to a large degree. There were exceptions to this rule, however, including the largest scandal of my year in Golden Valley. A local man from a large and well-established family was charged with maintaining a drug house and providing marijuana, alcohol, and methamphetamines to minors, as well as requiring sex from teenage girls in return, leading to both statutory and forcible rape. The charges went back nearly a decade. This horrifying discovery came as a shock to most in the town, even though the family was known to have struggled with alcoholism and drug problems for generations. The desire to believe that only outsiders were capable of selling drugs led many to ignore and deny the existence of locally born drug dealers. But regardless of their roots in and ties to the community, the outsider status of drug dealers, along with the intense social disdain for their activity, made them such pariahs as to be generally absent from most of the more conventional social settings and personal networks. Their marginalization may also help explain why drug dealing was a survival strategy that was seldom chosen by those with long-standing community ties.

Unlike in the urban setting,[46] in Golden Valley there are no competing cultural norms that sanction the drug trade. Being associated with drugs in any way—including as a user—is hugely stigmatized in Golden Valley and considered antithetical to its work ethic. While it is not uncommon for teenagers to "party" during high school, adults are expected to quickly end this behavior. Continued use, and in particular any association with selling drugs, is highly damaging to an adult's reputation. Thus, most poor individuals who are integrated into the community do not consider drug dealing to be among their possible strategies for surviving poverty.

Because of the community's high cohesion, most people's coping activities are known in Golden Valley and substantially influence their status as upstanding citizens versus deadbeats. Maintaining reputations for high moral standing can be immensely important to the poor because moral status is tradable for social and economic capital. Those who are believed to be morally upright members of the community are much more likely to be beneficiaries of ad hoc community charity in times of need. As discussed in chapter 1, when asked why they stayed in Golden Valley, subjects commonly talked about feeling secure in the knowledge that "the whole town will stand behind you in a time of need." Twenty-five-year-old Nicole Goodman, whose husband is employed by a local business and has long-standing ties within the community, explained:

> If your house burns down, like somebody's did recently, everybody's like, "What can we do, what can we do?" They come right over and start donating and helping. There's not money here, but everybody teams together to take care of everybody.

But the charity is not equally available to everyone. Julie Mitchell, a 26-year-old day-care provider and married mother of four, talked at length about the community organizing pie sales and spaghetti feeds to raise money to help residents with serious health problems. But her husband interrupted her to explain, "But see, that's for only the known people in town. . . . You want to be known in a good way." In Golden Valley, social capital and moral capital can together be traded for economic capital when a poor family or individual is truly in need. But the lack of either closes these doors to the community's generosity.

Similarly, perceptions of moral worth often play a significant role in deciding who gets jobs in Golden Valley, particularly among the low- and semi-skilled. Employers frequently complain about the lack of hardworking applicants who can be trusted to come to work each day. Those who are considered less than hardworking are seldom taken seriously. During my year in Golden Valley, I spent time observing at businesses in town. In multiple instances, employees commented to me on the likelihood of the applicant receiving a job. His chances generally rested on the impression they had of him, including his perceived work ethic, his known history as a drug user, or being from a "troubled family" that was known for long-term welfare receipt. While it is possible for individuals to transcend their families' negative reputations, this is generally done only through some combination of cutting ties and clearly manifesting behaviors that contrast with those of the larger family or clan. Generally, only those individuals who had better reputations and higher moral capital were considered for jobs in Golden Valley, regardless of how sincere they might have been in their desires to work. For those with low moral capital, the stigma of their pasts and presents became barriers to their futures.

The following three case studies illuminate the ways in which the poor struggle to survive and how the strategies they choose determine their moral capital in the community. The particular combination of work activities and government aid that an individual or couple chooses heavily influences their status within the community, which further influences their likelihood of receiving jobs and in-kind forms of community help. All three examples are married or cohabitating couples, the still-dominant family form in Golden Valley, and they are presented hierarchically from most to least social status. The three cases were chosen from among twenty-nine couples in the sample because they represent typical patterns that were found throughout the interview sample and ethnographic work in Golden Valley. Each case represents a different space on the continuum from most to least moral capital and helps illustrate the ways in which coping strategies combine with other behaviors to produce or reduce moral capital. The examples also illustrate the consequences of the addition or subtraction of this form of symbolic capital.

"Not Real into Handouts": *Liza Wright and Tommy Patterson*

Liza Wright and Tommy Patterson are a young couple in their late 20s who are well known and well liked in Golden Valley. They are not married, although they have a child together and they refer to one another as husband and wife.[47] They plan to get married someday but are waiting until they have enough money to afford a "real" wedding. Their names had been provided to me by several informants, who described them as nice people, good role models, and hardworking employees. Although both drank and used drugs during high school, they cleaned up as soon as Liza became pregnant, positioning themselves for responsible adulthood. This transition away from substance abuse occurred early and completely; by the time Liza was ready to look for work, she was known as a responsible and stably "married" mother rather than a partying teenager. They are now considered to be among the pillars of Golden Valley's younger generation, and their participation is often sought for community-organized events.

I knew Liza somewhat already because she worked as a clerk in one of the local grocery stores and was friends with a few of the women I knew in Golden Valley. When I arrived at their small house on a Saturday afternoon, Tommy was dressed to go riding on his ATV (all-terrain vehicle) with a friend, one of his favorite activities. Their 2-year-old son, Benjamin, and several of his cousins played in the front yard. Their rented house was small and dark, with sparse furnishings. It felt like the temporary home they planned it to be, since they hoped to buy a house of their own in Golden Valley in the near future. Both had lived in other places at times but planned now to stay. As Liza explained, "As long as we can survive here, we will."

Liza and Tommy survive through a combination of work and informal strategies that mostly exclude any form of government assistance. Liza works part-time as a receptionist in the local doctor's office and part-time at the grocery store. Tommy worked in logging like his father until the bottom fell out. Now he does construction work locally, which is seasonal and insecure but pays enough for them to survive most of the year when combined with occasional side jobs and Liza's income. There are times when they are not able to cover all of their expenses, but somehow they always get by. According to Tommy, who was raised to be independent and hardworking, the trick to survival in Golden Valley is really wanting to work and being willing to do even the less desirable (men's) jobs. For the truly hardworking, there will always be work of some kind.

> LIZA: There's been times when, you know, you kind of penny-pinch or wonder how you're gonna pay your next bill or whatever. But it's never been to the point where we said that we have to leave.
>
> TOMMY: The people that have a hard time surviving here are the people that nitpick their jobs, that can't set their pride aside and do certain jobs because they're beyond that. If you pretty much do what's available, it's not that bad. You just gotta hit it every day, usually five or six days a week. But you can.

For a while Tommy worked in the Bay Area, where he made a great deal more money than he could in Golden Valley. However, when Liza discovered she was pregnant with Benjamin, he decided to move back to be with her. Now Liza is the one with the more stable employment, but Tommy doesn't worry about finding work despite the seasonality of almost everything he's ever done. There is always something for a man like him to do: "Somebody always needs their driveway shoveled, or some firewood, somethin' like that. You just gotta do it." Tommy believes that with the right work ethic and an open mind, anyone can find work in Golden Valley:

> Well, everything's seasonal layoffs, but I haven't been without a job since high school. It's worked out pretty good. It's not easy. You gotta, like I said, you gotta just take what's available. You can't be real picky about what you'll do. You can't hold out for management, you know. You just do what's there, even if it doesn't pay as much as what you'd like to make or what everybody's making around the state. Everybody always says, "Well, I won't do that," you know, "Well, that's just too cheap." Well, you know, rent here, you can't compare it to the rest of the state either. It's so much cheaper to live here. So it all equals out.

For Tommy and Liza, there seems to be just enough work to get by. This does not mean that they can always afford to pay their bills, however. Seasonal work makes it difficult to stay on top of the expenses, since, as Liza put it, "unemployment [insurance] will never pay what your wages are gonna be like." They admitted that the seasonal unemployment to which Tommy is subject often makes it difficult for them to be self-sufficient. Luckily, they have their families to fall back on. Liza's mother provided all of their son's diapers and wipes until he was toilet trained, an expense she estimated at $60 per month. And Tommy's parents often help them through crises, including bailing them out when Tommy incurred major fines and expenses due to a drunk-driving arrest. It was after this traumatic experience, and before Benjamin's birth, that Tommy and Liza decided to stop their drinking and drug use. His parents' support helped turn his accident into a catalyst for change rather than an event that pushed them over the edge. For Tommy and Liza, economic capital borrowed from family helped them to begin to access moral capital as independent adults. They are grateful for this kind of help, although since the accident and the birth of their son they have come to relish their roles as responsible and independent adults.

> LIZA: His parents pulled through for us because they loaned us the money to pay off one of the fines, which really could've been, you know, meaning him going to jail. But for the most part, we just kind of made it on our own. And yeah, you know, every now and then you miss a bill and the collector will call. But you know, we always catch back up eventually on our own.

Although they try to take care of themselves and be independent, Tommy and Liza feel a certain security in knowing that their family will be there for them when they need it, and both are grateful: "We're fortunate that we have family that helps us in the real tough times." They compare their lives against those of people who lack this kind of support and feel that they are lucky. Like many young couples in Golden Valley, Tommy and Liza's needs are modest, and they feel privileged to have their basic needs met most of the time:

> LIZA: On Christmas Day we were drivin' to the Bay Area, and we were on Route 7. And out in the middle of nowhere, Christmas morning, there's this guy layin' on the ground.
> TOMMY: Yeah, this guy's sleepin' in the pullout on the side of the road.
> LIZA: On Christmas morning.
> TOMMY: And I just said, "We got it good. We're not layin' in the dirt on Christmas with nobody." You know, we don't know why he was there. It could'a been his fault, I don't know. But still, we're lucky. We're fortunate.
> LIZA: Yeah. I mean, we're goin', drivin' down to the city to spend a big Christmas with my family. It could be a lot worse. Like, well, we didn't . . .
> TOMMY: We're healthy. We have all our arms and legs, you know.
> LIZA: We eat every night.

For Tommy and Liza, the good life is to be found not in material success, but in the security of knowing that they have social support, both
from their families and the community at large. They can rely on this
continued support in part because their choices and lifestyle provide
them with high moral capital. The only government assistance they
regularly accept is unemployment insurance, which in their minds is
earned and deserved. They have never accepted welfare, disability, or
food stamps, and had only briefly received Medi-Cal, California's subsidized health insurance, when Liza was pregnant. As soon as they could
afford to, they purchased health insurance for Benjamin on their own.
The same set of beliefs that lead Tommy to take any job he can find
also make him wary of accepting government aid of any kind:

> It makes me feel better that we're buying insurance, anyway. I'm not
> real into handouts. But if my family needs 'em, I'll take 'em. But I'd
> rather not. I'd rather work an extra job or work a couple extra days or
> somethin' and take care of 'em myself. But that's just the upbringing
> I have.

Living near the edge is a source of some stress but not a source of
humiliation for Tommy and Liza. By focusing only on survival strategies that are consistent with Golden Valley's ideal work ethics, they are
able to provide for themselves not a life of affluence, but of self-respect
and social standing. Their strategies tend toward the most socially acceptable; they combine seasonal work and family support with unemployment insurance and Liza's full-time, low-wage work. The result for
them is access to both economic capital in the form of jobs and social
capital in the form of community ties and support. They still have trouble
making ends meet at times. But because they stay firmly tied to the paid
labor market and avoid the more stigmatized coping strategies, they are
able to maintain good reputations and high self-esteem as well as high
moral capital within the community (see Figure 2). They are proud of themselves and happy with their lot and are well respected in Golden Valley.
Their high moral and social capital mean that both Liza and Tommy
are able to feel secure in their abilities to find jobs there, and neither
has ever been unemployed for longer than a few months in Golden
Valley. Because they are so well liked and their work ethics are so ad-
mired within the community, it is unlikely that either will ever be out
of work for long. Although they are happy with their situation, they
hope that their hard work will pay off someday in the form of a home of

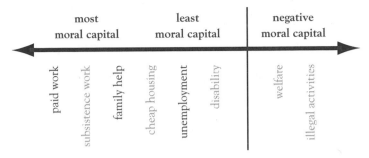

Figure 2. Tommy and Liza's strategies: high moral capital.

their own, in which they can manifest their pride outwardly. As Liza explained, buying a house takes priority over having a wedding: "You know, if we get a house, we'll be able to do [the wedding] in our backyard, and how cool would this be?"

"You Worked for What You Got": Joyce and George Woodhouse

When Joyce Woodhouse returned my call about sitting for an interview, she told me that she and George had just come back from a five-day salmon-fishing trip. I asked her what might be a good time to do the interview and she replied, "Well, we're home now." A half hour later I approached the Woodhouse home, a small, boxy cabin with additions tacked onto it on several sides. The siding was not painted to match, giving the house a patchwork effect from the outside. The front yard was filled with several vehicles that appeared to be in working condition, including a camper, a truck, a large SUV, and a dune buggy. The backyard was littered with heavy equipment, the remains of George's failed construction business. The neighbors on all sides were trailer homes. Inside, the house was cluttered and crowded, and we sat in a small living room area that wasn't fully distinct from the kitchen. Clothes hung along one wall in the open room. Several windows had blankets drawn across them rather than curtains. The wall above the couch was filled to capacity with pictures of their family, including children of their own as well as numerous children they had helped raise and shelter over the years. George and Joyce were both in their early 50s, and their large frames contrasted with the low ceilings and tight rooms of the small house.

Neither Joyce nor George has ever known a life much different than this one. Joyce grew up in this very house, and they are proud of the additions they built, which took it from a single-room cabin into a house with a separate bedroom and bathroom space. She inherited the cabin from her parents, and thus the additions represent most of what they have ever invested into their home. Joyce and George have always lived in cramped conditions but consider themselves to be among the respectable and hardworking poor. When they were younger, Joyce worked as a waitress and George worked in the mill. Eventually an unfortunate series of car- and work-related accidents forced Joyce out of the workforce and onto disability. She fought hard to continue working despite the string of health problems, but eventually gave in and accepted her disability. As George sadly observed, "So now she sits home and watches TV."

George also worked for most of his life, and for a while his mill salary kept the family afloat. Unfortunately for the Woodhouses, the "family" grew to unmanageable sizes at times and his salary was not sufficient for feeding so many extra mouths. Like many other poor but morally upstanding couples in the community, George and Joyce regularly took in children whose parents were physically abusive or drug and alcohol addicted. The question "How many kids did you have?" elicited the following response:

> JOYCE: I had two kids, a girl and a boy. They were four years apart. How many kids did we raise? About two hundred or more.
> GEORGE: That's no exaggeration. That's, we were the—didn't drink and do drugs and stuff like that. So everybody that was havin' drug problems and alcohol problems [at home] and domestic violence, stuff like that, would come to our house because they could sleep here and eat.

The Woodhouse home became known as a safe place for teenagers to go to to escape from troubled families. Joyce and George remembered during holidays like Christmas and New Year's having as many as thirty-five children staying with them at one time. I had a difficult time imagining how the small home could have possibly accommodated so many people. The Woodhouses accepted their roles as community parents with some ambivalence, but it was clear through their stories that they cared deeply for the children they took in. However, providing food for so many people put a strain on them financially, to which Joyce responded by increasing their subsistence activities. Without a job, she contributed to the family's diet by catching as many fish as she could, even when it meant exceeding the legal catch limit:

> GEORGE: I would go to work at the mill. And most all of my paycheck was going for groceries and stuff to feed all of 'em. Well, Joyce would go up to the reservoir, the lake, and fish. If she caught fish, then we'd have fish and, like, potatoes and stuff like that. If she didn't fish, then we'd have potatoes. Well, then the kids got started gettin' her up in the morning and sayin', "Let's go to the reservoir." So they'd go up and fish and stuff, you know, as a family-type deal.
>
> JOYCE: To tell you the truth, I was goin' to the reservoir [at] six in the morning. I set there till dark. And there was some older men that was settin' there, and they knew I was catchin' more than what I should. The kids would come up and check on me and everything, and they'd take the limit home with them. And I'd just stay there and fish.

As they got older and their own children moved out, the Woodhouses stopped taking in other children as regularly, although they still continue to help feed and occasionally house the children of their poor, alcoholic neighbors. Even with fewer mouths to feed, though, their financial situation has not improved. There were better times in the recent past, during which a number of the vehicles in their front yard, including the camper, were purchased. Their days of relative security and ease turned out to be short-lived, however, and Joyce and George now regret having spent so much of their money rather than saving it for the future. George worked at the mill for twenty-five years until an accident there forced him to take a year off. By the time his back healed enough for him to return to work, the mill was preparing to close and would not rehire him. Instead, George invested in construction equipment and tried to start his own business. While he had enjoyed some success at first, by 2003 there was little work left and the Woodhouses were seriously struggling again:

> GEORGE: [We've got] no money, we're broke. Well, we got, we got our own business, a backhoe business, but there's very little backhoe business anymore since they put the sewer system in. So it's getting tough. We were considering halfway moving to Hillview or something like that, just to get employment.

Joyce and George are getting older now, and George worries that it is too late for any change in career. He has looked for other jobs but was unable to find anything locally and complained that no one would hire him to do decent work. Their finances are being stretched thinner than ever, and both worry about how they will survive retirement, particularly with Joyce's failing health. But for now they survive as they always have. Their house is paid for, although there is no extra money available for upkeep or improvements. George still makes a little money with his backhoe business here and there. As for food, they rely heavily on deer they shoot in their yard and fish they catch on trips like the one from which they had just returned. Particularly for Joyce, fishing for food is an integral part of the only lifestyle she has ever known:

> JOYCE: Now, when I was a kid, I was raised on salmon and deer meat. And last year we brought home twenty [salmon], and one of 'em was fifty-four pounds. So we had about six hundred pounds. But that was why we went, was to smoke it and can it so we had it for the winter, to help, you know, with things.

George and Joyce survive poverty through a strategy that focuses on the more highly regarded and traditional of Golden Valley's options. They rely on subsistence food, low-cost housing, and disability assistance in addition to sporadic work—strategies that even when combined are barely enough to keep them clothed and fed. Joyce and George remain among Golden Valley's more respected and valued community members and are active in several local organizations. Joyce accepted disability assistance only after multiple attempts at working proved her unable to continue. And the Woodhouses still work for their food and take care of themselves as best they can, as well as continuing to help those even less fortunate and proactive than themselves. In Golden Valley, manifesting this kind of work ethic, even while living in poverty, is enough to be considered productive community members, although they do not receive quite the same respect as more stably employed couples like Tommy and Liza, nor does George have the same faith in his own ability to be hired locally. His age, combined with his recent time out of the workforce, makes him less attractive to local employers. And while they may contribute to self-esteem and social standing, informal charity activities are not considered on par with work activities. Paid work still remits the highest amount of exchangeable moral capital, and the lack of it is stigmatized by Golden Valley's choosy employers.

Yet despite their obvious poverty and need, their pride and loyalty to local cultural norms compels the Woodhouses to avoid the most stigmatized types of government assistance:

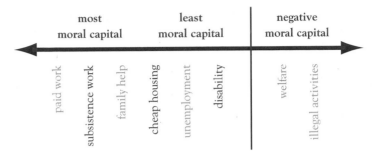

Figure 3. Joyce and George's strategies: medium moral capital.

GEORGE: We don't try to get food stamps or welfare or anything like
that. I mean, basically, we probably could. But I don't know—we
were always brought up that you worked for what you got, you didn't
have welfare and stuff like that. If you didn't work, then you cut
back on what you was eatin' until you got a better job.

JOYCE: It's embarrassing.

The Woodhouses' strategy for survival is socially rational despite seem-
ing economically irrational. While they could live more comfortably on
welfare, they believe—with some reason—that to do so would lessen
their worth as individuals and community members. Although they are
short on cash, their strategy does pay off to some degree in the form of
social capital. They know they can rely on help from the community in
times of need, whether it is the local deputies helping them to deal
with troublesome neighbors or friends helping out when Joyce is ill or
injured. For Joyce and George, being fully accepted members of the
community and the self-esteem that comes from being self-sufficient
outweigh the benefits that welfare income or food stamps might bring.
Ultimately, their strategy pays off in terms of social support, if not economic support as well.

The Taste of Poverty: Angelica (and Jim) Finch

Thirty-eight-year-old Angelica Finch has lived on both sides of the
social acceptability line and has experienced firsthand the ways in which
welfare use and substance abuse are often entwined. Angelica met me
alone as her husband, Jim, did not want to be interviewed. She is a thin
woman with an infectious laugh and an incredibly positive attitude despite all that she has lived through. Angelica's childhood was difficult,

and both her father and later her stepfather were alcoholic and abusive. As a teenager she drifted between her divorced parents' households in Golden Valley and Hillview, eventually settling in Golden Valley for good when she got pregnant at age 17. She soon dropped out of high school under pressure from the school administration that feared, she joked acridly, that pregnancy was contagious. While pregnant she met the man she would eventually marry. Jim Finch was twenty-seven years her senior, had been married and divorced twice already, and had four children with his previous wives. He had worked in the woods for years, but by the time she met him he had gone on disability due to a serious injury. He has never worked much in their twenty years together, and thus any income beyond the disability check has been earned by Angelica herself. Since the couple later had two additional children together, and at times supported his children as well, a disability check alone was never enough money for them. They also had serious drug and alcohol habits to support for their first decade together, which added further expense to their strained budget. According to Angelica, such habits were a common part of life in Golden Valley.

> There's nothing else to do in this valley but drugs and sex. That's how I got knocked up at 17, you know? Really, there's just nothing else to do around here. Even in Hillview you could go to a skateboard park or a movie, or pizza parlor, bowling—there's options.

Despite her substance abuse problems, Angelica was no stranger to work. But as many researchers have found, low-wage work often isn't enough to support an individual, let alone a family.[48] It was difficult for her to find fulfilling and well-paid work, particularly since she had not finished high school. She eventually did get seasonal work with the U.S. Forest Service, which she loved. Unfortunately, after the spotted owl ruling, she was permanently laid off. At that time she began working at one of Golden Valley's remaining grocery stores. Although she hated the environment and the work, she remained in the low-wage and thankless job for nearly a decade. She eventually became so depressed there that she quit working, partially to spend more time with her children. Meanwhile, she had also been attending community college in Hillview and Miner's Gulch to finish her high school equivalency and begin work toward her associate's degree. Pursuing her education put an incredible strain on the family, yet she steadfastly clung to her dream of improving herself. The eventual receipt of her degree boosted both her self-esteem and her earning potential and helped her to land her current job as a low-level administrator at Golden Valley Elementary School. With the higher-paying job, she was able to pull her family out of intense poverty. The worst of her experiences with poverty were now behind her, but she was still haunted by the memories of her days at rock bottom.

Angelica described her life in deep poverty, when her meager salary and Jim's disability check were simply not enough to meet their family's needs. In the beginning their home had been a frequent hangout for her husband's heavy-partying friends, an environment that she felt was conducive only to substance abuse:

> We were so poor. Our home was so miserable. It was just a mobile. My husband owned it free and clear, but it was just a nasty, old, thrashed mobile. It had been the party house. I can remember coming home from the hospital with my daughter, and they had moved a foosball table into the kitchen. And here I am, a brand new mom, 18 years old. If I hadn't had a friend stay with me that first week, I don't know if we would've made it.

In those early years, survival was a constant struggle for Angelica and Jim, particularly while she was going to school full-time. While Jim never worked in the formal sector, he did contribute to the household in the form of subsistence activities, although not all of them were legal, let alone respectable. According to Angelica, his contributions included gathering wood for heat and providing them with stolen electricity:

> He would climb this tree, and he spliced this wire and tied into the other—not anybody else's bill, just the main pole. And he would be out on this limb in the rain. Yeah, because when it would get windy and stormy, it would blow it loose. So he'd go up this tree and out on this limb in the rain, in the winter. It was so scary. It was so awful. And it was the first thing I changed as soon as I could. But for four years all we had was some food stamps and, I don't remember, like $100 in cash aid or whatever. I was trying to go to school in Hillview. I would hit the top of Gold Mountain and turn my engine off and just coast down into the valley to save. I mean, it was that—we were that poor, you know— it was that desperate. If it hadn't been for food programs, the WIC program, food stamps, Medi-Cal, we wouldn't have made it at all. Or I wouldn't have been able to get my education. You know, I would've had to work year round. And I worked seasonally as it was. So, but, oh man, there were some hard times.

In addition to these less socially sanctioned survival strategies, Angelica and Jim also augmented their diet through hunting. Although it was a source of less shame and humiliation, she nevertheless recalled their subsistence diet with distaste:

> And that was one of our other survival tricks, was that deer out the back door. Back when times were hard we had to eat venison. In most places, venison is like a delicacy, a treat. Up here—and I'm not the only one who feels this way—venison is what you eat when there's nothing else to eat, and then that's all you eat. It gets real old real fast.

Therein perhaps lies the difference between hunting as a sport and hunting for survival. For Angelica, deer meat would always be a symbol of poverty, and she hoped never to have to taste it again.

During those hard times, Jim and Angelica's drug and alcohol problems both resulted from and contributed to their misery. When asked if being poor had been stressful for them as a couple, she replied, "Yeah, yeah, and it just leads to that desire to go medicate because you can't see any way out. You're so destitute and struggling, and it's such a struggle." Between the substance abuse and the desperate survival strategies, Angelica suffered much shame during those years. She described feeling marginalized by the community and internalizing a self-hatred so intense that she did not want mirrors in her house, because she could not stand to look at herself. While poverty was the main source of their struggle, and her ultimate goal was to end it, she was well aware that their drug and alcohol abuse would prohibit them from achieving the lifestyle reversal that she desired. For Angelica, ending their addictions was the prerequisite for the substantive changes that occurred afterward. It was not an easy thing for her or Jim to do, as it entailed isolating themselves from all their former friends in addition to quitting the addictions themselves. It was a transition that took four years before it was complete, but in the end it allowed her to make other necessary changes in her work life, her relationship, and eventually her physical environment.

Angelica focused first on ending their addictive habits one by one, then improving their financial situation by seeking better-paid work, and finally improving the conditions of their home. For her, the journey out of addiction and poverty was also a passage from non-personhood into humanity:

When I got our credit all straightened out we got a HUD loan, a $40,000 HUD loan, and we built an addition and brought our trailer up to code. And this was after, this was way after, the major changes in our life. This is what brought us up, brought us up into society, instead of being down pretty much in the gutter—brought us up to be a part of society.

The combination of her education and her current job, along with the changes in their lifestyle and the improvement of their home, meant Angelica and Jim could move from the margins of Golden Valley society into the mainstream. It also meant she could finally come to accept herself:

In the last—since I left the grocery store three years ago, took this job, I have mirrors in my house. I never had a mirror in my house except in the bathroom, ever. And now it's like, they're in every room. I—well, it's trying to lighten the environment, and also I don't mind seeing myself now. I really don't.

Unlike the Woodhouses and Tommy and Liza, the Finches had relied on strategies that were not socially sanctioned in Golden Valley (see Figure 4). Although like the Woodhouses they had relied on subsistence food and disability assistance, and like Tommy and Liza they had relied on unemployment insurance and Angelica working, they had also relied heavily on illegal strategies and means-tested welfare programs. Despite combining all of these strategies at times, they still had endured grinding poverty along with social disdain that made it difficult for them to garner either social support or economic opportunities. With such low moral capital, they were denied access to both living-wage job opportunities and social capital within the community. Changing her lifestyle meant that Angelica could eventually find some acceptance and respect within the community. Had she not invested in her moral capital, she would have faced more barriers to cashing in on her upgraded human capital; it is highly unlikely that Golden Valley Elementary School would have hired a known drug user. Despite her schooling and her many years as a reliable worker for the grocery store, she was unable to find a better-paying job while still using drugs. It was only after clearly establishing herself as clean and sober for several years and cutting most ties to her drug-addicted friends that Angelica was able to find a more respectable job. Although she described the process as lonely and difficult,

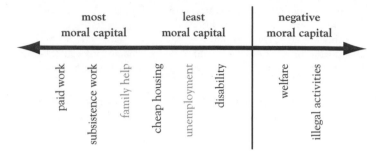

Figure 4. Angelica and Jim's strategies: low moral capital.

she believed it was worth it. While she and Jim now have few friends, they have greater access to economic and social capital than ever before. Over time Angelica has felt increasing acceptance and support from the community and is now less afraid to appear in public. Angelica and Jim's history remains a scar on their reputations, but Angelica has at least finally proved herself worthy of a decent job in Golden Valley.

A Place on the Continuum: Behaviors, Social Status, and Family Background

When Andrew left the office, the personnel manager commented to me that he was from a troubled family, but that he was different from the rest of them. She said he was a good, responsible guy, a hard worker, and the kind of person they might want to hire. (Field Notes, April 15, 2004)

Andrew told me that word had gotten back to him that he was likely to be offered the job that he had applied for, but that his brother James was not. He had heard through a friend that while he was considered responsible and trustworthy, James was seen as a partier with a reputation for having problems. Andrew reacted angrily to this information, explaining to me that his brother was trying hard to clean up his act and be responsible, especially now that he had a child on the way. Andrew, on the other hand, had already decided that he didn't want the job—or any job. (Field Notes, May 1, 2004)

The Value of Family and Social Ties

As the preceding comments and stories suggest, individual behaviors are important factors determining the social acceptance of poverty in Golden Valley, and behaviors that are considered immoral or inconsistent with local work ethics can seriously damage one's moral capital in the community. Yet while individuals' or families' access to moral capital is heavily influenced by their behaviors, behind each set of behaviors is a combination of personal choice and agency as well as preexisting family status and social ties. Thus, it is not random that Tommy and Liza, who both had relatively supportive families, made a much quicker transition from teenage partying to adult moral capital than did Angelica and Jim, whose families were abusive and neglectful. On the other hand, both Joyce and George came from families plagued by alcoholism, neglect, and shifting adult relationships, which nonetheless did not cause them to repeat the same behaviors. A person's place on the continuum is clearly influenced by his or her starting point but not fully predetermined by it. While acquiring moral capital was much easier for those who came into the world with it, the bulk of subjects with high moral capital did not come from families with high amounts of it.

Particularly in this time of transition, in which the meanings of drug and alcohol use have changed rapidly, multiple factors affect people's chances to build or destroy moral capital. These factors include the social ties and economic advantages provided to them, but also personal strengths and choices and their strategies for coping with challenges wrought by the changes the community has been through. One of the hardest pitfalls for many to avoid is the cycle described by Angelica, in which poverty, desperation, and self-hatred coalesce into a spiral of substance abuse and retreat from social and civic life. Substance abuse— and particularly alcohol abuse—is not new to Golden Valley, and both have been endemic for as long as anyone can remember. Nonetheless, as the economic landscape has changed, so has the acceptance of alcoholics and drug addicts, who are now demonized much more than in the past. The shame engendered by being an addict in the community is often similar to that experienced by welfare recipients and drug dealers there, and often similarly isolates individuals from mainstream social networks. Known drug users and alcoholics like Angelica and Jim often find themselves accepted only by others with similar problems and lifestyles, and thus lacking support for ending their addictions as well as for securing better jobs in Golden Valley. Regardless of where or how their substance abuse issues originate, for those with less family and social support to begin with this cycle can be extremely difficult to break.

Spiraling Out of Control: Jeremy Fletcher

I first met Jeremy when he arrived unexpectedly at my door on a Saturday afternoon, looking for my house's owners. He was a scruffy-looking
man in his mid-20s, with long, matted hair and a beat-up down jacket
that he would be wearing every time I saw him subsequently, regardless
of the heat or cold of the day. Jeremy grew up in one of the neighboring
houses and had long known my landlords and their daughter. Being as
vulnerable and isolated as I was out in Deer Run, I did not open the door
for Jeremy but spoke with him through the glass. Despite my refusal to
open the door and my curt answers to his questions, Jeremy engaged me
for quite a while through the glass door, asking me about myself and
sharing with me random details of his own life. The information he
volunteered included the story of how he had been incarcerated for
marijuana growing soon after finishing high school. He had been away
from Golden Valley for years, but had recently returned and wanted to
settle down and make a life for himself there. He spoke optimistically
of finding a job and a place to live. When I told my landlords about the
encounter, they expressed great concern. They explained to me that they
had known Jeremy since he was a child and had witnessed his sad decline into drugs and alcoholism since his high school years. They further
confessed that one of the main reasons that they wanted a caretaker in
their house was that they had long been worried about Jeremy returning to Golden Valley and trying to move into it. They said that he was
troubled and dangerous and that I should not allow him to come near
the house again.

Although I did not, in fact, encounter him again at my home, I did
continue to run into Jeremy throughout my stay in the area. I picked him
up as a hitchhiker one day on my drive from Deer Run to Golden Valley.
As I drove him into town, he spoke rapidly with the manic cadence of
someone high on methamphetamines and told me in a disjointed, un-
focused way of his struggles to get himself together. He began to describe how upon returning to Golden Valley he had immediately fallen
back into his old habits, namely partying too much. He said he knew
that his behavior was destructive, but that he wasn't able to resist the
pull of drugs while living there. He described his current living situation as unstable. For the moment he was staying in his father's house in
Deer Run, but it wasn't a long-term situation since the house was actu-

ally being rented to another family who wouldn't tolerate him squatting there for much longer. Before that he had been staying at his stepgrandparents' house in town, and he expected to return there soon. He did not think that it was a good living environment, however.

Former friends of Jeremy's, who worried about him, concurred with regard to his stepgrandparents but did not step in to help. Most felt that he was in bad shape and untrustworthy and they wanted to avoid interacting with him. Jeremy's family had few resources with which to help him, be they economic, social, or moral. His father was widely considered to be mentally unstable, and no one seemed to know his current whereabouts. Jeremy himself told me that the stepgrandparents with whom he had been staying were also drug and alcohol users, and said he worried about their preteen granddaughter, who lived with them. He expressed a desire to get his own place as soon as he found work, although he couldn't quite articulate what kind of job he expected to find. First, he explained, he had to focus on fixing his broken car. Then he would worry about finding steady work.

Over the months that followed, Jeremy did not appear to get himself together as he had hoped. I often saw him at the bars in Golden Valley and Riverbend, both on weekend nights and during the middle of the day on weekdays. He began to put in applications for work locally. At one business, where he applied for summer field and brush work, I witnessed prospective employers laughing at him after he left the office. They then explained to me that they would never hire someone like him. Their reasons included his history of welfare receipt, along with his basic appearance and poor hygiene and lack of known work history. They also mentioned awareness of his jail time and the reputation for instability that preceded his entrance into their office. To my knowledge, he received no job offers in Golden Valley.

As the months went on, Jeremy continued on his self-destructive path. His appearance continued to deteriorate, and it alone signaled to almost everyone who interacted with him that he was unreliable and untrustworthy. The last time I saw him, he was in line in front of me at the grocery store, paying for his groceries with food stamps. A liquor bottle protruded from the shoulder bag he carried. When I asked him how he was, he immediately launched into a long story about his recent car accident and DUI arrest. He was driving home drunk on the narrow and winding road from Riverbend when a police car approached him from behind. Jeremy panicked and took a turn too fast; he ended up driving his car over the riverbank and destroying it. His injuries didn't stop the police officer from charging him with drunk driving and revoking his license. When I asked him his plans for the future, Jeremy was less certain than ever about what to do next. He said he was seriously considering skipping his court date and leaving town and mentioned both Florida and Alaska as possible destinations. With no car and no money it was unlikely he would make it that far. However, it was also unlikely that he would pull himself together in Golden Valley. The community, which will do so much for its well-respected members in times of medical crisis, often has little help to offer to those with obvious drug and alcohol addictions and seemingly poor work ethics. With little family support and no one else who seemed interested in helping him get his life back on track, it seemed unlikely that Jeremy would ever cross back over from the side of the drug-addicted welfare recipients in Golden Valley.

Changing Conceptions of Substance Use

Stories like Jeremy's are not unusual in Golden Valley, and he was certainly not the only person I met there for whom substance abuse fed into a cycle of desperation that deepened his marginalization and further cut him off from sources of both social and economic capital. In this way the connection between substance abuse and welfare use is often reinforced. As his negative moral capital helped to cut him off from the paid workforce and made community members uninterested in helping him, welfare became the only option left for Jeremy. Thus the cycle continues, and the connection between the two behaviors is further solidified in the minds of Golden Valley's residents.

As discussed earlier, welfare and drug and alcohol use constitute the antithesis of Golden Valley's moral norms. Substance abuse, once common among the hardworking, is now a stigmatized behavior that diminishes the moral value of the individual and separates the deserving from the undeserving poor. While Joyce, George, Liza, and Tommy provide examples of poor families who do not use drugs or alcohol, substance abuse is nonetheless common among Golden Valley's poor and unemployed. A number of my subjects referred to "partying" in their testimonies.

When Angelica Finch used the term several times, I asked her to explain what it meant to her. She replied:

> It's the whole Golden Valley thing. I don't know how many people you've interviewed, but we have huge problems with drugs and alcohol in this community.

Drug and alcohol problems were pervasive in the lives of my subjects. Nearly half said that they had grown up with at least one alcoholic or drug-addicted parent or stepparent. Nearly half had also at least gone through a phase of partying themselves, although most of the more socially integrated subjects had stopped early in their adult lives, like Tommy and Liza had. Most had quit their substance use for similar reasons, believing it would damage their marriages or family lives.

This incompatibility between alcohol and respectability did not always exist in Golden Valley. According to my subjects, back when the woods and sawmills were in full production, Golden Valley's then multiple bars were frequented religiously by the community's hardworking men. At this time, regular drinking was not viewed as antithetical to work ethics in the same way that it presently is. Fifty-five-year-old Jake Robbins grew up with an alcoholic father who was physically and verbally abusive to his wife and children. As an adult, Jake has purposely tried to be a different kind of man than his father. But when asked if he considered his father to be a negative role model, he replied, "Yeah, in a lot of respects. But he did teach me good work ethics." For working men of his father's generation, even serious drinking did not necessarily undermine respectability and was directly connected to the working-man's masculine image. As George and Joyce Woodhouse explained:

> GEORGE: It used to be, when you worked in the woods and all that stuff, you got off work and you went to the bar, and even if you didn't drink you went to the bar. And that's where everybody and all that stuff was.
> JOYCE: You worked hard, you knew how to work hard to make money for the family things, but then again you knew how to play hard, you know. Because you had one way, you did the same the other way. You just had a good time at everything you did.

For the loggers and mill workers of Golden Valley's recent past, masculinity was wound up securely in work. As long as a man worked hard in the woods or mill or similar types of "honest" manual labor, neglect and abuse of family, as well as frequent drinking and even alcoholism, were tolerated as acceptably, and even respectably, masculine flaws.

Vestiges of this form of masculinity are still alive in Golden Valley, although the shifting nature of work in the community has changed the relationship between masculinity and work, as well as the meanings of drug and alcohol use. Alcohol use was once part of a workingman's leisure time and thus synonymous with the work ethics that are still so important to social standing in Golden Valley. Use of stimulant drugs such as methamphetamines, while not widely talked about in those days, was also common among men trying to stay awake through long, tedious mill shifts. Nowadays, however, these activities have taken on new and darker meanings. They are no longer the accepted vice of the workingman, but rather the dysfunction of the deadbeat who lacks sufficient drive and work ethic to compete for the few remaining jobs. As Joyce Woodhouse put it, nowadays "alcohol is basically involved more in the situation of not having a job, not being productive, not being able to have good shoes and clothes for your kids, and food and things." Methamphetamine use, which has grown substantially over the years, is considered even more deplorable than alcoholism. To be respectable, it is now less imperative than before that a person have a paying job (although work status is still important), but he or she must nonetheless have a proper work ethic. Escaping into drugs and alcohol is viewed as giving up on oneself and taking the easy way out, which is inconsistent with hard work.

There was a strong tendency by the sober to create a social distance between themselves and the drug addicted, which had deleterious consequences for individuals like Jeremy Fletcher. The two groups seldom interacted, and the addicts and alcoholics were so often pointedly ignored in public that many were reclusive, and those who did venture out were easy to spot. They would look down when meeting others, thus avoiding eye contact and the friendly greetings that were requisite parts of Golden Valley's social etiquette. The social separation was so entrenched that many of my respondents argued, and seemed to truly believe, that the bulk of drug- and alcohol-addicted people were newcomers to Golden Valley and thus not similar to themselves at all. This was despite abundant evidence to the contrary, and common knowledge that many of Golden Valley's most established families also had the most established drinking and drug problems.

For many residents of Golden Valley, both old and new, partying is a way of life and can be both a response to and a cause of unemployment and poverty. The connection between poverty and substance abuse is well established by researchers[49] and generally taken for granted in Golden Valley, although subjects differed in their opinions on cause versus effect. Research has linked poverty to a number of abusive behaviors as well as to higher incidences of child abuse and neglect, which are then translated into higher risks of substance abuse in adults.[50] While many respondents believed that unemployment and lack of motivation caused people to turn to substance abuse, I also found evidence that having a drug or alcohol problem contributed to unemployment. Not only are the drug and alcohol addicted less likely to be reliable employees, but in a town as small as Golden Valley, they are much less likely to be hired in the first place. Particularly now, in the community's constricted labor market, moral capital plays an important role in deciding who gets the available jobs. Once a man has garnered a reputation for being morally degenerate, it is hard for him to find anyone to invest in him as an employee. In a place of this size, almost everyone's story is known and low moral capital can be a serious deterrent to finding a decent job there. While a recognized family name might help to some degree, if the family as a whole is known to be troubled, name recognition will only hurt a man's chances of finding decent work.

Although this kind of labeling does keep people out of the workforce, it is clearly not the only reason that people are unemployed, and unemployment does appear to be a factor that sometimes contributes to drug and alcohol abuse as well. Jake and Barbara Robbins are in their early 50s and have lived in Golden Valley for most of their lives. Unlike many of Jake's coworkers, he kept his job with Northwest Timber when the mill left and moved with it to Adams, a suburb of Sacramento five hours away, for several years before returning to Golden Valley. When I asked them how the community had changed over their lifetime, Barbara replied that they had fewer friends now than they used to. I asked if this was because people had left, and she replied that the ones who remain are also different now:

Some have left, some have changed their lifestyle, and it doesn't fit ours.

What do you mean by that?

How do you put that? Drugs and stuff.

People you were friends with got into drugs?

Oh, yeah. A lot of them. I don't think—they didn't go [to Adams], a lot of them, and they were too young to retire, you know. Didn't know what to do . . .

What caused them to turn to drugs in your opinion?

Lack of jobs, I think. Yeah—hard on people. It's not that easy, you know.

Jake and Barbara had watched a number of their high school friends' lives deteriorate into drug and alcohol abuse after the mill closed. According to them, these people had once had a decent standard of living and a good work ethic but were unable to cope once they lost their jobs. Most had never known any kind of work other than the mill and didn't know what to do next. Having witnessed their friends' lives fall apart, Jake and Barbara, like many in Golden Valley, believed that substance abuse was a common effect of unemployment there.

On the other hand, many people, including many of Golden Valley's employers, believed that drug and alcohol abuse were the causes rather than the effects of unemployment and clear signs that an individual lacked a proper work ethic and was unworthy of a job. Regardless of where the cycle begins for people, substance abuse creates and reinforces barriers to social and economic capital in Golden Valley. These barriers are then frequently augmented by the lowered self-esteem that many marginalized individuals felt, further contributing to a cycle in which welfare becomes a more viable option. With fewer social ties, individuals are less able to access certain morally acceptable coping strategies. Others, such as paid work, are also inaccessible for most known drug addicts and alcoholics. For some, even subsistence work becomes difficult, as substance abuse inhibits both their health and the motivation necessary to do the required physical labor. Meanwhile, since low moral capital is already established, the perceived repercussions of welfare receipt are further eroded, making it less odious as a remaining survival option. The tendencies of the drug addicted to choose welfare and welfare recipients to turn to drugs contribute to the stigma of both activities, further entrenching the cycle.

Conclusion: Poverty and Moral Worth in Golden Valley

There are those ones that, just their history and what their family's done and what they're doing, you know, you just see the same pattern of going the wrong way. It's kind of hard, especially since you know the families so well. . . . They're just fallin' into a route, into a hole that they'll never get out of. 'Cause nobody'll ever in this town give 'em a chance. (Jeff Taylor, 33-year-old mechanic and married father of two)

Golden Valley is a community in which hard work is believed to be its own reward and is infused with moral value. Although culture is no more static than are structural conditions,[51] Golden Valley's current culture focuses hard on perceived continuity with the community's past. Unlike in the urban setting, within this small community there are few competing cultural repertoires from which to choose. Thus work ethics have come to define who is and who is not an upstanding member of the community, particularly with regard to who is worthy of employment. Behaviors that are inconsistent with the current understanding of what constitutes hard work decrease a person's moral value in the eyes of the community. As this chapter has illustrated, these behaviors include both welfare use and drug and alcohol abuse. Although these are two different issues, in the collective understanding of the community they are inextricably linked through their similar associations with laziness, dependency, and passivity.

As the stories presented here suggest, often the desperately poor and unemployed turn to drugs and alcohol as a solace when things are at their worst. However, they also suggest two mechanisms by which pre-existing substance abuse acts to deepen and exacerbate the experience of poverty and unemployment. It is generally assumed that the substance addicted will be unable to be reliable, steady workers, and my research definitely uncovered numerous cases in which this was true. Often when a drug- or alcohol-addicted individual was hired, he would be less likely to show up to work regularly and more likely to be belligerent and uncooperative with his supervisors. In a tight job market like Golden Valley's, individuals who do not prove to be the best workers rarely keep their jobs for long. On the other hand, as stories like Angelica's illustrate, not all drug addicts or alcoholics are necessarily poor workers. For many it is not their work performance as such, but simply their perceived lack of moral capital that means they are unlikely to be considered for most jobs. For these stigmatized individuals, the combination of unemployment and social contempt undoubtedly helps reinforce whatever substance abuse problems they may have already developed. Over time they are marginalized not only from the formal labor market, but also from the mainstream culture that links hard work with masculine and moral values. Whether or not they originally desired a life without work, they often end up on that side of the divide, permanently identified as deadbeats who are not worthy of the few work opportunities Golden Valley has to offer.

On the other hand, for those people—particularly those men—who are sufficiently tenacious in their desire to work and to prove themselves hardworking, there are social rewards even if their economic situations are not substantially better. A common saying among Golden Valley's working men is, "I was looking for a job when I found this one." This obscure aphorism means simply that the jobs in Golden Valley go to those who are active in their pursuit of work, not to those who sit around waiting for something to find them. Thirty-four-year-old David Lewis, who works at the local hardware store, moved back to Golden Valley in 2002 without fearing that he would be unable to find work. When asked why he had been so sure of himself, he answered:

> Just because I know a lot of people and I'm not afraid to work. That's the biggest thing. You can get work anywhere if you're not afraid to work.

Hard work, combined with moral and social capital, often pays off in Golden Valley in the attainment of more hard work, as well as the increased moral, social, and economic capital that work provides.

However, in this simple equation, personal agency on the part of the worker is taken to be the only important variable, and the roles of preexisting social status and economic resources, as well as mental conditions and physical addictions, are considered unimportant. Golden Valley's more successful residents have come to conceive of the local labor market as a Darwinian fight in which only the strongest and most morally superior survive. Rather than looking critically at the larger macro forces that have created an environment in which only those with the most resources—be they social, economic, or moral—can find jobs, they instead blame the individuals who are out of work for their own unemployment. Lost is any real conception of just how few jobs are truly left, and the obvious but easily ignored fact that in such a tight labor market there will necessarily be some people who cannot find jobs. Men like George Woodhouse, for example, end up being judged as inferior for the simple fact of not having a job, when in fact they are willing and able to work as hard as those who have been fortunate enough to find one. There *are* people who truly are looking for a job but still haven't found one.

Blaming the victims is often easier, and seemingly more productive, than lashing out at invisible hands that cannot be controlled. Furthermore, in a community as racially and economically homogeneous as Golden Valley, there are few other means available by which to create distinction among members of the community. It is for this reason that culture and its moral norms have evolved into a moral form of capital that functions in much the same ways as do other forms of symbolic capital.[52] It separates the deserving from the undeserving and creates social boundaries that can be policed and controlled. When employers have to decide between numerous job seekers, it can be called upon to help distinguish between similar applicants with basically identical human capital and work experience.[53] An individual's perceived moral worth can thus be translated into both social and economic capital. While it does nothing to address the underlying forces at play, it at least provides Golden Valley residents with a sense of control and agency over their lives.

These findings suggest that community setting can affect the behavior of the poor in numerous ways, including dictating appropriate means for surviving economic hardships. Although we are long past accepting culture of poverty theories that blame the cultural characteristics of the poor for their own poverty,[54] we have not invested much into newer theories to explain how culture and setting interact with poverty, particularly in the rural setting. The evidence from Golden Valley suggests that rural areas may operate according to very different social rules than urban areas. It further suggests that in order to alleviate poverty, we must first understand the different social milieus in which poverty is prevalent and the ways in which setting interacts with culture and behavior. Assumptions based in evidence from very different types of communities—or sometimes in no evidence at all, but simply popular stereotypes—lead to poverty policies that are inadequate for addressing the needs of a community like Golden Valley. To effectively address poverty in such places, it is necessary to understand both their structural conditions and their cultural preferences.

The preoccupation of the rural poor with such issues as moral and family values often seems perplexing to both academics and political analysts.[55] Popular mainstream books often question why working class and poor populations vote against what we perceive as their interests and describe middle-American voters as ignorant victims of a false consciousness imposed upon them by conservative elites.[56] When the rural poor prioritize issues such as gun control over economic concerns, they are often dismissed as uneducated and backward. But in marginalized places like Golden Valley, economic issues often seem distant and untouchable. Rightfully so, most of its residents feel that their economic concerns are largely ignored by politicians on both sides of the fence. They see that the political right prioritizes the interests of corporate industries, such as the large logging companies that clear-cut the woods in previous decades. On the other hand, the political left prioritizes the interests of urban liberals, such as the reviled environmentalists who are blamed for Golden Valley's current impoverishment. Most residents feel that neither side has much interest in their material well-being and economic sustenance. However, the right-wing agenda, with its focus on moral and personal issues, hits much closer to home. When your hunting rifle is a major source of your ability to engage with your children in a masculine activity, reproduce your unique culture, and provide for your family, gun control will likely seem a serious threat. Similarly, when moral capital is one of your main sources of tradable capital, the agenda that stresses moral issues will be the one that resonates better.

3

Family Life:
Tradition and Safety

The Family as a Social Structure

I came from a family of seven. So yeah, I wanted [kids]. I just wanted a
boy and a girl. Because, you know, you want that. I mean, that's part of
life, I guess. Like, most people have kids, you know, and lots of people
that don't have kids are schoolteachers or they're around kids. I mean,
they're fun. (Emily Richards, 40-year-old secretary and married mother
of two)

I think everybody figures that they will have a family. (Ted Dorsey,
42-year-old small business owner and married father of two)

One of the hardest aspects of moving to Golden Valley for me was the
lack of a peer group. Single, childless, 30-somethings like me were rare
there. The community lacked appropriate activities and social spaces
for someone in my stage in life. Even the two bars, once centers of
adult social activity, had been quietly abandoned since the mill closure. I
quickly discovered that most social and leisure time in Golden Valley was
focused expressly around children and family. While the exceptional
single or childless adults did exist there, they generally felt somewhat
isolated in this community in which family was so highly prioritized,

and most had their own parents, siblings, and extended family in the area around whom they structured their social lives. My unusual situation was generally treated with pity by young mothers—who were often ten or more years younger than I—and I was frequently subject to slightly patronizing comments that questioned my choice of career over family. Although I had not previously been aware of having made such a choice, or that life had presented me with such a dichotomy, it was clear that in Golden Valley a woman—and, I would discover, a man as well—who did not prioritize family was an anomaly that many found confusing and even threatening.[1]

I rarely met a childless couple in Golden Valley who had specifically chosen not to have children. Of the twenty-five women (between the ages of 25 and 60) whom I interviewed, only three did not have biological children, and two of them said that they had health or fertility problems.[2] All three had also helped raise the children of friends or relatives at some point. Similarly, twenty-four out of thirty men in my sample had biological children (including a number of noncustodial fathers), and among the six who were not fathers were two married men with fertility issues and two unmarried men in their early twenties who hoped to have children someday, when they were more settled. Only two out of thirty men claimed to have chosen not to have children. Both of these "childless" men had unstable romantic histories that included having lived for significant amounts of time with women who were raising children of their own and having played father roles in these children's lives.

As a social institution and means of structuring social life, the family was crucial in Golden Valley. Most of my female respondents were young (late teens to early twenties) when they had their first child, and many were married young as well. Most respondents of both genders professed to having always wanted children and focused their lives around their family responsibilities. Respondents consistently described Golden Valley as "a good place to raise kids" and referred to themselves and their community as "traditional" with regard to marriage and family. But the community has unique traditions with regard to family life. While early marriage and childbearing are common there, the "traditional" focus on marriage and family has long included numerous family structures outside of the nuclear family that is commonly associated with the term "traditional." There are many common family structures in Golden Valley that may resemble the nuclear family but that nonetheless include many unrelated or extended family members. Additionally, often those whose current families are the most "traditional" are themselves coming from families whose structures were different from the nuclear families of their adulthoods.

What exactly then were the meanings of tradition and family values in Golden Valley? Why were these terms so pivotal to its residents? In the introduction to her 1996 book *In the Name of the Family*, Judith Stacey asserts:

> The uncertainty principle that now governs our work lives—who will have employment, for how long, and with what risks and rewards?—also governs our most intimate relationships, severely disrupting domestic tranquility and seeding nostalgia for those better times which The Family has come to symbolize. . . . From this perspective the contemporary appeal of family-values parlance is quite easy to comprehend.[3]

In this passage, Stacey makes an important connection between intensifying economic concerns and the growing political and ideological importance of "family values" in the United States. Yet, although the passage suggests a focus on why individuals engage in nostalgic idealizations of the family, two pages later she instead turns her attentions to the political realm and comments that "Republicans and Democrats alike now compete to promote their politics in the name of the family—meaning one particular kind of family."[4] Like Stacey, many educated liberals are concerned with the implications of the growing importance of "family values" rhetoric and the apparent increasing strength of the conservative political backlash to which it is connected.[5] While this discourse has clear meanings in the political realm, its success, I argue, is due not necessarily to its clear reference to a specific family type but, on the contrary, to its vagueness and malleability.

"Tradition" and "family values" are terms that are loaded with moralistic overtones yet are imprecise enough to have multiple meanings. Few Americans, whether rural or urban, liberal or conservative, consider themselves to be anti-family. The importance of these terms, and their ability to motivate political support, are due more to their wide-reaching appeal than to their exclusionary qualities. They are terms that can take on different meanings in different contexts and that can be used to differentiate within and between populations, dividing the morally righteous from the morally bankrupt. Like the discourses around work ethics discussed in chapter 2, family values discourses can also prescribe norms of acceptable behavior and provide a sense of superiority to the economically inferior. As Stacey suggests, in times of economic uncertainty, belief in the goodness and righteousness of the family—however it is defined—can provide a rare source of social stability and personal satisfaction.

Most literature—both academic and popular—that addresses the family values debate looks at it from the top down. The assumption is that these ideologies are being crafted by politicians and intellectuals and fed to ignorant middle Americans who accept the ideas without critical thought.[6] There is scant attention paid to the ways in which individuals and communities constitute these discourses for themselves and shape them to fit their own needs. As Rubin contends, "Few people today would argue with the notion that what happens in the social, economic, and political world outside the family affects life inside. But we too often overlook the other side—that is, that people in families respond to those external forces in ways that change both the institutions and the discourse of public life."[7]

For Golden Valley residents, family values are being constituted in reaction to the changes the town has undergone. In this community, "traditional" is a term loaded with meanings that imply neither continuity with past behaviors nor a single specific family structure. Similarly, the belief that Golden Valley is more family oriented than other communities, and thus "a good place to raise kids," obscures several underlying issues that help justify the town as home and glorify its unique culture, population, and practices. The belief in their own traditionality and family focus provides a conceptional framework around which Golden Valley residents structure their lives, goals, and senses of self and community. Bourdieu states that "social identity is defined and asserted through difference."[8] In Golden Valley, discourses around tradition and family are being created and morphed to provide moral categories that produce this difference, both within the community and between it and other communities. They are concepts that create distinctions among residents, provide boundaries for self-protection, and give them a positive sense of their uniqueness as a community at odds with the outside world of cold and uncaring urban life.

In Golden Valley the terms "traditional" and "family-oriented" refer to three key divisions both within the community and between it and the world outside: (1) the prioritization of family stability over individual needs and pursuits; (2) clearly marked boundaries between functional and destructive behaviors; and (3) the endorsement of this isolated, impoverished, and homogenous community over more diverse places with larger ethnic and racial minority populations. All of these distinctions are attached to the term "traditional" and the underlying family focus and moral stance that it suggests. The first two divisions emphasize the local understandings of family structure and conduct within the family setting. The third division is focused instead on the uniqueness of Golden Valley as a location and particularly the shelter it provides from the evils of urban areas, such as the violence and crime stereotypically associated with poor ethnic minorities. As Newman argues, "While tradition is often seen as a conservative force, it can also be a powerful resource for criticism."[9] In this case, it provides a language for Golden Valley residents to critique both modernity and the urban society that has become politically and culturally hegemonic in the United States.

The concepts of family values and tradition are vital to Golden Valley's social structure in that they provide a framework for social control, creating enforceable boundaries between acceptable and unacceptable behaviors. They also establish an alternate route to success for people who have little chance for economic achievement, allowing them to find instead their sense of accomplishment through the moral advantage that can be attained via the creation and sustaining of "traditional" families. The concept of "family orientation" also validates for Golden Valley residents the choice of a place and lifestyle that are very much at odds with the American mainstream. Being "traditional" and "family oriented" gives them a sense of their own success in moral terms as opposed to the unattainable economic terms of the American dream. Exploring the role of family values discourses in Golden Valley can help us understand why they have become a refuge for so many struggling Americans. Only in so doing can we hope to find a way in which to draw these disenfranchised populations back toward policies that may help, rather than hurt, their chances for survival.

Myths and Traditions: Family Structures in Golden Valley

> We always wanted to do it the traditional way. I mean, we lived
> together...but we always thought it was important to be married
> before we had kids. So we got married, bought a house, had Brian,
> and then had Ashley. (April Layton, 32-year-old guidance counselor
> and married mother of two)

> Ours would be considered more in nowadays' terms the traditional
> family. You know, I was fortunate enough to be home when the boys
> were home, and I worked a work schedule around being able to be
> home with the children. We took foster children also, so they were an
> important part of our lives. (Susan Elders, 50-year-old day care provider
> and married mother of two)

Most Golden Valley residents believe that their community is significantly more conventional and conservative than most modern urban
communities. The word "traditional" was generally conflated with what
most subjects viewed as the primacy of family life in Golden Valley. Yet
their testimonies do not suggest a community in which family structures were ever homogeneous, nor did they ever tend to be extremely
stable or strictly nuclear.[10] As Coontz points out, the nuclear family is a
relatively new structure, which was "based on a unique and temporary
conjuncture of economic, social, and political factors,"[11] which, if they
ever existed in Golden Valley, are no longer all prevalent there. Stacey
contends that among the working class, despite popular portrayal as
"traditional," family formations have always been varied and fluid.[12] In
Golden Valley this certainly has been the case. While the nuclear family
is an important structure there, both in the recent past and in the present,
it is a goal that was not and is not always attained. In this community
family structures have always been somewhat fluid, and they continue
to change despite the significance of the family as a symbolic and real
structure.

Most subjects described the families in which they grew up as "traditional." For them this generally meant a mother who did most of the
housework and a father who did most of the material provision. Although
these families were not always either stable or nuclear, the division of
roles and gender spheres helped to define their traditionality in my subjects' minds. Thus, a "traditional" father was one who was often unavail-
able to his children and whose relationship with them focused mostly
on working together for basic family provision. Many women just didn't

interact with their fathers very much as young girls. Most of my male respondents saw more of their fathers, but generally only through helping with subsistence activities such as wood gathering, hunting, and fishing. A traditional mother, on the other hand, was centered in the home and available to her children. She did the cooking, cleaning, and child care. As chapter 4 will explore, these particular gender roles are changing rapidly under Golden Valley's current conditions. Nonetheless, its residents continue to conceive of themselves as traditional.

Separate gender spheres were perhaps the only part of "traditional" family life that was consistent within my Golden Valley sample. Among respondents, only about half grew up with biological parents who were married to each other and stayed married—and this figure includes several common-law marriages, which have generally been regarded as identical to legal marriages. The other half of subjects grew up with divorced parents, stepparents, unmarried mothers, and foster parents. A number of these included mothers who were never married to the subjects' biological fathers. As in many similar high-poverty communities, marriage and family in Golden Valley have seldom been overly stable or homogeneous in form. Stacey asserts that "rising divorce and cohabitation rates, working mothers, two-earner households, single and unwed parenthood, and matrilineal, extended, and fictive kin support networks appeared earlier and more extensively among poor and working-class people."[13] What she fails to point out, however, is that despite these realities, it is often the poor and working class who portray *themselves* as more dedicated to family life than their middle- and upper-class counterparts.[14] In Golden Valley the term "traditional" appears to be malleable enough to encompass several family types, despite its common association with the nuclear family, both in Golden Valley's and in America's larger cultural and political discourses. Thus, despite the diverse family arrangements that prevail there and have prevailed in the past, its residents still conceive of themselves as more family oriented than their urban counterparts. Yet while in its own mythology Golden Valley may conceptualize itself as a community of stable nuclear families, its reality has always been more complex than a single dominant family form implies.

When interacting with the inhabitants of Golden Valley, I was seldom entirely clear about what was meant by tradition or what constituted a nuclear family. Underlying the discourse around traditionality and family values are two distinct sets of meanings: that the first refers to family structure, stability, and care, and the second refers to the unique rural setting. As the quotes that introduced this section illustrate, according to the first meaning, "traditional" may imply either a stable nuclear family or a family form in which the care of children is a major priority, whether or not they are one's own. The second sense of traditionality is deeply tied to the place and rural lifestyle, which many Golden Valley residents believe to be uniquely able to foster "family values." This place-centered sense of "tradition" is illustrated by the following quote from Fred Graham, a 50-year-old U.S. Forest Service employee:

> The ones that have stayed and stuff, I'd say their values have stayed pretty traditional. Because when you're in a small town . . . a lot of the things are family oriented. We went to softball tournaments, everybody camped together, and their kids played in the park and went skiing and went fishing and went to the ball games, and everybody did everything as a group. So I think that helps to establish the family values and responsibility. . . . I think in a rural community it's much different than in a metropolitan area.

The ideas of family values and family-oriented behavior are commonly associated with conservative political arguments and undoubtedly contribute to the popularity of such politics and politicians in Golden Valley. But these terms also have a salience and a symbolic weight that cross political affiliations and religious stances. For this community, the "traditional" primacy of family life is one of its most important social structures and unifying identities. It is a concept that is normative in nature, yet the norms dictated by the traditional family are neither strictly nuclear nor strictly related to the community's history. Tradition as an idea has taken on a meaning all its own, which includes particular standards of care and behavior for responsible adults. It has in many ways less to do with either previous behaviors or the nuclear family than it does with sustaining a particular set of values and practices that are constructed in contrast to those of the undeserving poor, ethnic and racial minorities, and even the urban middle class. The focus on family life and "traditional" values in many ways helps the people of this struggling community to protect themselves from the worst problems associated with high poverty and unemployment while simultaneously creating distinctions between one another based on their adherence to local norms and family-centered values.

Breaking with Their Own Traditions

For a number of respondents, their current dedication to the goal of a stable nuclear family stands in stark contrast to their lack of such stability in childhood. Many people grew up with unmarried, divorced, or remarried parents, several of whom had multiple volatile relationships. For many Golden Valley residents, their adult goals were created in direct opposition to the family life they had experienced growing up. Such comments as "I knew about my real father leaving quite early in life, and you know, I never wanted to be like that" frequently were offered to explain subjects' strong adult commitments to their children and families. Often people whose natal families were the most chaotic aimed for the most calm and secure family lives as adults, and their abusive or unstable parents served as negative role models that guided their behaviors.

Andy Newton is a 60-year-old retired mill worker who considers himself to be family oriented. He and his wife have been married for twenty-six years and neither was married previously. In contrast to his relatively stable adult family life, Andy described a tumultuous childhood full of moves and multiple stepfathers, as his mother remarried several times after his parents' divorce. His mother remained the only constant in his life as male figures came and went. When asked about his role models for marriage and family, Andy mentioned only one stepfather who had taken an interest in the family and who had briefly played a fatherly role to him. Other than that, his experiences with family stability were limited:

> I never really [had a] family life, and then moving so much, and there was a lot of drinking and different things in the family. But there was really, other than this one stepdad, there was really never a relationship between father and son.

Despite never having experienced it, Andy yearned for the two-parent family that he had so often romanticized during his youth:

> Something I wanted, I remember as a kid, like, when you started in school you get these books, *Dick and Jane*. Oh, and you see the kids, that they're riding on their dad's back and things like that. That's a thing we never had, you know. As a child I kind of longed for that kind of life but never did, you know, experience it.

For Andy, lacking early family stability made it more of a goal in his adult life. The mythical nuclear family that he had not experienced growing up would become the focus of his energies as an adult. To that end, he and his wife created a life together that was not only stable, but in which "everything was built around the family." For Andy, the creation of a successful nuclear family was one of his life's greatest achievements.

Andy's story was not unusual in Golden Valley. Similar tales were told by several of my subjects there of all ages. Forty-year-old Bud Richards recounted a similar story of a transient life following the death of his father when Bud was age 3. His mother remarried an abusive "raging alcoholic," and the family was moved from location to location because of his insecure jobs. Eventually his stepfather kicked teenage Bud out of the house after a particularly bad fight, and his mother agreed to accompany him back to his birthplace of Golden Valley. He finished high school there while living with her and supported her as well as he could with after-school jobs; she had never worked or learned how to drive. Bud got married right out of high school; he and his wife have been together for eighteen years and have two teenage children. Like Andy, Bud focused his life on being the kind of father he never had and providing the stability and family structure he had lacked. When asked what his life goals had been, he answered, "You know, raise my family right, that's all I really wanted."

Thirty-year-old Kim Clark is yet another example of a similar trajectory from childhood turmoil into orderly adult family life. Her mother never married her biological father but cohabited with another man who had three children of his own. While living in the joint household of six children, Kim experienced some amount of neglect. Things worsened substantially when she was 13 and her mother and stepfather separated, plunging her family into chaos from which it never recovered:

> After my mom split with her boyfriend there wasn't really, like, a family structure. You know, there was food in the house—she just didn't cook it. So if you were hungry, you just ate whatever you wanted. And you made sure you had clean clothes and that type of stuff. . . . She just didn't want to be mom anymore and was going through, I guess, her own crisis. But we just did whatever we wanted when we wanted. You know, we knew we had to get up and go to school, we knew we had to do our homework, we knew that there was just certain rules we had to follow, but if you don't break 'em, you could do whatever you want. You know, you make sure you're home by one or two. So that's pretty much what I'd do.

At times Kim moved in with friends to escape the disorder of her mother's household, a practice that is not uncommon in Golden Valley among the children of more troubled families. Kim described her reasons for choosing to live at her best friend's house during periods in high school:

> I liked being at her house because she had two parents in her house and she had to check in, and she had dinner on the table, and, well, I wouldn't say got to wash the dishes but had to. But it was more of a family than it was at my house.... I enjoyed being at Stacey's house because, regardless of how her mom would get, you just deal with it, because that was a family. Her parents treated me as their own kid. So when I was there I had to abide by those rules; that was the way it was.

Like Andy and Bud, Kim idealized and longed for the family structure she lacked and has focused on achieving a nuclear family as an adult. And thus, despite her "nontraditional" upbringing and a divorce in her 20s, she is currently married with two children and determined to remain married, despite mounting tensions and frustration with her husband.

As these stories illustrate, for many people there, the importance of the nuclear family structure in Golden Valley has more to do with its idealization than its actualization in their personal histories. Despite the fact that nearly half of its residents did not grow up in stable families, Golden Valley continues to conceive of itself as a community that traditionally was made up of secure nuclear families with similar focuses and values. While it was never the sole—and was barely the dominant—family form there, the nuclear family has taken on great significance for many people because it symbolizes all the opportunities for love, stability, and social acceptability that their natal families lacked. For so many of Golden Valley's most "traditional" families, the creation of two-parent, biological nuclear families is actually a break from their own family histories of divorce, remarriage, nonmarriage, and extended-family households. Their idealization of this particular family structure provides them with a clear set of norms to follow so they can escape from the abuse and volatility of their pasts.

For these families, the idea of tradition has a meaning that is clearly something other than continuity with their personal histories or the community's norms. The conceptions of traditionality and family values instead describe a certain ideal, one that both was and is difficult to sustain under the stressful conditions caused by persistent poverty and unstable employment. The nuclear family structure is one that, for many, is associated with the opposite of poverty and dysfunction; it is indicative of stability and moral fortitude and of adults who are in control of themselves and their lives. For people like Andy, Bud, and Kim, the "traditional" family is one that lacks the worst trials they suffered as children, including transience, substance abuse, physical violence, and neglect. For Golden Valley as a whole, it describes an ideal rather than the most common family type or average family history.

How does tradition come to mean its opposite? A key theme in all of these stories is the creation of an ideal-type of family and the moral ownership of that form. For these families, the creation of stable nuclear families out of the disarray of their personal histories represents more than just an opportunity for stability and love. It also sustains a mythology around their moral fiber and the moral character of the community. Connection to "tradition" through family structure allows them to claim moral and personal success when they have few other opportunities to achieve some version of the American dream. It allows them to establish themselves as part of Golden Valley's morally upright society rather than existing on its degenerate fringes. While they may not realistically hope for economic success, fame, or power, there is a clear set of norms they can follow to achieve moral success in terms of their personal and family lives. Thus families like those of Andy, Bud, and Kim, who barely live above the poverty line, can nonetheless conceive of themselves as rural success stories due to their stable marital and family situations. Their ability to rewrite their personal scripts as a return to traditional values allows them to connect themselves to the morality of the American middle class while simultaneously creating a sense of moral superiority over other groups of poor Americans both within and outside of Golden Valley. To do this, they rely on discourses that originate not simply from their own pasts, but rather from a set of shared cultural mythologies that are idealized both in Golden Valley and in national debates and political arguments. Connecting to these larger trends allows them to further establish the idea of themselves as successful according to both local and more universal moral standards.

Our Kin and Beyond: Creating Family through Caring for Nonfamily

This prioritization of nuclear families among those who lacked them as children does not mean that the diversity of family forms has diminished in Golden Valley. For many there, the importance of family and the sense of responsibility for children still extend beyond their own biological children and nuclear families. Situations like Kim Clark's high school experience, in which one family helps raise another family's child, have long been and continue to be common in this high-poverty community. Nearly half of my subjects had cared for children who were not their biological offspring at some time. This responsibility to others extends to both the children of relations and to those who are not. In many ways the networks that formed to take care of children in Golden Valley resemble those found in urban areas, such as those documented by Stack.[15] But while kin care in particular is common in poor urban communities,[16] there are distinct differences between the care networks documented in urban areas and those that are found in the rural United States. Most important, adults in Golden Valley who care for others' children are often unrelated to the children and do not generally expect any reciprocity from the children's biological parents or legal guardians. Frequently the caregivers are not even socially connected to the children's parents and prefer to distance themselves from them since they are viewed as morally deficient in their family lives. Instead, the caregivers' rewards come in the form of personal satisfaction and the moral and social status produced by being "good parents."

Caring for others' children is professed to be done because it is believed to be the right thing to do and to benefit the children involved. It is also one of the main ways in which the poor distinguish among themselves in Golden Valley and create a clear delineation between the moral and immoral poor. Moral discourses around the family allow individuals to conceive of their behavior as motivated solely by altruistic concerns, which it certainly is, in part. But caring for others' children is about more than providing a stable family structure for all children in need. It simultaneously helps establish a family on the moral side of the divide, often despite joblessness and extreme poverty.

Residents of Golden Valley have multiple reasons for taking in extra children, all of which are consistent with their view of themselves as family focused and morally upright. Yet their understandings of these moral obligations, as well as their conceptions of what caring for children entails, are unique and distinct from common beliefs and practices found in most urban and suburban parts of the United States. Golden Valley parents do not necessarily feel it is their duty to provide either economic stability or life opportunities for children in their care. Considering the economic constraints they face, such goals are sadly unattainable for most of them. Instead, they profess to believe strongly in the importance of providing a safe and supportive environment for their own children as well as any other children who may find themselves in difficult or dangerous situations. This belief spawns a number of creative family situations in which children are raised by people who are not their biological parents, either for brief periods of time or on a long-term basis.

Sometimes children are raised by people other than their biological parents because the parents are unable to care for them due to lack of resources or other constraints. Rod and Julie Mitchell are a young couple; she is in her mid-20s and he is 30. They met while she was in high school, and when she became pregnant at 16 they got married, planning to create a nuclear family of their own. Julie's first pregnancy had multiple complications, and due to these problems their son was born disabled. They took care of him until he was a toddler, at which time they transferred custody to her parents, who are still raising the 10-year-old boy. According to Julie, their original reasons for the custody change were financial:

> Our oldest son was getting Social Security and stuff, and they were gonna cut him from Medi-Cal and Social Security because of his dad's income. And I said, "That's not right." I said, "That's not the kid's problem. That's to take care of him and meet his needs." I can't believe they would do that. But they do it. And so we asked what other ways we can go about doing this. . . . You know, we couldn't fathom that doctor's bill, taking him off Medi-Cal, because we knew how often he was gonna have to be seen. And taking that Social Security away would mean that he wouldn't be able to get the things he needed. And the only way we found to go about it was to shift guardianship to my mom and dad for him. So they have legal guardianship of him.

Julie's parents live nearby, and the couple still interacts with their son frequently, although they do not have any of the main caregiving responsibilities for him. Since his birth they have had three more children and have their hands full taking care of them while Rod works full-time an hour away and Julie works part-time at the local nursery school. They have no plans to regain custody of their oldest son and gave no indication that her parents have any interest in changing the custody arrangement, which they felt was to the benefit of everyone involved.

In Golden Valley, as in poor communities throughout rural and urban settings, it is common to find grandparents (and often stepgrandparents) taking care of children whose parents are unable to care for them properly.[17] However, permanent custody changes like Julie and Rod's are generally not the norm in the community. It is more common for couples to take in other children on a less formal short-term or semipermanent basis. Fred and Cathy Graham, both stably employed and in their early 50s, had no children of their own due to health and fertility problems. They had wanted to be parents, however, and did not let their physiological constraints stop them from playing parental roles in multiple children's lives. As both described in separate interviews, they were close to their numerous nieces and nephews and had actually cared for many of them, as well as several unrelated children, at different times. Fred explained:

> We've been able to spend a lot of time with nieces and nephews and we've got other kids we've taken under our wing that we're really close to, who have no father, in one case. And then we took care of a couple of kids, had foster kids. And my niece, when her dad died, we were real close and spent a lot of time with her. And then she lived with us for the last year of high school—sort of transitioned from being under her mom's wing and got used to being on her own.

Taking care of less fortunate children became one way in which Fred and Cathy could share their relative prosperity, as well as experience the family life they desired. Almost all of the childless men, women, and couples with whom I spoke had had similar experiences and at least for periods of time had created families through taking care of children who were not their biological offspring. Thus, some couples manage to achieve their ideal of a "traditional" family through the creation of extended family and nonfamily households and the temporary care of others' children.

For many of the families who take in other people's children, however, neither available resources nor the need to create family are their main motivations. Many of the Golden Valley couples who take in others'

kids are poor themselves and do so despite the financial burden it adds
to their already strained budgets and families. Chapter 2 shared the
story of Joyce and George Woodhouse, who repeatedly housed, fed, and
clothed children and teenagers who needed a haven in which to escape
brutality, substance abuse, and neglect at home. They explained that
they took care of kids in need because they believed that all children
deserved to live in a safe, stable home environment—even if it meant
expanding their definition of family responsibilities far beyond their
nuclear unit and stretching their material resources dangerously thin.

Laura and Eli Jordan, a couple in their late 30s and early 40s respec-
tively, have had a similar family experience to that of Joyce and George
Woodhouse. Eli began working in logging when he was a teenager, but
he has been out of work and receiving disability since the mid-1990s
due to increasingly serious health problems caused by various work-
related injuries. Laura has entered the workforce instead, but with only
her GED[18] and no college experience her salary at her full-time secretarial job is only $16,000—the most she's ever made in a year. To-
gether their income does not equal the $24,000 needed to keep them
above the federally established poverty line for their current family of
six.[19] When asked to name the biggest source of frustration in their life,
Laura answered, "Money, definitely money. You just can't earn enough
off of disability and my little job, no way." Eli echoed her sentiments:

> Well, it makes you worry. Are you gonna be able to put enough food
> in the refrigerator for your kids and stuff like that? Are you gonna eat
> dinner? Are you gonna have to eat ramen noodles?

Daily provision is definitely one of their most pressing concerns. Yet
one of the mouths that they are currently feeding is not one of their
own. Their household includes an "adopted" teenage son who, Eli explained, is "not really adopted. He's [just] staying here." My request for
more information on this arrangement elicited the following exchange:

> ELI: Well, he's from a...
> LAURA: Not so normal family.
> ELI: Abusive type.
> LAURA: He just needed to stay here.
>
> *How long has he been here now?*
> LAURA: Since June [six months earlier].

And you'll let him stay for . . .

LAURA: As long as he wants. He'll decide what he's gonna do. He's gettin' more healthy all the time.

So you guys are one of those families that takes care of kids?

LAURA: Oh, yeah. If you come to our house any given day, we probably have people scattered all over the couch. Any friend of the kids, they'll come and stay if they need to.

Does that happen a lot?

LAURA: Yeah. We're just solid, solid foundation for a lot of the kids that don't get it at home.

ELI: Well, there's no abuse, you know. They see what it's really supposed to be like. You know, they get to go fishin' or go out in the woods. This kid here, he's never been around anything like that, you know, so it's a big change for him. So if it helps him, then we did something.

Eli and Laura cannot truly afford to feed one more teenager. Laura described their situation as "less money, more kids, older kids, growing boys, empty refrigerator." Like Joyce and George, they supplement their diet through hunting and fishing, which the boys mostly do now that Eli is too unwell to be very active. Yet despite the strain on their finances, Eli and Laura believe it is important to provide a stable family life for kids who lack one, even if they can't quite provide for that family. Like George and Joyce, they explicitly contrasted their caregiving with that of the abusive families from which they were rescuing kids.

For the many Golden Valley couples like George and Joyce and Laura and Eli who take in relatives' children, friends of their own children, and foster children, the importance of providing a "traditional" family takes precedence over such basic needs as material provision and economic survival. When asked to describe how these arrangements arose, almost all of them described the decisions as growing organically out of their perceptions of the children's needs, and few seemed aware that this response is much less common among urban and suburban families, whether middle class or poor. The types of care networks documented in urban settings differ from those found in Golden Valley in several important ways. Urban care networks are generally described as being mostly kin-based, requiring reciprocity of some kind, and focused on the care of young children who need nearly constant supervision.[20] The caregivers are also generally chosen by the biological parents of the children, who have some say over who does and who does not care for them.[21]

As the examples provided illustrate, care for nonbiological children in Golden Valley often occurs outside of such informal networks and does not always require either reciprocity or social contact with the biological parents. It also is frequently extended to older children, whose needs are not so much constant care but simply more stable households in which to live semiautonomously. According to Nelson, rural cultures of self-sufficiency often make parents reluctant to ask others for help, which may contribute to the phenomenon of care networks that are focused on the children's situations rather than their parents' needs.[22] While kin care is common, as illustrated by the stories of Julie and Rod Mitchell and Fred and Cathy Graham, it is not the only or even the most common form of care, nor is reciprocity generally expected. Even when caregivers are taking care of close kin, they generally frame the decision as benefiting the children rather than the parents. Also, unlike the networks of care described by Stack[23] and Hansen,[24] caregivers in Golden Valley do not necessarily share parenting styles or values with the biological parents, but often are "saving" children from parents whose styles they feel to be inferior or injurious.

Thus, in Golden Valley, several unique forms of informal care exist alongside those more commonly documented in urban settings. Fred and Cathy engaged in multiple caregiving networks, providing basic care for young nieces and nephews but also fostering older, sometimes unrelated children who were having problems with their parents. Generally caregivers do not distinguish between these different types of informal care and simply provide whichever form is deemed necessary. Dawn and Keith Bartlett are a married couple in their late 20s and early 30s. They have no children of their own and are unsure whether they face a biological constraint. They do, however, frequently care for their nieces and nephews when needed. Keith explained, "You know, we've had kids in our family that we get to kinda take." Currently they take care of their young nephew one full day and night each week to help out his single mother. This type of arrangement looks very much like those commonly described in the urban literature, in which single parents rely on kin for temporary help with child care. However, according to Keith, he and Dawn would be willing to do more than provide occasional child care for kin. When I asked him if they would consider adopting a child should they be unable to have their own, he explained that he felt formal adoption would be unnecessary:

> You know, I'm not sure as though we would run out and look to adopt. In Dawn's family it's always been [if] a kid's in a real hard position or a real hard way, and the parents can't get anywhere with 'em, [you take care of them]. Dawn's parents have taken on many kids like that. And it has had just a total beneficial effect for all of the kids that are taken in by them. So I could totally see something like that happening. I would not object to anything like that.

While such non-kin care is not unheard of in urban and suburban America, it is not the dominant form of "other mothering" in these settings.[25] While the forms of care in Golden Valley differ from those in urban poor settings, it is also important to note that the *standards* of child rearing also differ from the current American middle-class mainstream. According to Rosenfeld and Wise, among the white middle class in the United States today, "many parents are acting as though life can be planned and children programmed, the ultimate goal being admission to a prestigious college and the supposed success that invariably follows."[26] These "hyper-parents" are described as being obsessively concerned with making sure that their children are provided with every opportunity and advantage possible to help them achieve their parents' goals. Warner similarly describes the American upper-middle class's contemporary parenting climate as causing parents to believe that "if we don't do everything right for our children, they may be consigned, down the line, to failure. To loserdom."[27] Lareau characterizes these different parenting styles as "concerted cultivation" among the middle class versus "accomplishment of natural growth" among the working class and poor.[28]

Rather than consisting of providing opportunities meant to optimize their children's future outcomes, Golden Valley parenting often focuses more on creating a safe environment for their present survival. There is a pervasive belief in the community that providing this type of basic care for any and all children in need is the responsibility of all good parents and morally responsible adults. Like the choice of subsistence work over welfare described in chapter 2, the choice to take care of nonbiological children is often economically irrational. However, it is clear that it provides some payoff in terms of moral worth and self-worth for these families. It allows poor, unemployed men like Eli Jordan and George Woodhouse to feel like "we did something." It distinguishes them clearly and powerfully from their drug-addicted and abusive neighbors who may nonetheless be equally poor. It also distinguishes them from the self-centered parents of the urban middle class, who are much less likely to sacrifice their own children's material well-being to provide for an extra child in need.

Family values provide a sense of moral worth and access to some social capital, although it is not the same as the moral capital discussed in chapter 2. Neither George Woodhouse nor Eli Jordan has had much luck with the labor market, and their family values are not interchangeable for work ethics. Yet on a more personal level these choices clearly have some payoff. This conception of family responsibility allows the poor to still feel successful with regard to their children; calling it tradition gives it the sense of moral superiority that it might otherwise lack. Thus, the myth of the traditional family in Golden Valley dictates a standard of care unknown to most of the United States; good parents may be ones who stretch their economic resources to the breaking point to care for children who are technically not their responsibilities and are often not even kin. Although it is most certainly not identical to the "traditional family" in other parts of the United States, it nonetheless functions in this community to create distinctions between individuals, just as more economically based conceptions do for the urban middle class.

What Family Values Aren't

> I was never going to be dependent on a man. I watched my mom get beat up once a week because she didn't want to leave him. She didn't think she could support us, she didn't think it was good for us not to have a father. She was wrong! (Angelica Finch, 38-year-old school administrator and married mother of three)

As several quotations in the previous section suggested, the concept of family values and tradition extends beyond dictating a focus on family togetherness. While it is normative in the positive sense of suggesting what kinds of behaviors a good parent and good family should engage in, it also has a clear negative normative value. Certain behaviors are excluded from the definition of traditional and family-oriented, despite the fact that many of the subjects I interviewed had been raised in families in which these specific behaviors were prevalent and considered normal, if not necessarily healthy. The current definition of family allows

individuals and the community to protect women and children somewhat from many of the most destructive behaviors typically associated
with poverty. For women, it allows them to refuse certain forms of male
abuse while still conceiving of themselves as moral, traditional, and
family focused. It has allowed them to rewrite certain gender scripts
without having to acknowledge any kind of gender or feminist awareness that might threaten their idea of themselves as traditional, feminine women. Thus, to fully understand the meaning of family values in
Golden Valley, it is also necessary to understand what they are not and
which behaviors are excluded from the definition that is so central to
social life in the community.

Although separate gender spheres and the homemaker/breadwinner
divide were the only real attributes common to most of my subjects'
"traditional" natal families, these separations and the need for a man to
be working no longer define the traditional family in Golden Valley.
The most significant way in which the definition of the traditional family has changed is that it no longer clearly excludes out-of-work men.
Chapter 2 explored the ways in which a man can still be perceived as
hardworking in the absence of paid work. Chapter 4 will look in depth
at the ways in which masculinity and fatherhood are adapting to the
new labor market conditions in the post–spotted owl period. Much previous research has explored the ways in which fatherhood and masculinity are tied to working and providing, particularly for working-
class American men.[29] In Golden Valley, the ideal family myth still
assumes a working husband. However, it no longer strictly excludes a
man who does not have a job or who cannot support the family on his
own. Instead, the behaviors that are currently considered antithetical
to family values are those that are considered most inconsistent with
the values of hard work identified in chapter 2: namely drug and alcohol use and the domestic abuse that often accompanies it.

As discussed in chapter 2, in the days of the mill and the woods being open for business, both (semi-)functional alcoholism and domestic
violence were common in Golden Valley, and neither was considered
particularly immoral or emasculating. While many marriages fell apart
because of these issues, many more stayed together and weathered the
problems. Nearly half (44 percent) of subjects mentioned either alcoholism or physical abuse having played a significant role in their daily
lives growing up. The abuser was almost always a father or stepfather.

While most subjects felt that abuse was not easy to live with, it often did not mean that they disrespected their fathers or believed them to have been bad parents. Thirty-four-year-old Linda Cole described her father as a good man and "a real fighter" whom she loved dearly and missed terribly after his death. She spoke to me for more than an hour before mentioning her father's alcohol problems, which constituted a trial for her that she believed contributed to her strength as a person, but which did not undermine her respect for him:

> He was a drinker and stuff, I remember [from] when I was younger. And some of that lifestyle wasn't the best for a child to grow up in. But I think a lot of it has to do with the individual. I mean, you can wallow in it, or you can take that and realize how much character that builds and run with it. And I think that's kinda what I've done.

Linda described without anger her father's weekend drinking sprees, which were so intense and so regular that her mother included them in her monthly household budgets. For Linda these binges, although unhealthy, were understandable for a man who worked hard all week in the woods: "You work as a logger all week long, who's gonna begrudge you to go out on the weekend?"

Linda's husband is not a logger, but he does have a steady—albeit seasonal—job with a local woodworking cooperative. Yet when asked what the biggest source of stress was in her marriage, she answered, "Well, drinking used to be." She went on to describe her husband's occasional binges and explained:

> I grew up with that, and I grew up with the dynamics that alcohol in a home can cause. So I didn't have a lot of tolerance for it.

The same behaviors that Linda tolerated with so much understanding in her father were not acceptable to her in her adult relationship. She recalled, "It caused a lot of fights; it caused a lot of problems for us." Finally, after years of arguing with him, she successfully convinced her husband to stop drinking and thus was able to salvage her marriage. Linda, who could not begrudge her father his weekly binges, refused to live as an adult with these same behaviors, which she believes "take years off of the amount of time that we can be together."

Much has changed in Golden Valley since the days of the woods and mills, and as chapter 2 illustrated, alcoholism, drug use, and physical abuse are no longer considered to be consistent with hard work or masculinity, but are instead associated with laziness, emasculation, and welfare receipt. They are also no longer believed to be compatible with family values and good parenting. Both men and women—but especially women, who are more likely to have been subject to an abusive partner or spouse—cited drug, alcohol, and physical abuse as among their main reasons for ending previous relationships. For women, these three forms of abuse were the most common explanations for previous relationships' demises, and there were few other reasons given for why their relationships had ended.[30] Drug and alcohol use was cited most frequently by couples as the main source of past stress in their relationships and the issue that brought them closest to breaking up. While it appears that a good father and family man does not necessarily have to have a paying job, he can no longer abuse either substances or his spouse and still be considered an upstanding man or a good husband. Abusive parents are not only scorned by the neighbors who take in their needy children, but they are often abandoned by the partners who realize how incompatible their behaviors are with the mythical family life they desire.

I spoke with a number of women who had left their ex-husbands and boyfriends because of drug use and physical abuse while remaining with men who were under- or unemployed. Allison Butters is a 30-year-old mother of two who survived a rough childhood that included foster care and abuse. The father of her children is the man with whom she currently cohabits, an out-of-work logger. She is also helping to raise his two children from a previous relationship. Allison was married in her early 20s to another Golden Valley logger, but the marriage was short lived and they had no children together. She described her divorce simply: "There were drugs involved and abuse, and I left." Although she had used drugs for a time as well, she insists she has been clean for years now and does not want to return to that lifestyle. She is happy with her current partner, who is not a drug user, and has encouraged him to stay home with the children rather than leave Golden Valley to find work. For Allison, an out-of-work man is much better than an abusive one. While she expressed concern for her partner's self-esteem, she did not criticize him for being out of work, nor did she think he was a bad father for not providing for his children. Instead, she described with pride his active role in his children's lives: "He has my baby all day. They just go out, drive around, visit his friends, get wood, whatever's going on." For Allison, being dedicated to one's family means staying together even in the absence of work and avoiding abusive behaviors.

Thirty-year-old Kim Clark, whom we met earlier in this chapter with regard to her own childhood neglect, gave a similarly concise explanation for the demise of her first marriage: "I met my husband and we dated for five years. We got married, and I decided I wasn't going to stay because he was a drug addict." When Kim realized that his drug use was increasing, not decreasing, she decided to call it quits. Like Allison, she had no children with her first husband and did not believe him to be adequate father material. For Kim this is in contrast to her current husband, with whom she has two children. Al Clark is a difficult and controlling man, according to Kim, but he is nonetheless a good father and family man who "loves his kids." Although he is also out of work for much of the year, in Kim's view this does not negate his ability to be a good father. Drugs, on the other hand, are irreconcilable with the stable family life she has chosen for herself.

Substance abuse was blamed more than anything else for relational troubles, while many women seemed more or less unconcerned about whether their husbands had jobs, as long as someone in the family was able to provide an income. We met Angelica Finch in chapter 2, whose husband never worked, and she was saddled with both breadwinning and the entire second shift at home[31] for most of their life together. Yet despite the intense poverty she described, it was not his lack of employment but rather his "partying" that finally caused her to leave him for nearly two years after a decade together. When Jim asked her to come home again, she agreed on one condition: that they stop their drinking and drug use and give up their addictions for good. Despite the struggle that this decision imposed on them and the years it took to implement, when asked what her life would be like if that transition hadn't occurred, Angelica replied, "We wouldn't be together—we wouldn't be together. I wouldn't be in Golden Valley." In response to a question about what would cause her to leave a relationship, she replied:

> Emotional abuse. And that's what drugs and alcohol lead to. Because your self-esteem goes down because you're all wasted. And so you don't feel good. So why should anyone around you feel good? Emotional abuse, definitely.

As the stories in this chapter have suggested, family values do not always meet a single definition in Golden Valley, and they do not necessarily suggest a strictly nuclear family with a male breadwinner and stay-at-home female. However, they do clearly exclude the kinds of substance abuse and domestic violence that just a generation ago were considered an undesirable but acceptable part of "traditional" family life. It appears that as poverty and unemployment have worsened in Golden Valley, the community has reacted protectively by redefining fatherhood and family to control and exclude the most dangerous behaviors that are often associated with male unemployment.[32] As circumstances have forced women into more independent roles and often into the workforce, they have begun to refuse to accept the worst problems from their pasts. While the myth of traditional masculinity and family still remains, the requirements of masculinity have changed to focus more directly on work ethics than on breadwinning itself. And, as chapter 2 illustrated, drug and alcohol abuse in particular have become the antithesis of work ethics. While on the one hand the current definition of family creates moral divisions within the community, on the other hand it allows women to protect themselves against abusive partners without losing their sense of femininity or traditionality with regard to gender roles. It may be that such a definition of family values was not possible a generation ago, when women were more likely to be centered and isolated in the home and had fewer options for easily leaving men who were abusive to them and their families.

When people in Golden Valley talk about their traditionality and family values, they are not just invoking a specific family form, but additionally suggesting a community-level sense of responsibility for children and a belief that neither children nor women should be subject to the various forms of abuse that are so often the results of economic and social stress. Tradition in Golden Valley is a protective umbrella under which people can shelter themselves from the worst problems endemic to their community. It simultaneously provides categories according to which they may garner the moral and social standing that comes from embodying its most noble ideals. In defining their community as traditional and family focused, they are also able to claim for themselves an identity substantially different from the one that urban and suburban America might impose on them. Instead of seeing themselves as the uneducated hicks and rednecks of rural stereotypes, they instead construct themselves as morally and socially superior to other groups of Americans. They believe they are different not because their family practices are unusual, but because they are more "traditional" than those of the urban middle class and poor.

Home Is Where a Safe House Is

> I feel fortunate to live, be able to raise kids, have a job, own property, and not have to live in the city where it just seems so crazy and so go-go-go-go-go, and it seems like the anxiety is higher and stressful. I just feel fortunate to be able to raise my kids in a safe place and have some of the pleasures of life. (Emily Richards, 40-year-old secretary and married mother of two)

> I don't think I'd wanna raise my kids anywhere else. Here they all know who their parents and grandparents are. But I think my favorite thing is the continuity. It's where I grew up. (Grace Prader, 45-year-old administrative assistant and married mother of two)

> I think the city's no place for kids to grow up. . . . This is a good place to have a family and kids, I think. (Sam Acton, 33-year-old disabled, single, noncustodial father of one)

Although the understanding of family in Golden Valley is complex and fluid, it remains concrete enough to both validate and motivate the choice to stay there. While family in the community implies a certain set of behaviors, it also implies a physical stability and a tangible place called home. Chapter 2 illustrated the importance of the state of one's home as an outward manifestation of work ethics. The home is also in many ways the physical embodiment of the concept of family in Golden Valley and the symbolic manifestation of safety and shelter from the frightening realities of the world outside the isolated community. For many it is difficult to separate home and family from each other and from Golden Valley. Thus, many families have made major sacrifices to keep the three together. Family is one of the main reasons residents give for their decisions to stay there, whether it is being close to extended family or raising their children in a "safe" environment. The ability to own a home is often the other main reason people give for remaining in the community. Many claim to have chosen to stay because, even though they may struggle for income, they are able to afford a house in which to keep the family stable and rooted in a safe place.

When the mill closed, most of Golden Valley's working men were faced with a serious dilemma and the choice between moving their families away or staying put without solid job prospects. Many families did move away permanently, and many others moved away but tried to hold on to their homes through renting them out or setting up caretaking situations. Many families chose instead to move only the working male away and kept the rest of the family in Golden Valley. For these families, splitting up seemed like a better way to preserve their sense of family than did moving to a more "dangerous" community. In time, however, most found the arrangements too stressful to sustain. Fifty-year-old Susan Elders, who remained in Golden Valley for more than five years while her husband, John, worked in a neighboring county, explained that, like her husband, most of these men eventually gave up job stability and incomes to return to their families:

> One by one they ended up deciding that it wasn't worth it, and one by one they came back. And those particular people were go-getters. They would do like we did—they would've accepted any job just to keep going. And so they're not living on as much now, but they're here. They're not paying $250,000 or $300,000, whatever it is, for a house.

For Susan, this scenario is all too familiar. She worked at the mill for years and was offered a job in Adams when the mill closed. She described her decision to stay as being for the benefit of the family: "Well, they offered whoever wanted to, to go elsewheres, but we had already made the decision as a family we were staying here and do what we could." She took a part-time job with Northwest Timber in Hillview, more than an hour away over the mountains but nonetheless a seemingly acceptable commuting distance. She commuted there two days a week for five months that she described as "miserable." Nonetheless, despite her distress at the time, she insisted that "moving was just out of the question." Eventually she was laid off and decided to look for work in Golden Valley, while John took the only job he could find, which meant he could be home only on weekends. At this point they finally considered moving the family to be near his work, but in the end they decided that financial constraints would not allow it:

> We spent days doing the house hunting, and we were just miserable. What we could not afford up there we already owned here! So finally after just days and weeks of trying to figure it out, we decided God was trying to tell us just stay put. And I will just keep the home fires burning. We just couldn't afford—we just couldn't afford to leave.

Susan admitted that keeping "the home fires burning" by herself for five-and-a-half years was stressful but described it as "a family commitment that we made that this was a long-term betterment of our family." Both she and John asserted this belief, despite the marital and personal strain the arrangement created:

> SUSAN: It's not ideal for a marriage. One time—and this probably hurt him more than anybody—a man said, "I guess I'd make more money if I moved away, but I'm not ready to abandon my wife." And that really bothered John because he wasn't abandoning us. It was a decision to live like this for the ultimate benefit of the family.

Both Susan and John described the difficulties of this separation, which included frequent fighting during his brief visits home. But both ultimately believed that what mattered most was continuing the lifestyle that they had in Golden Valley, in their case particularly with regard to having a home of their own, a physical manifestation of their family life. Thus, in their minds they were maintaining a stable family, despite living separately.

Numerous couples had experiences similar to Susan and John's. Many had tried to endure separations and long commutes and eventually decided that being together as a family and keeping their homes in Golden Valley were more important than being stably employed. For most, the importance of family came to symbolize concerns beyond family ties to Golden Valley, including the lack of social networks in other places, unfamiliarity and dissatisfaction with other physical environments, and the inability to afford housing in more competitive markets. Although all of these issues were concerns that contributed to these families' decisions, ultimately the stories they told focused on family and community as the motivating factors.

When the mill left, 55-year-old Jake Robbins followed it to Adams, where he lived for five years while his wife and daughters remained in Golden Valley. He and his wife, Barbara, described the experience as "miserable" and "not good." Jake elaborated, "It was hard. I think it was probably a mistake. I was very unhappy being away so much." He and Barbara further expressed regret over his absence in his younger daughter's high school years, as well as the loneliness he experienced living so far away from his family. I asked if they ever considered moving the family to Adams. They explained:

BARBARA: Yes, we did. We talked about that. I don't know why we
didn't end up, besides the youngest one throwing a fit.

JAKE: We didn't want to, really. I had envisioned that in a year or two
after the mill left that things would kind of level off, and I would be
able to get back up here with a logging job or something. It hasn't
happened. So it just kept . . .

BARBARA: . . . getting worse . . .

JAKE: It just kept going along. I was making good money. I made really
reasonable money there. So it was about the money. But finally it
got to the point where I decided it wasn't enough. Yeah, it just
wasn't worth it.

In the end, Jake returned to Golden Valley to be with Barbara. In so
doing he gave up a well-paid job in a career he found interesting and
challenging. As it was for Susan and John, for Jake and Barbara the
dual ideals of home and family were forever tied to their community,
and they were not willing to give up both, not even for financial stability and Jake being able to maintain his breadwinner role.

As their stories illustrate, most of Golden Valley's current residents
have given up many opportunities to remain there. The importance of
place to them outweighs many other concerns and conveniently conceals their inabilities to easily adapt to unfamiliar circumstances. They,
unlike most Americans, are unwilling to move away from their homes
to follow work and do not prioritize moneymaking over other quality-
of-life concerns. The importance of family and homeownership are
generally cited as the motivating factors behind their decisions to live
in Golden Valley. But the desire to remain in the community is born
out of several concerns. In addition to the economic strain of moving
and the social isolation of living so far from their limited networks, for
many the fear of what lies outside the isolated valley is also a strong
motivating issue in their decision to remain.

The choice of Golden Valley as home is not just indicative of a positive desire to live there, but also a negative reaction to living in other
kinds of places. While it is clear that being near extended family is one of
the important issues involved, and that having a home for one's family is
another, the idea of Golden Valley as "a safe place" to raise a family is also
loaded with darker meanings that vaguely or specifically reference urban
concerns such as violence, crime, and racial and ethnic tensions. Safety
issues were mentioned repeatedly among the reasons that respondents

chose to remain in Golden Valley. The following quotes represent just a few of the many similar references to safety matters:

> Even if I'm poor and way below the poverty level, I don't mind for what it grants me. We don't have to worry too awful bad about drug dealers or really weird people. It's just—it's fifty years ago, basically, if you compare it to L.A. We live fifty years ago, a safer, calmer, slower pace. And it's well worth it. (Kenny Blake, 25-year-old gas station clerk and cohabiting father of one)

> There's a big pull back to Golden Valley. A lot of people leave and come back. There's something about staying in a safe community, even in poverty, that's easier for them than it is elsewhere. Some of them are generational poverty. It's easier to live poor here than it is in the big cities. It's safer. (Cathy Graham, 50-year-old married schoolteacher)

> We pretty much want to raise our kids here, even if there isn't no work. Just because of how the rest of the world is, you know. With kids and drugs and gangs and guns, and stuff like that. (Randy Taylor, 35-year-old disabled, married father of two)

> I like it here 'cause I feel safe with the kids, raising them here. I don't have to fear, like, walking out the door and shots or somethin' like that. I mean, it's already happening in Hillview, and, you know, I just, I feel safe raising them here. (Julie Mitchell, 26-year-old nursery school teacher and married mother of four)

As these statements and numerous others like them suggest, part of the "family orientation" that keeps people rooted to Golden Valley has to do with safety concerns. Yet just as the meaning of "traditional" there is not exactly its textbook definition, the meaning of "safety" is also not entirely self-evident. While many parents mentioned being safe from gun threats, they were apparently ignoring the obvious fact that gun ownership is extraordinarily common in Golden Valley. I did not have to even walk out my door to hear gunshots that were constantly reverberating across the lonely landscape in Deer Run, the sound of my neighbors' almost religious target practice. During the fall hunting season the sound of gunshots was even more persistent and more of a cause for concern, as hunters were known to cross onto private property at times when tracking game. Most people in Golden Valley own numerous guns; most teach their children how to use them and occasionally guns do end up being used in unsafe ways by kids. During my year there, a teenage girl from a large local clan, drunk and high on methamphetamines, took her life by using one of her father's guns to shoot herself in the head. While parents often mentioned drugs as another one of the urban-based evils from which they were sheltered in Golden Valley, drugs and alcohol were nonetheless acknowledged to be major problems there for teenagers (and adults). Several parents of teenagers remarked that it was difficult to keep their kids away from these temptations when there was so little else for them to do and so much peer pressure to "party." Likewise, although quotes like the preceding ones suggest a community in which it is always safe to walk the streets, the same people who chose Golden Valley for its safety advantages often also repeatedly chided me for choosing to live in isolation out in Deer Run "without a gun or a dog."

While Golden Valley most certainly does have a lower crime rate than most inner cities,[33] the sanctuary the community provides is not just shelter from guns, drugs, or violence, but from particular forms of racialized crime and violence—modern evils that are perceived to be rampant in more populated parts of California. Jeanie Mayer, a single mother in her 40s, was one of the few subjects who openly discussed racial and ethnic issues among her "safety" concerns. Jeanie had spent several years living outside of Golden Valley as an adult while she was attending college and described her distress over trying to raise her children in one of California's small Central Valley towns:

> It had a very high Hispanic rate, a lot of gangs, a lot of drive-by shootings, violence. My son's fifth-grade class was more than 50 percent Hispanic, which I don't have a problem with in itself. He had some good friends who were, um, Mexican. . . . But no 10-year-old should have to deal with taking on a gang of friends that might want to beat him up. . . . So needless to say, we were out of there that next summer.

On tape, few subjects were as open about these concerns as Jeanie, although racial comments of the "not that I have anything against black people" sort often came up in more informal settings. In the formal interviews, they were rarely discussed except by the occasional subject who found the community's stance offensive. Angelica Finch, who spent part of her childhood in the Bay Area, was one of the few who explicitly problematized Golden Valley's lack of diversity and negative attitudes toward minorities. She recalled, "I actually remember the very last time that an African American family was run out of Golden Valley, and I was so deeply, horribly ashamed of this town." She further commented, "This town can be so incredibly redneck and so horribly, horribly judgmental." On occasion offhand remarks illustrated her point, such as mill worker Rod Mitchell's comment regarding a job he had refused because he felt it was beneath him. After telling me that he would try to use "polite" language, he described it as a task "for black people and Mexicans."

Although such comments made it clear that racial and ethnic differences are not tolerated in Golden Valley, due to its relative homogeneity it is easy for most residents to ignore these issues most of the time. For most, such concerns lurk unnamed but just below the surface, leaking out through such comments as, "In the city... we'd probably have to keep [the kids] in and locked up so that they didn't turn out like a lot of kids do." For many the "safety" of Golden Valley represents a haven in which to shelter their families from people of other races and ethnic origins. While it may not be as safe as they perceive it to be, it is at least isolated from the problems of many poor urban minority populations. The valley's seclusion means that such concerns remain a relatively distant threat that can be avoided by choosing to live there versus most other parts of the state. It also means that few residents have enough contact with people from different backgrounds to create a basis for any kind of mutual understanding. Hence their fears and prejudices are reinforced through stories they hear on the news and tales their friends may tell, while few real-life examples exist to challenge their stereotypes. On the rare occasion that a minority family who moves into Golden Valley is acknowledged to be an asset to the community, they are treated as exceptions to the rule rather than the norm. While people may express pleasant surprise with regard to a specific individual or family, it does not change their view of ethnic minorities as generally violent, anti-family, drug dealers, alcoholics, criminals, and welfare parasites. The generally negative reception that minorities experience in the community undoubtedly helps to keep their numbers there low.

Thus, part of what makes Golden Valley a "traditional" place is that, as a community, it has remained relatively homogeneous and consistent, while the rest of the state has gone through major demographic and cultural changes over the last fifty years. Many of those who choose to stay do so out of a combination of logistical concerns, community ties, and aversion to the world outside. Golden Valley is for many of them a haven from a tumultuous and increasingly complicated modern world. Focusing on the positive attributes of its sheltered, family-oriented lifestyle and working to reinforce those positive aspects allows them to justify accepting the negative sides of life there. Their love of the physical place, the rural lifestyle, and the community itself masks for many the downsides of this economically ravaged community. Although they often acknowledged that Golden Valley is thought of as backward and "redneck" by people from other places, its focus on positive family values and lifestyles is enough to convince most residents that living there is a justifiable and valid choice made for the right reasons. Its racial composition and lack of urban amenities allow its residents to not only construct Golden Valley as more "traditional" than the modern urban world, but to also feel superior to other groups of poor Americans because of their traditionality.

Conclusion: What Family Really Means

> [What makes someone] a good parent? Just the small things. Just taking the time to ask your child, you know, how was your day, and what do you think about this? Or if you run to the store, sayin', hey, do you wanna come with me? And of course there is a certain amount of being a good parent by making sure they at least have clean clothes and, you know, breakfast, lunch, and dinner. But you know, just sort of taking the time to let them know that they matter to you. (Kate Burton, 30-year-old hairdresser and married mother of one)

In Golden Valley, family is the pivot around which social life turns. Most people's lives focus on providing for and sustaining their families, and even their free time is generally spent engaging in family activities versus solo pursuits. This focus is taken for granted and assumed for most people; often when asked about their aspirations while growing up, the one goal they could articulate was starting a family. Parents there take enormous pride in being good mothers and fathers and in raising their children in what they believe is a safe and wholesome environment, both inside their homes and within the larger community setting. Though many acknowledged the opportunities that their children might miss by living in Golden Valley, they have constructed their discourses to reinforce the belief that living there is nonetheless in the best interest of their families. For most, living within a safe rural community and providing a stable and abuse-free environment for their families is proof enough that they are successful parents with traditional values, uncontaminated by the ills of the modern world.

As an outsider to Golden Valley, one quickly realizes that familiar terms like "tradition" and "family values" are often loaded with complex meanings that change depending on the particular cultural context in which they are invoked. The meaning of family values to middle-class whites living in the Bay Area may be very different from those of working-class and poor whites living in rural Northern California. Like morality itself, these concepts are important, not because the terms are clear but because their fluid meanings imbue them with the power to create and enforce social order and social boundaries. These discourses are more than just words and concepts. For Golden Valley residents, they are vital sources of social standing and self-worth.

As this chapter has illustrated, parenting and family in Golden Valley are very much distinct from most of California and much of the United States in both form and content. While in urban and suburban America the current generation of competitive middle-class white parents wear their nerves thin making sure their children have all the material advantages necessary to get ahead,[34] Golden Valley parents instead focus their energies on making sure that their children, and any others in need, are provided with the very basics. Often this does not even mean sufficient food, but simply an abuse-free environment in which to sleep at night and parental figures who will support them in their endeavors. Most Golden Valley parents are more or less unconcerned about whether their children attend college at all, let alone whether they attend prestigious universities and end up with high-status careers.

Although within Golden Valley parents generally define themselves against their urban and suburban counterparts, Lareau argues that the parenting divide is a distinctly class-related phenomenon that occurs throughout the United States and crosses racial lines. Her work finds that middle-class parents focus on "a deliberate and sustained effort to stimulate children's development and to cultivate their cognitive and social skills." Meanwhile, working-class and poor parents "viewed children's development as spontaneously unfolding, as long as they were provided with comfort, food, shelter, and other basic support."[35] Her description of this latter form of parenting does describe Golden Valley parents with some degree of accuracy, although there are also practices that are unique to the rural setting. Nonetheless, her point is important: both parenting styles are focused on the well-being of children but with conflicting definitions of what this means. Although Golden Valley parents think of and portray themselves as more family oriented than urban parents, the reality is that their family priorities are simply different and rooted in class differences that are symbolized for them by community size and racial/ethnic diversity. In this particular community, a parent's worth is not measured through the success of his or her children, but rather through the degree to which that parent prioritizes family values.

Few of my respondents, when asked what their goals were for their children, could articulate anything concrete. Much more common were vague statements like the following, from 33-year-old mechanic Jeff Taylor: "I hope that my girls go out and do something to support themselves if they need to. I'd like 'em to have an education." While such things as education and future employment might be referenced, there were seldom more specific goals or plans for children. Most Golden Valley parents believe that the best way to raise kids is to teach them to be independent and self-sufficient and to let them make their own decisions regarding their futures. They tend to support their children's decisions and accomplishments but stop short of having expectations or of making much attempt to influence their children's lives. And few Golden Valley parents ever seemed to be focused on having children who were superior to anyone else's. Their children's achievements were perhaps a source of pride, but they were seldom a main source of a parent's self-worth. More important were the moral achievements of the parents themselves.

In Golden Valley, parents find their competitive edge through manifesting their moral worth and "traditionality." Rather than defining success through the employment and income achievements of their children, they instead take pride in their abilities to create and sustain functional, abuse-free home environments despite the employment and income challenges they face. They work hard to pass on their unique culture and way of life, teaching their children skills and customs that are of little use outside of the rural mountain environment. Their discourses on family and tradition allow them to distinguish among themselves who is or is not succeeding and to distinguish their unique community and culture from competing cultures and places that might scorn and judge Golden Valley as a place where only uneducated rednecks would choose to live and raise children.

According to Bourdieu, class distinctions do not form a single continuum across a society, but vary according to a subgroup's "position in social space, and . . . the relationship between its distribution in geographical space and the distribution of scarce assets in that space." He further explains that the "exchange rate" for the various types of capital—that is, social, economic, and cultural capital—depends on these spatial and distributive factors and differs according to them.[36] In Golden Valley, the general lack of economic and cultural capital has led to a devaluation of these forms and a greater value being placed on social and moral capital, the only forms that are still abundant there. The community's isolation from the larger society has allowed it to evolve a set of standards and norms that are separate from those of the world outside and are constructed in direct opposition to it. Instead, Golden Valley's cultural norms focus on retaining its exclusivity and preserving its particular lifestyle in opposition to other modern lifestyles. As discussed in previous chapters, "class" distinctions have come to be based more on who is morally upright and hardworking than on who has the most money, education, or access to high culture. Those forms of capital that are highly valued and pursued by the white middle class in urban and suburban America now have little value in Golden Valley, where they are nearly impossible to acquire.

Thus, family is significant and important in Golden Valley, not just because the community has a history of focusing on family, but because it is the one area left in which its citizens can define themselves and their community as a success story. Golden Valley exists on the margins of U.S. society. As the country has rapidly changed, it has not taken isolated places like Golden Valley with it. Instead, this community finds itself left behind the times, both culturally and economically as well as in terms of infrastructure and opportunities. It is no wonder that the community's response is to cling to "tradition" and to elevate in status those few arenas in which it can still create the mirage of success. Moral strength, in the form of work ethics and family values, is all that this community can hold onto in this shifting structural and cultural terrain.

In addition to their discourses and strict hierarchy of morality regarding work ethics, Golden Valley residents have produced a complementary discourse around family and tradition that also creates boundaries between themselves and the world and between the deserving and undeserving poor within their community. Family values and family-oriented behavior, like work ethics, have been elevated to moral categories that perform normative functions. To achieve moral success by Golden Valley standards, it is not enough to have the appropriate work ethics—although as chapter 2 illustrated, this is a necessary condition for moral success. But to be successful, an adult in Golden Valley must also be able to demonstrate proper family values and "traditional" behaviors. This means the creation and sustaining of a stable home environment where one's children and others' children as well can feel safe and supported. It means restricting substance abuse and domestic violence to a bare minimum and focusing one's free time on family activities versus individual pursuits such as drinking or socializing with friends. Adults who adhere to this code of family orientation are able to distinguish themselves from those who do not. Although the "bad parents" may not have any less money or live in any worse conditions, they are known to most community members and scorned for their irresponsible, selfish behaviors.

Once again, it becomes clear the ways in which certain political arguments have taken on intensified salience in places like Golden Valley: when moral values, family, and tradition are the main axes along which you define your own and your community's strengths, the agenda that stresses these issues more will be the one that resonates better. These are the issues that upper-middle-class Americans tend to misunderstand or refuse to acknowledge. For those who feel more in control of their economic destinies, family values are much more likely to be tied to economic success issues than to more vague moral concerns such as those that dominate in Golden Valley. Yet most Americans do not recognize the degree to which their own definitions of family values and tradition may differ from those of people from different race, ethnic, and class backgrounds. In Golden Valley this perspective is lacking as well. However, the terms there have an importance that cannot be underplayed. They have a weight and significance that elevates them beyond simple concepts to be the scaffolding upon which much of social life and social distinction rests.

4

Remaking Masculinity:
Losing Male Breadwinners

Family Instability in Golden Valley

> When I first started it was fairly certain that most of your kids had a
> mom and a dad, got breakfast in the morning, came to school, backed
> by parents who thought school was important, who made sure that
> homework was done, who put them to bed at a reasonable hour, and
> then got them up the next morning and started the cycle again. Now,
> if you looked at my class, probably 40 percent of them are still coming
> with those things in place. (Cathy Graham, 50-year-old married
> schoolteacher)

Some of the statements quoted in chapter 3 give the impression that
Golden Valley is a community that models itself on television shows from
the 1950s, in which every family has two parents and at least a couple
of kids. They suggest that time has passed them by, and that while family values and family norms have changed drastically in the rest of the
United States, their community has remained—or more accurately,
become—a rare bastion of family stability. This is, of course, far from
the full truth. While my subjects discussed the importance of family
values and the goal of stable families, there was always either an implicit,
or often an explicit, reference to those families that were unstable and
those poor children who were growing up without two parents present.

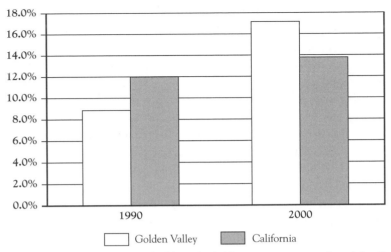

Figure 5. Single-parent households with children as percentage of total family households, in Golden Valley and in California. *Source:* U.S. Census Summary Files (1990, 2000).

Schoolteachers in particular often bemoaned the lack of two-parent, stable families in Golden Valley, and many talked about increasing numbers of children who were transient, who had multiple siblings with different last names, and whose parents were constantly changing partners and moving households.[1]

Despite the importance of family in Golden Valley, and the prominence of the nuclear family as an ideal, it is nonetheless difficult to sustain stable, two-parent families there, now even more so than in the past. During my year there I met many single mothers (and several single fathers), often struggling to make ends meet and sharing housing and child care with relatives who were willing to help. Depending on the relationship a person had to the particular single parent, they were discussed with pity, disappointment, and sometimes scorn. Yet their presence persists, despite the judgment and stigma they endure. Over the decade from 1990 to 2000, the percent of family households in Golden Valley that were headed by single parents rose substantially. In 1990 single-parent households with children made up just 8.7 percent of total family households there, considerably less than the state average of 12.0 percent. By 2000, their incidence had nearly doubled to 16.6 percent, now higher than the state average of 13.9 percent.

What accounts for such a dramatic rise in single-parent families, particularly in a community which by its own accounts is extremely traditional, conservative, and family oriented? This is a place where marriage is the norm and pregnant teenagers are more likely to have shotgun weddings than to have babies out of wedlock. In Golden Valley the rising rates of single parenting reflect increases in both nonmarriage and divorce/separation over the period. During the same time period, California's divorce and nonmarriage rates remained stable. However, nonmarriage occurred at a much higher rate across the state in both 1990 and 2000, while divorce rates in Golden Valley began higher and continued to rise.[2] Since married couples are more likely to have children than are never-married individuals—particularly in Golden Valley—marital breakup is likely a larger contributor to single-parenting statistics in Golden Valley than in California as a whole.

Academic research has long found evidence of a correlation between poverty and family structure, specifically a high likelihood that single-parent families will be poor and vice versa.[3] Golden Valley residents have their own anecdotal evidence to link economic decline with family changes, and most believe that families have become less stable since the mill closed. Few have neat theories to explain exactly why family instability has accompanied labor market collapse, but they generally point fingers at the same forces that are to blame for their community's decline in all arenas: drugs, alcohol, and welfare receipt. Many residents talked about the difficulties of sustaining families under the conditions caused by the mill closure, including the separation of husbands from their families when they chose to follow work, as well as the drug and alcohol abuse to which many men fell victim when they were out of work indefinitely. Thirty-year-old Allison Butters, whose common-law husband is out of work, gave this explanation for the breakup of many relationships since the mill closure:

> I would say that I'm pretty lucky and that lots of people who've been infected [sic] by the timber industry are not so lucky. I do believe that when their husbands lose jobs things become very hard. They don't know how to cope with it or to train themselves in something else. So drugs and alcohol becomes a very big deal.

There is a large literature that explores the causes behind the link between poverty and family structure and numerous ways of explaining

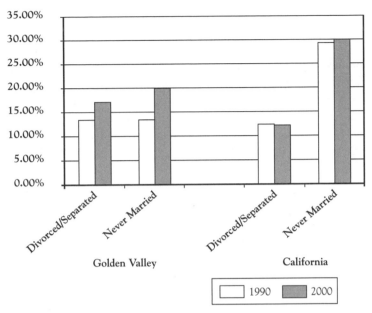

Figure 6. Divorce/separation and nonmarriage rates for adults age fifteen and older, in Golden Valley and in California. *Source:* U.S. Census Summary Files (1990, 2000)

it. In urban poor settings, much literature focuses on nonmarital child-birth versus marital breakup as the dominant pathway to single-parent families. In these settings nonmarriage is often explained as the result of a "retreat" from marriage, which occurs mainly due to women's economic concerns and lack of interest in marriage to poor or unemployed men.[4] Researchers who study inner-city poverty have argued that poor women find unemployed men "unmarriageable," preferring the independence offered by welfare or low-wage work to marriage with jobless men.[5] While nonmarriage has not been studied in the same depth in rural communities, there is some research that suggests that rural women's choices with regard to family structure are the same as those of urban women and for mostly similar economic-based reasons.[6]

However, there is also ample evidence to suggest that poor women are as concerned about the behaviors of poor men as they are about their financial status. Edin and Kefalas, for example, find that regardless of race, the poor women in their sample choose nonmarriage both because of economic concerns regarding men's employment and financial status and because they fear men will be unfaithful, abusive, incarcerated, and drug and alcohol addicted.[7] There is abundant research from the urban poor setting that suggests that nonmarriage may be linked to men's personal issues with regard to unemployment and poverty as well, which often contribute to the development of "protest masculinities."[8] The threats to masculinity and male dominance created by job loss and poverty can result in misogynistic behaviors,[9] gender distrust,[10] and refusal to accept responsibility for children,[11] all of which contribute to nonmarriage.

For those who are already married, the type of job loss and job insecurity found in Golden Valley can contribute to marital and family problems that seriously threaten families' long-term stability as well.[12] Family dysfunction can be the result of identity crises and loss of self-esteem for the unemployed, who experience shame and guilt as well as threats to their senses of masculinity or femininity.[13] Job loss and the resulting downward mobility have been linked to numerous negative outcomes for families in various settings, "including stress, high levels of alcohol consumption, marital tension, and depression . . . [as well as] physical brutality, incapacitating alcoholism, desertion, child abuse, the complete disintegration of the family, and in some instances, suicide."[14] Men tend to experience these symptoms more violently than women because both their self-images and masculine identities are often tied to breadwinning.[15] Segal explains that "male unemployment and the restructuring or dismantling of old industries create new crises in traditional patterns of male authority. Such disruption connects up in turn with cultural struggles over the meanings of 'masculinity.'"[16]

Unemployment and job loss can be particularly devastating for rural men, whose masculine identities are often tied not only to paid labor and breadwinning, but also to work in specific, historically established industries like farming or logging.[17] Rural research from divergent communities has shown that the loss of employment in traditional sectors can create a profound sense of loss and personal failure for men,[18] which can translate into problems such as increased strain and hostility between spouses,[19] as well as between men and women in public spaces.[20] Large-scale job loss has even been linked to the emergence of reactive protest masculinities,[21] which arise in some affected rural communities as the traditional complementary gender roles are undermined by men's lack of work.[22] Hostile gender relations are in turn linked to rising rates of divorce as well as drops in marriage and birth rates for affected rural communities.[23]

Even when economic crises do not result in such antagonistic and predatory gender relations, gender often remains a tense and contested sphere for many families. Norem and Blundall explain that for families affected by the U.S. farm crisis of the 1980s, marital discord often occurred "when a lack of flexibility in roles prevented adaptation to the changing family and economic situation and it was not possible to renegotiate role definitions accordingly."[24] Nelson and Smith similarly find that among households where economic strain is the worst, and traditional gendered divisions of labor the most threatened, gendered responses are generally the least flexible and often devolve into "sheer assertions of male privilege."[25] Researchers find that the entry of women into the workforce, rather than being met by increased gender equality, is often devalued and underplayed in importance by both men and women who are uncomfortable with new gender roles.[26] Hochschild argues that women's rapid entrance into the workforce has not been accepted by men, leading to a "stalled revolution," which creates tensions that lead to the retrenchment of the traditional breadwinner/homemaker divide or resistance to marriage itself.[27] Traditional gender roles and norms often become the most rigid and unshakable at exactly the point where circumstances require them to be the most innovative and flexible, leading to marital and family tensions that exacerbate economic strain.

The stalled gender revolution is not the only possible outcome for families that must take on new gender roles, however. A few studies have found evidence of some amount of change in rural gender roles, such as women's increasing workforce participation being met by male willingness to take on a limited amount of household chores rather than simply the devaluation of women's work.[28] Mederer notes the importance of such gender flexibility to rural families' survival in times of industrial crisis:

> Families whose paradigm includes the ability to share roles, as well as less traditional attitudes toward gender and family, are better equipped to adapt their lives to the new economic and interactional circumstances, such as instituting new definitions of breadwinning and parenting. Flexibility in roles leads to less marital tension under conditions of economic uncertainty.[29]

In Golden Valley, this type of gender flexibility is emerging as one possible response to the changes the community has undergone and does appear to be key to the long-term sustainability of family units. But this type of flexibility still exists alongside its opposite: rigid gender norms like those described above, which result as part of an attempt to re-create the past rather than adapt to the present circumstances. These rigid gender norms are in turn linked to the types of negative outcomes found by previous researchers, including power struggles within families and other types of gender antagonism. Although they have different underlying ideologies, each of these sets of gender strategies is accompanied by specific discourses around masculinity and family that help justify the stance as both masculine and moral. The discourse and ideology adopted by a family has serious consequences for the quality of marital relationships and the satisfaction of both spouses.

In the absence of work but in the presence of a strong cultural tradition with regard to work and breadwinning, as well as social pressure to marry and create two-parent families, men are under increasing amounts of stress in Golden Valley. Understanding their experiences with the structural changes and the confusion and ambivalence that result can help explain why family instability is becoming more common in the community despite how important "traditional" family values are there. The dissonance that the economic collapse has produced between men's ideals and their realities has created an enormous challenge for them. For many of Golden Valley's men, the moral imperative of a "traditional" family has come into conflict with the masculine imperative to be the sole breadwinner for such a family. The ways in which families navigate and bridge the divide between their moral beliefs and their gender identities have an impact on their economic survival, happiness, and ultimately their abilities to remain together as family units.

Secondary Breadwinners and Stay-at-Home Moms: Women's Flexible Gender Roles

[If we have kids, hopefully] he'd be working. Yeah, but if not, then I would work and he would stay home. Keith has no problem being a stay-at-home dad. When I did my student teaching he was on unemployment, so he wasn't working at all. So he did all the housework, he made dinner, he did all of it. That he took care of the house, which was great, showed us that, that we can do this. We work well, and those stereotype roles do not exist. Definitely not! (Dawn Bartlett, 26-year-old married schoolteacher)

Women's reactions to Golden Valley's structural changes, as well as their reactions to men's roles and behaviors, play a significant role in families' abilities to adapt to the economic collapse. For women, the changes generally have been less catastrophic to their senses of self than they have been for men. Most of the jobs lost in the wake of the spotted owl ruling were men's jobs. For women, the main change has been not job loss, but the need to enter the labor market to help make up for the income shortfall caused by men's lost jobs and wages. While not as devastating as the loss of work is to men, this change nonetheless represents a major transformation in many women's gender expectations. Just one generation ago, Golden Valley's women were predominantly stay-at-home mothers. Thus women, as well as men, have needed to adjust their expectations of gender norms, family responsibilities, and breadwinning responsibilities. The ability to do so also has been essential to the success or failure of the community's families. To make these adjustments, women call on discourses from family values to feminism, combining them in ways that justify their new choices while stressing the ways in which they are still "traditional" and family focused.

As their stories and comments will illustrate, Golden Valley's women have shown a dedication to remaining in two-parent families despite the new burdens placed on them. They have often taken on both first- and second-shift responsibilities[30] within their households and have been surprisingly understanding of out-of-work men. Far from losing interest in marriage with unemployed or underemployed men, many of the women have learned to take pride in being successful earners as well as wives and mothers. This does not mean that they are willing to forgive all behaviors, however. For some, the destabilization of gender norms in Golden Valley has resulted in a tense dance between men and women within the family and between old and new conceptions of family roles and responsibilities. While many women may be willing to bend their expectations, they can still eventually reach a breaking point. However, the issues that cause them the most concern are not always those predicted by previous researchers, particularly those working in urban settings. Golden Valley's women are generally less concerned with men's unemployment and seldom fear infidelity.[31] On the other hand, many react with frustration to men who are controlling and oppressive in their attempts to retain traditional male breadwinner and head-of-household positions within the family, and some eventually find these situations intolerable.

Working for the Good of the Family

> When he worked at Northwest Timber and he was here, he made really, really good money and I didn't have to work. You know, I didn't really have to. But the pay is different over there in Miner's Gulch. . . . I always felt bad if I, you know, if things might have been tight, then I felt like, if I was working it kinda helped make it not be so tight. (Julie Mitchell, 26-year-old nursery school teacher and married mother of four)

> Let me work. I have to work. If I won the lottery I would still work, because that's how I get my self-esteem. It's not—you know, I'm not the best housekeeper in the world, and my house isn't a pigsty or anything, but it's not something I love to do, you know? So I work, because that makes me feel good about myself. Cleaning my house doesn't. It's just something I have to do so I can go work. And you can only get so much self-esteem off of cooking a good meal, you know? (Angelica Finch, 38-year-old school administrator and married mother of three)

In Golden Valley the urban-based finding that women are uninterested in marrying poor men[32] is not consistent with women's testimonies regarding the breakups of previous relationships. Over my year there, I met only one woman who explicitly referenced economic concerns as a reason that she remained unmarried. Jeanie Mayer, a 45-year-old single mother of two, lived in Golden Valley until her early twenties and then returned again a few years later after completing her AA degree elsewhere. She has had two long-term relationships with two different Golden Valley men, both of which she eventually ended because neither man held a job or contributed regularly to the family's collective living expenses. She described her frustration with her children's father:

> He worked, he worked some, but it wasn't steady. He was pretty laid-back—you could say lazy, you know—and he's my opposite. I'm more the overachiever, workaholic type. So we definitely never ever saw eye to eye on work, you know. And I'm not one to sit and watch TV, you know. It's a waste of time. Even if he did work, then he'd be sitting and watching TV all night, work's done. Yeah, not with two kids, you know. So we managed to keep it together until Carrie was about a year and a half, two years old. And then at that point it was just like, "I'm outta

here. You know what, it's easier to do it on my own than to never have your support."

Jeanie's second relationship had similar problems, as the second man also had trouble keeping jobs and managing money responsibly:

He couldn't keep a full-time steady job, and he didn't have a GED. And so, basically it was like I was taking care of him as well. You know, I had kids and animals and I was in school. I was still having to pay his portion of the rent because he didn't have the money, and, yeah, it was like, OK, I can't do this, I've got too many other things. And I don't mind paying for food, but I'm not paying for all his bills. He should know how to take care of himself. So I ran out of patience after a while, and I have been very happily single ever since. It's been three-and-a-half years now.

When asked if these financial issues were the main source of stress in the second relationship, Jeanie explained, "Yeah, that and then he started drinking a lot. But I think that was because of the stress we were having with everything else."

Jeanie's story illustrates that even in Golden Valley a man's lack of "marriageability" in economic terms can cause relationships to falter, particularly when a man demonstrates traits or attitudes that cause him to be perceived as lazy and lacking the work ethic necessary to keep a job. However, Jeanie's story also brings up another important perceived moral deficiency that can damage a relationship: excessive drinking. Alcoholism and drug abuse were the core issues that most women mentioned as their main frustrations with previous relationships. As was discussed in chapter 3, substance abuse and domestic violence issues came up much more often than did unemployment or poverty in explaining from the woman's perspective the disintegration of their relationships. Poverty is something that many of Golden Valley's residents grew up with and can tolerate. Very few of my respondents, particularly the women, had ever aspired to much beyond simple economic survival and being able to meet their most basic needs. Serious substance abuse and domestic violence, although also problems that many of them grew up with, are issues that most are not willing to live with as adults.

While women were often intolerant with regard to substance abuse and physical abuse, they were generally willing to compromise regarding traditional gender norms and breadwinning responsibilities within the family. Most were willing to take on paid work if the family budget required it and did not blame out-of-work men for their inabilities to find jobs. None besides Jeanie ever suggested that a man's lack of work made him unmarriageable, but rather they adapted to the situations as they arose. Some women were pleasantly surprised by how much they enjoyed working, despite the fact that many had originally envisioned themselves being stay-at-home mothers. Others had grown up in poor families in which working was a necessity for all children and had pre-existing identities built up around working. While some women portrayed themselves as secondary earners, others called on pop-culture versions of feminist ideologies that helped them to justify feeling empowered by their status as major contributors to the household finances. For some, their discourses on working matched their current circumstances, but for others the discourses justified the situation in ways that identified them with the gender norms of the past. Yet whether they professed to prefer to work or to be primarily stay-at-home mothers who were forced by circumstances to work outside the home, most Golden Valley women accepted their responsibilities to contribute to the household finances and did not express anger or frustration with their husbands' inabilities to fully support them. Regardless of their original expectations, the women showed extraordinary flexibility with regard to gender norms and showed little resistance to taking on most breadwinning responsibilities.

Forty-five-year-old Grace Prader is an example of a woman who had always imagined being a stay-at-home mother but who adapted to financial realities without blaming her husband. Bill Prader had worked in the mill, but they decided together that he would not move with it to Adams. Since the mill closure, however, he has struggled to stay in the workforce and has been laid off repeatedly. At the time of our interview, Bill was out of work again and Grace was working to support the family as well as she could with a low-wage secretarial job. She explained, "If I didn't have to, I would prefer to stay home with the kids. But there wasn't a choice." For Grace and Bill, there simply wasn't the luxury of set roles with regard to breadwinning; survival mattered first and foremost. Grace described their recent financial stresses:

> Last year we made $17,000, you know, and so by the time you take taxes out that's twelve hundred bucks a month. So yeah, it was tight. This year's not much better because Bill got hurt in February, and the most he's worked since then is like three or four hours a day. And now he's laid off.

Despite the difficulties imposed upon them by Bill's labor market struggles, Grace did not blame him or even seem to expect him to be able to
provide on his own. When I asked her if it was difficult to be the main
breadwinner for their family of four, she replied, "Oh, well, Bill's had to
support us the last three years," suggesting that in their household breadwinning had come to be a shared responsibility. Grace expressed regret
over having spent so much of her two children's lifetimes in the workforce, particularly since Bill's parenting was not quite equal to her own.
Nonetheless, she found ways in which to justify her "nontraditional"
gender roles within the family:

> I have a lot of regrets in that [our son] Aaron has been extremely inde-
> pendent, but he's been basically taking care of his brother since he was 4.
> You know, because I was working, and Bill was around the house a lot,
> but he was busy doing his stuff, so the kids were there, they had adults
> around—you know, for safety purposes—but for the most part, they took
> care of themselves. And I have guilt about that, but at the same time it
> really made Aaron independent and he relies on himself. It's really nice
> if I get sick now that I can be sick now. I don't have to feel like a lot of
> other women—"So you're sick. Where's my dinner?" He cooks.

Many Golden Valley women, like Grace, accept the need for both
partners to contribute to moneymaking as much as they can, even when
it conflicts with their original gender and parenting expectations.
Thirty-two-year-old April Layton has worked since she was a teenager,
but still hoped to be able to stay at home with her children while they
were young. Financial necessity forced her back into the workforce, as
her husband's low-wage job was not sufficient to support the family.
April adjusted her expectations and went to work. She described the
transition as difficult, but not overly traumatic for anyone involved,
and eventually she came to enjoy her job as well:

> It makes it a little more hectic when I'm working because then there's
> less time to get stuff done around here. But after I got the job and got
> adjusted to my hours and working and what I was doing, the kids and
> getting them used to what's happening with that, then it's a lot easier.
> I like it a lot right now. So, you know, if the house doesn't get picked
> up one night, then, you know, it doesn't get picked up one night. That's
> just the way it has to be.

Like Grace, April focused on the positive aspects of her new gender
roles and relied upon a discourse that helped to rationalize her decision
to work full-time as part of a woman's responsibility to her family.

Generally, even women who believed a mother should not work were able to find peace with the situation when financial need required it. Often they justified their work as secondary and thus still conceived of their husbands as the main breadwinners. Twenty-five-year-old Nicole Goodman, who makes nearly as much money as her husband through several part-time jobs, explained, "I don't mind doing the part-time to supplement the income, but I don't wanna be the one that does the main income." She made it clear throughout her testimony that she considered her work to be only supplemental and secondary to her husband's job. This downplaying of the importance of women's work has been noted by a number of scholars of gender relations in rural as well as urban areas.[33] I found it to be common among couples for whom sending wives into the workforce presented a major challenge to their preexisting gender norms.

Like Nicole, 32-year-old Rosemary Taylor entered the workforce reluctantly because her family needed the money. She maintains that her work is secondary and done only out of necessity. When asked if she would work if she didn't have to, Rosemary replied:

> No, I'd stay home. 'Cause when you go and do something, you know, earn a little extra money, something goes lacking at home. No, I wouldn't do it if I didn't have to. As long as [the kids are] home. When they're gone, I can see myself doing that and, you know, staying busy and stuff, but it's harder now.

While both Rosemary and Nicole went to work mainly because they felt it was necessary for the family's survival, both nonetheless accepted their responsibilities to contribute to the family budget, albeit with resignation rather than enthusiasm. Both women dreamed of staying home but realistically acknowledged that life would be much harder if they were to currently prioritize gender norms over financial survival. Like Grace and April, neither Nicole nor Rosemary blamed her husband for being unable to support the family. Instead, they adopted discourses around women's work as a family-level survival strategy and as a necessity versus a calling. In their cases, the downplaying of work helped to bridge the distance between their original expectations and current realities.

As these stories suggest, women in Golden Valley do not generally consider a man's employment status to be either a main requirement or a deal breaker with regard to his marriageability. They consistently choose to marry and cohabit with men whose jobs and labor market attachments are tenuous, and they react not with scorn for their struggling partners but with a pragmatic sense of responsibility to help make up the earnings deficit. Most women have taken on work responsibilities without fully losing their sense of themselves as "traditional" mothers, thus allowing them to continue to perform traditional gender displays[34] despite changing roles. Like working-class and rural women in a number of different contexts, they maintain their sense of traditional femininity through downplaying the importance of their contributions, through claiming that they work only out of financial necessity, and through working in occupations that are generally feminized, such as child care, in-home care, and service and secretarial positions.[35] Although a few working mothers call upon popular American discourses around women's work and empowerment to justify enjoying and prioritizing their work, most still tie their gender identities to mothering and the household. Thus, while they are often strained by their numerous responsibilities both at work and at home, most do not struggle with gender identity issues and do not have problems conceiving of themselves as appropriately feminine.

Women tend to understand that men's jobs aren't available in Golden Valley anymore and that men's unemployment is generally caused by structural problems rather than men's personal shortcomings. Several women suggested that it is men, not women, who are more bothered by the structural changes and in particular by a man's inability to be the provider for the family. A telling example of this came from Eli and Laura Jordan, who have struggled with poverty since he fell out of the workforce in the 1990s. He described the difficult time he experienced when his injuries first forced him onto disability and particularly his fears about his changing roles within his family. The following exchange between him and Laura illustrates how much more seriously he took these issues:

> ELI: I was afraid I was gonna lose my family and my wife, more than anything, from bein' hurt. It was a really depressing time, it was— that was my biggest fear probably.
> LAURA: He says that all the time. He's stupid.
>
> *Because you weren't going to leave him?*
> LAURA: No! No!
> ELI: No, but it's your fear, you know. It's you're not doin' anything, it seems like, for the family or anything else.

LAURA: So we make him the house bitch and make him clean up.
[laughs]

Women were generally able to adjust their gender expectations to accommodate the labor market changes and were forgiving of men's lowered status, even when slightly uncomfortable with it. It was for the men whose status moved from breadwinner to "house bitch" that these changes were far more commonly fraught with anxiety and threatened gender identities. As Allison Butters explained with regard to her breadwinning status and her unemployed partner:

> I don't mind working. But I would hate to see him think he was less of
> a man because he wasn't.
>
> *Do you think that's what's happening?*
> No. Well, I think that's what he thinks sometimes.

As both of these sets of comments suggest, while women may be flexible with regard to their own gender roles and forgiving of men for being out of work, they also struggle with how to redefine masculine identities for unemployed men. While Laura Jordan may have had no intention of leaving Eli, her comments nonetheless portray her discomfort and frustration with his nonworking status. Allison Butters, although less aggressive in her implicit criticism of her husband, is similarly aware that his job loss makes him less of a man—to some at least, if not to her. For men like Eli, these small comments and observations undoubtedly carry more weight, adding insult to the injury of being out of work in a community where work ethics are synonymous with both masculinity and morality.

While women may not always be entirely at ease with nonworking men, they are nonetheless quite forgiving and generally willing to contribute financially themselves. In Golden Valley it is still considered the norm and mark of financial success for a woman to stay at home while the man works. Yet the current economic and labor-market reality makes this situation increasingly unattainable, and thus growing numbers of women there do work outside the home and many enjoy the experience. In many families the woman has the more secure job or is the main breadwinner for most of the year. It is not extraordinary on nice afternoons to see men in flannel shirts and hunting caps pushing baby carriages down the street, either alone or with buddies. Between the lack of acceptably masculine jobs and the high rate of serious injuries among men who have worked in the mill or the woods, it is becoming normal for men to be at home while women go to work. Disabilities in particular are seen as valid reasons for men to not contribute much financially to a household, and women tend to be accepting of and sympathetic to men who are not in the workforce due to debilitating injuries. Although disabled men may be viewed as slightly emasculated, they are nonetheless still supported by their wives.

However, women are generally supportive and understanding even with men who are physically able but who cannot find work. Despite the fact that women can and do support themselves and families in Golden Valley just as well as men, no working married woman suggested that she would rather be on her own than married. For most of the town's wives and mothers the focus is on family survival, and they understand that circumstances there sometimes demand that whoever can find work takes responsibility for supporting the entire family. Most women's top concerns are material survival and family stability, not gender norms. This sense of equal responsibility for breadwinning was reflected again and again in women's testimonies, with few exceptions. For those women who are divorced or single, economic struggles were seldom the main factor leading to the dissolution of previous relationships, although economic struggles remain a serious source of stress in many current relationships. But a working man, though an asset if you are lucky enough to find one, is perhaps too much to demand in a place like Golden Valley.

Few women consciously acknowledge feminism as an influence, yet many borrow its more popular concepts from the larger culture to construct their family values around gender equality with regard to work and financial responsibility as befits their situations. The women, more often than the men, tend to be extremely flexible with regard to gender expectations and generally make whatever changes are necessary in their ideals to stay afloat and keep their families intact. They often construct their feminine identities through a combination of traditional ideologies and modern feminist ideologies, picking and choosing only those necessary to best explain and justify their situations. In a sense, women are the lucky ones in Golden Valley with regard to changing gender norms. Within a culture that so heavily prizes work and work ethics, they are gaining increased access to moral authority. Thus, their only struggle is to find ways to integrate their new culturally and morally acceptable activities with their preexisting gender identities. The increasing mainstream acceptability of working wives and mothers throughout the United States over the last fifty years provides them with multiple discourses from which to choose. Thus, most are willing to trade homemaking for breadwinning as their families' circumstances and their husbands' employment experiences require. Some ended up enjoying working, while others wished that their situations would allow them to stay at home.

Similarly, some husbands openly acknowledged their wives' contributions as vital parts of the household budget, while others downplayed them as simply extra spending money. However, no woman openly criticized her husband for not being able to provide for the family on his own. As their comments suggest, for women the changing gender norms have been less traumatic than for most Golden Valley men. On the contrary, for many Golden Valley women it has been harder to maintain more traditional stay-at-home mother roles than it has been to enter the workforce. With the current economic conditions, it has become much harder for families to keep a woman at home, and the attempt to do so often results in both economic strain and personal frustration for women.

Frustrated with Tradition: Women at Home

> I would have to say that money is a big source [of stress]. I spend it, though I don't know what the heck I spend it on. And he's making it, and says, "You don't make the money," and "You don't know what it's like having to go out there and work." Well, you know, I don't. But if I had the opportunity to make the money you could make at the moment, believe me, I'd be out there and *you'd* be sittin' at home! (Stacey Morris, 30-year-old married mother of two)

While it is common now for Golden Valley women to enter the workforce, there are still many who stay at home despite the financial strain it often causes. These financially questionable choices are often made jointly, and many women who stay at home did desire, at least at first, to be at home with their children. However, as will be explored in the following section as well, these arrangements often persist despite the struggles they impose because of men's desires to be the sole breadwinners and heads of the household. In these homes tensions often run high, between the financial stresses and what women often perceive as their husbands' controlling behaviors. Compared with women who have entered the workforce, those women who stay at home are often less understanding of their husbands' plights and more frustrated with both their strained budgets and their lack of power within their families. While women are likely to leave men who are obviously abusive, they are less sure about how to deal with men who are simply controlling and oppressive in their behaviors. In my volunteer work with young (generally stay-at-home) mothers at the Family Empowerment Alliance (FEA), I sat in on many conversations in which mothers with more "traditional" family structures complained bitterly about their husbands' extreme behaviors and their feelings of powerlessness within their families.

Particularly for those families in which the men are still working with some regularity but earning incomes that are not particularly high, the semblance of a traditional family is often created and sustained through strategies that emphasize male dominance and power within the family and often expressly disempower their wives. In these families, husbands generally do not share housework or child care and often hold strict control over finances. Most of these young mothers, including several who do work part-time or informally, have no access to money except the cash allowances that their husbands dole out to them for living expenses. They have neither credit cards nor checkbooks in their own names, and any money they make goes straight into their husbands' bank accounts. Thus, their husbands are able to achieve a traditional breadwinner form of masculinity even during the months when they are out of work. They generally do not spend those months off helping around the house, but rather are out in the woods with their friends, hunting, fishing, and gathering wood until it is time to go back to work again. These "traditional" homes were generally the unhappiest ones that I entered, with bickering and arguing, frustration and resentment expressed in front of me on the occasions when they were interviewed as couples. More often than not, more traditional couples declined to be interviewed together, and often these individuals discouraged me from interviewing their partners at all. When the women were interviewed separately, they were often more frank about the sources of their marital tensions.

We met Kim Clark in chapter 3. She is 32 years old and married to Al, once a locally employed logger who now works seasonally in logging outside of Jefferson County. He is away from the household for most of the spring and summer months. Kim does not work outside the home, although she did for several years before she married Al. During the off-season from work, Al is habitually away on hunting trips and thus still mainly absent from the home. His increasing absence has put considerable stress on Kim, who is left alone for long periods of time to care for their two young children. However, Al does little housework or child care even when he is present. As Kim explained with some frustration:

> He can't seem to pick his stuff up or clean up his own dishes. Oh, but he's real good at telling me to do it and having me [do it]. His good one is, "You know, people need to eat three square meals a day." That's the good one.

In casual settings such as the FEA, Kim tends to come across as negative and angry. She spends a lot of time complaining about Al, who she often describes as a "pig." One of her most common complaints is with his absolute control over their finances. She explained in her interview:

> We don't have, like, a bank account together. All finances are in his name. And we just pay bills as they come. When I need money, I get money, he provides. I don't know, I'd say he gives me whatever I want or need or—we don't really fight over that. Sometimes I buck up over it because it's just the damn principle of having a damn checking account! It's just the principle. I'm 32 years old and I'm not *allowed* to have a checking account?!

Kim's close friend Stacey Morris had similar complaints about her husband and joked, "Yeah, we forgot to mention, we both have three children: two actual children and our husbands that act just as bad." Although she works part-time providing informal child care for her friends' children, both Stacey and her husband, Bruce, consider her to be a stay-at-home mother for their two kids, who are both in school. Bruce controls their bank accounts and finances, and according to Stacey, "My husband gives me $20 a day, and you know, the kids eat at school, so that's supposed to buy dinner and whatever else needs to be done." Like Al Clark, Bruce Morris is also seasonally unemployed and spends much of his time off trying to avoid the household and its chores. Stacey expressed a desire to go back to work full-time, which she said Bruce would allow. However, she feared that it would be difficult because she couldn't trust him to help around the house even when he was out of work. She explained:

> I have no doubt that he would open up a can of soup and the kids would be fed. But the dishes would not get done, the laundry would not get done, the house would not get cleaned. He would make sure his kids are fed and probably homework done. That's probably as far as it would go.

Like Kim, Stacey was somewhat frustrated by Bruce's refusal to help with daily household chores, which he avoided through both active and passive forms of resistance:[36]

> He will not vacuum. He won't do the dishes, he won't do his laundry— you know, he won't do stuff like that. He'll make the mess, but he won't clean it up.

According to Stacey, his refusal to help is not because Bruce doesn't know how to do household chores, but because he believes they are not a man's job: "He wasn't choreless when he was growing up. He just feels now he's an adult, he has a wife, and he shouldn't have to do that." However, particularly during the months that he is out of work, Stacey finds this rigidity with regard to gender norms inappropriate and irritating:

> You know, it's "I bring home the money." Well, no, you haven't brought home anything in two months. Yes, you have brought home unemployment, but you haven't actually worked for that. So I understand that you're bringing home the money, but you're really not, so get off your butt and go get wood or whatever. You have not worked all day; you have not come home tired.

For women like Kim and Stacey, it is hard to remain in their traditional gender roles while their friends go to work and receive more help at home from their husbands. Yet it was in households like theirs that both the men and their wives cited financial responsibility as a father's main task, often regardless of whether the women expressed a desire to be working outside the home. In most of these families money was a major source of stress and tension, yet most did not seriously consider either moving away or having the women take on full-time jobs to ease the stress. But as the repeated complaints of Kim, Stacey, and other women like them illustrated, these tensions frequently cause frustration and unhappiness among the women, despite the fact that they tend to be complicit in the arrangements. While they may still be tied to the old gender norms in terms of daily life, their ideologies have begun to change despite their own and their husbands' reluctance to adapt their lifestyles. Although many have not fully adopted the gender discourses of their working peers, they do appear to be influenced by them. Thus, they find themselves mired in a conflict between old and new ways of thinking about women's roles, freedoms, and financial responsibilities.

While a number of women in Golden Valley expressed a desire to have the "traditional" two-parent family in which the wife stays at home, only a handful were able to attain this goal. For them life was generally more difficult for those who worked, and most stay-at-home mothers expressed a desire for a more flexible family structure, either wishing that their husbands would allow them to work outside the home or that they at least would treat them more as equals with regard to housework, child care, and access to money. While those women who were in the workforce generally either took household chores less seriously or received help from their husbands, most who stayed home did not receive any help from their husbands at all. For those whose husbands were unemployed either temporarily or permanently, this was a particularly difficult situation to accept, and they struggled like Kim and Stacey to reconcile their ideas of breadwinning and homemaking with their current situations. Thus, they struggled on the brink of the uneven gender revolution.[37] Most were dedicated to remaining married despite their mounting frustrations and felt that they had no real reason to leave a man who did not drink, use drugs, or physically abuse them. But as we will see in the next section, often this pattern of male control and female submission was linked to underlying frustrations and self-esteem issues for out-of-work men, who were not only controlling but also depressed, angry, and eventually abusive as well.

Taken together, the women's testimonies in this chapter and the previous one suggest that in Golden Valley single parenting and family instability are seldom caused by women choosing not to marry men who are poor or unemployed. Instead, single-parent households are more often created by the breakup of relationships and marriages in which substance abuse, physical violence, and controlling and oppressive male behaviors are major problems. This pattern looks similar to that found by researchers of divorce, such as Demie Kurz, who argues that women generally leave marriages "because of discontent with male control and traditional gender roles, violence, and their husbands' use of drugs and alcohol."[38] Unfortunately for Golden Valley women, its current circumstances exacerbate all of these problems. As the next section will explore, men who are unable to find work are likely to experience internal doubt and self-hate, along with the desire to reassert their dominance through the types of controlling behaviors described earlier. However, it will also demonstrate the importance of discourses around fatherhood and masculinity for creating a space in which both men and women are able to change their gender expectations to better fit their situations and help support one another to sustain romantic and family relationships.

Men without Sawmills: Rigidity and Flexibility among Men

> I enjoy my job. It's a good job to have. . . . I do miss time with the kids, but you gotta sacrifice some things for others. It ain't gonna be free ever. (Rod Mitchell, 30-year-old sawmill worker and married father of four)

> I have to work. And that's the way I look at it, is I have to work. Whatever she wants to do, then that's what she does. We were both, though, when our kids were babies, said that she's gonna stay home with the kids until they get old enough to where we feel comfortable, or she feels comfortable, going back to work. So that's what we did. (Craig Layton, 32-year-old hardware store employee and married father of two)

For men, the changes in the labor market have been more threatening than they have for women. Chapters 2 and 3 explored several of the ways in which some of the local understandings of masculinity and expectations of men have persisted, while others have changed either subtly or significantly over the decade since the closure of the woods. They illustrated the persistence of the link between work ethics and masculine identity as well as the change in attitudes toward drinking and physical abuse. They also suggested that there is some amount of change in attitudes toward breadwinning as a man's job. While a good man should still be hardworking, it is no longer imperative in Golden Valley that he be the sole breadwinner. Men who have worked hard in the past, or whose current work doesn't allow them to fully support their families on their own, are becoming more acceptable in the community.

While this norm is changing for some, however, not all men are equally willing and able to accept new roles and identities or to redefine the tenets of masculinity. Letting go of breadwinning as an ideal can be difficult, particularly for men whose masculine identities have long been tied to it. As Kimmel and Ferber note, "Since the early nineteenth century American manhood has pivoted around the status of breadwinner—the self-made man who supports his family by his own labor."[39] For those men who still tie their notions of manhood to the power and authority that comes from being the breadwinner, working wives can seem threatening.[40]

Due to the loss of Golden Valley's most plentiful and masculine jobs, men are now being confronted by circumstances that preclude them from living the lives that most had imagined for themselves. Not only have most lost their abilities to be sole breadwinners, but changing moral norms have also resulted in the loss of the local bars as public spaces in which to enact masculinity and to separate themselves from the feminine domestic sphere.[41] Men are now increasingly present in the home, with fewer ways to clearly distinguish themselves from women. In a real sense, the loss of the old way of life has threatened their abilities to be masculine according to their own cultural traditions. While for women the changes have generally increased their freedom and power within the family and community, for men they have had the opposite effect. Additionally, while for women adapting to the new labor market conditions has required a change in gender norms, but not necessarily major changes in gender identities or the ideals of femininity, for men both norms and identities have been profoundly affected. It is hard enough for men to take on family and household chores that their own fathers avoided; it is a completely different thing to rework the expectations of the hegemonic form of masculinity[42] away from its focus on breadwinning and providing for the family. Not surprisingly, some men refuse to accept this combination of power loss, changing gender norms, and changing gender identities.

Yet many of Golden Valley's men have been able to adapt both their gender norms and identities while still claiming continuity with their community's moral values. My research has uncovered two significantly different patterns of reactions to threatened masculinity among men and their families in Golden Valley. The ways in which masculinity and gender norms are retained or remade, and the strategies chosen for family survival, reflect particular relationships to masculinity and particular discourses around work, marriage, and fatherhood. While some men and their families have shown surprising flexibility in their conceptions of fatherhood and the masculine ideal, others adhere rigidly to the old understandings and norms despite their shifting realities. I find that the particular discourse and gender strategy that a man and/or family pursues during this time of economic and gender crisis significantly affects the degree to which both partners feel satisfied with their relationship and marriage and ultimately influences the family's chance for long-term stability.

The following sections explore these two ideal-typical forms of masculinity and their implications for male gender identity and family life. The categories "rigid" and "flexible" describe patterns found within the sample and are constructed to reflect many of the differences found in men's conceptions of themselves and their attitudes toward gender roles, masculine identity, and family. The category "rigid" refers to men who insist on a gender power structure within the family that includes male dominance and breadwinning, limited female access to money and employment, and strictly segregated male and female spheres. In these households, men generally ground their identities outside the home and do little to no housework or child care. "Flexible," on the other hand, refers to men who have refocused masculine identity away from breadwinning and segregated spheres and who are more likely to share power, child care, and household chores with women. Like all ideal-types, these categorizations are imperfect, and there are men within one category who exhibit some characteristics of the other. Furthermore, gender identity is not static in Golden Valley (or anywhere else), and some men were somewhere in the process of transitioning from rigid to more flexible masculine identities. With these limitations in mind, subjects were categorized as one or the other type according to the category that best described them and the bulk of their actions and declarations regarding gender roles and identities. Although many shades of gray exist on the continuum between rigid and flexible, men generally did exhibit more tendencies of one type than the other. Thus, this ideal-type is a useful analytic tool for understanding the relationship between masculine identity and family dynamics in Golden Valley.[43]

Rigid Masculinity and the Fight to Preserve Traditional Gender Norms

> I don't do much at home. I sit around a lot, drink beer, watch football.
> I don't even get wood anymore because we have a [propane heater]. But
> that used to be what I did. And as the kids got older I shirked most of
> my jobs to them, like mowin' the lawn and takin' out garbage and goin'
> to the dump, doin' all that kind of stuff. (Ted Dorsey, 42-year-old small
> business owner and married father of two)

> I'm s'posed to be making the money and doing that, and I'm failing if
> we have to be on welfare. (Jeff Taylor, 32-year-old teacher and married
> father of two)

For men, the struggle with unemployment and poverty is often a cause
of greater emotional anxiety than it is for women, particularly if they
are strongly identified with breadwinning as a source of masculine identity. For those men who still cling to this previously dominant form of
masculinity, life is more of a struggle and relationships are often more
troubled and unstable. For men who are unwilling to let go of it, traditional masculine identity and gender roles can carry a high price tag in
Golden Valley and often create a struggle for them personally, as well as
for their wives or girlfriends and families. In a situation where work
that allows a man to be the main breadwinner is hard to come by, particularly for those who are not healthy enough to do strenuous physical
labor, breadwinner masculinity is an elusive and hard-won ideal whose
pursuit often causes more tension than it relieves.

Many men in Golden Valley are still uncomfortable with the concept of working wives despite how common they have become there. A
third of men in the sample (ten out of thirty) hold tightly to traditional
conceptions of fatherhood and masculinity despite circumstances that
challenge their abilities to achieve success according to these standards. Of these "rigid" men, three are unmarried. Most of them (seven
out of ten) are men who were raised in families with mothers who did
not work outside the home, and they carried these expectations forward
into their adult lives. Most of these families simply make do with less so
that the women can remain at home, while the men work seasonally in
the woods or with the U.S. Forest Service, doing odd jobs or hunting
while receiving unemployment insurance during the slow months.
Often their work takes men far from home for extended periods of time
or in some cases entails a lengthy daily commute over the mountains.
And as the previous section explored, many of these men employ mul-

tiple strategies to control their wives, including refusing to help at home and limiting women's access to money.

There are few other strategies available to men who desire a traditional form of masculinity in Golden Valley. Only the wealthiest men are able to sit securely in the breadwinner role without exerting some degree of pressure on their wives. Without high-paying jobs, it is difficult for a man to hold onto the power position that was once the breadwinner's entitlement. For men who are unable or unwilling to change their gender expectations, there are few choices besides these types of intra-family power plays. Most Golden Valley men are not lucky enough to have legitimate jobs that allow them to fully support a family. Thus, if they are not flexible with regard to their gender identities and norms within the family, they are left with few options and often end up with either lowered moral capital or lowered self-esteem, or both.

Greg Smith, a 42-year-old married father of three, is one example of a man who has found a way to keep his wife out of the workforce without enduring severe poverty. However, his moral value in the eyes of the community has suffered the consequences of his gender strategy. Greg met me in the public park rather than at his home and came alone. He drove up in a relatively new-looking truck with oversized tires. Greg has been out of work and on disability for four years now, spending much of his free time drinking and "partying" with his teenage children. He plans to return to the workforce only after they have moved out of the house. Despite his lack of job, his family has managed to live comfortably through this period without his wife ever working. They are able to do this partly through living in his parents' house rent-free, but the real secret is that before he hurt his leg, almost every job he had held was illegal in some way. He began by selling drugs in high school and "made a lot of money when I got out." His major work endeavors over the next twenty years included selling marijuana, poaching trees to sell to sawmills, illegally cutting costs and fudging the bookkeeping as a contractor, and under-the-table real estate deals. Needless to say, Greg and his family are not well regarded in Golden Valley, and several of my subjects expressed concern over their children's association with Greg's kids.

Although his financial successes allow them to live comfortably enough without another income, Greg admitted that his wife would prefer to work at least part-time outside the home: "Yeah, she wanted to get away from me for a couple of hours a day. Said she'd work for free." But he had been raised by a stay-at-home mother and said he wanted his wife to stay with him at home. He thus refused to let her take on outside work, asserting that since he and their sons do little housework, she already "has a job in [the home] taking care of the three of us." Greg achieved his ideal family through high-profit illegal activities, since he had neither the skills nor the opportunity to make as much money through more legitimate means. Although he was successful in a sense, the social toll was serious. Considering the amount of time he has spent out of work under the excuse of a questionable disability, in addition to his known history for engaging in illegal activities as well as drinking, using drugs, and encouraging teenage partying, it is doubtful that Greg will have much luck should he ever attempt to reenter the legal workforce in Golden Valley. Yet his refusal to let his wife take on a paying job has constrained his family to either living comfortably by morally questionable means or living in poverty on just his disability check. While he alluded to his wife's dissatisfaction with this arrangement, he would not allow her to meet with me and discuss her situation herself.

The struggle to keep women out of the workforce often has many personal and financial repercussions, particularly for men who are truly unable to work. Randy Taylor is a 35-year-old married father of two who has a debilitating work-related back injury that keeps him from doing physical labor. Like Greg, he chose not to meet me in his home, a trailer that he claimed was too small and noisy for an interview. Instead we met alone in a small, isolated cabin on Gold Creek that is owned by his landlord and is inhabited only in the summer. The cabin lacked heat, and it was a frigid November day. Randy turned on the gas burners on its small cooking stove in an attempt to warm the place, but the effect was imperceptible. He wore only ripped jeans and a short-sleeved T-shirt riddled with holes, and he sat with his hands in his armpits for warmth. I shivered in my coat while my toes went slowly numb. I later found out that Randy's wife was furious that he'd met with me alone in the cabin—not because she didn't trust me, but because she felt that he would never have allowed her to meet an unknown man alone in the woods like that.

Randy explained that he was already married with two children when his incapacitating accident occurred while working in the mill.

His employers there lied to him regarding the extent of his injury, and as a result he did not receive proper medical treatment. After going untreated for nearly five years he could barely stand upright, and he subsequently had a series of surgeries over the next five years just to retain minimal ability to stand and get around. His dedication to the masculine ideal of being the sole provider had kept him working for those first five years despite the pain:

> Well, you know, when I was working, I just—the way I dealt with it was, you know, I didn't have a choice, because they said it was nothin' serious in the first place. And then when the mill shut down and whatnot, you know, it was like, at that time I was about ready to take care of it. But then when I went to logging I didn't have no insurance or nothin' like that, so it's, you know, just try to block it out the best I can and try to do what I have to, 'cause, you know, I gotta provide for my family.

Randy has been on disability since 1999, and this has been the sole source of income for his family of four for the entire period. He described the experience of being out of work as personally difficult:

> It's been pretty frustrating. Especially at first, it's real hard to be—you know, you were workin' and now you're not workin', and you're not gettin' the money that you're used to and everything. All the responsibilities, you know, I believe it's the man's. I took 'em, you know. I told my wife I'd take care of her and whatnot, so it's pretty frustrating.

For Randy, self-esteem and masculine identity are strongly tied to providing, even in the wake of his accident. He grew up in a two-parent family with a stay-at-home mother and a father whose philosophy boiled down to, "Men earn their things, and girls, everything is handed to 'em." Randy feels that his inability to work has been a major source of stress and frustration in his marriage and that the lack of money is their most urgent problem: "The hardest challenge we face is making it from one payday to the next. You know, just to have enough food and enough kerosene to stay warm, enough food for our kids to eat, that's what our biggest challenge is." Unlike Greg, Randy has chosen more morally acceptable but less economically lucrative coping activities. His family's main strategies for survival include caretaking a trailer for very low rent, borrowing money from relatives, and "eatin' fish and deer" that he kills himself, thus allowing him to still be the main provider for his family. His daily activities, as he described them, center mostly on hunting, fishing, and spending time with friends. He also sometimes takes care of his 2-year-old son, Jared, although generally Jared is his wife's responsibility.

Although in his interview Randy asserted that the main sources of his marital stress were financial, his wife, Christine, told a different story. She was often frustrated and on the verge of tears at the FEA on the rare occasion that she was able to get there. He often took their one working car during the day without telling her where he was going or when he'd be back, leaving her stranded in their small trailer miles from town. Christine wanted to take on paid work, but Randy forbade it. She complained repeatedly that he was becoming increasingly controlling and oppressive as well as depressed and angry. Over the year that I knew her, Christine became less and less reliable as a volunteer at the FEA and her behavior was often erratic. Friends speculated that both she and Randy were using drugs, as they had been known to have serious methamphetamine problems during previous difficult times. However, neither Randy nor Christine admitted to having drug problems at the time.

Volunteer coordinators described Christine as a once-troubled girl who had built up her confidence and competence over several years. However, since her husband's job loss, her trajectory seemed to be reversing itself. Christine's apparent decline finally began to turn around four months after my interview with Randy, when she left him and filed for divorce, plunging herself into the ranks of Golden Valley's poor single mothers. In the months that followed, her moods vacillated from empowered to despondent. In her dark moments, she often blamed Golden Valley, and particularly the mill closure, for the failure of her marriage. However, at other times she described herself as feeling empowered by escaping the troubled marriage, once even proudly exclaiming to me, "I am woman, hear me roar!"

During our interview Randy said nothing to me that foreshadowed such serious marital problems, however, and claimed to have a relatively happy marriage. He told me that he had always wanted a wife and family and that he was grateful to have them. He felt lucky to have started his family back when he still had a job and said that he probably wouldn't have had the confidence to ask Christine to marry him if he had been out of work then: "I wouldn't have had nothin' to offer. Yeah, it would've been a lot harder." When asked if he thought he was a good husband, Randy replied, "Yeah. I'd be a lot better if I had a lot of money, though."

For Randy, being a husband and father meant being the provider and head of household, at whatever cost. Without that status, he was unsure whether he could have become either.

For men who have no job prospects at all, starting a family is, in fact, a lot harder. Sam Acton can't quite imagine ever becoming a husband and father, although he at one time thought that he would be by his current age. Sam is a 33-year-old single man who lives alone in a small rented cabin in the woods. He has been out of work and living on disability since a log crushed his shoulder and arm three years ago while he was working as a logger. Sam was raised by a stay-at-home mother and a stepfather whom he described as "a stickler for worrying about making the big money." Although he claimed that money wasn't particularly important to him, he described his worst jobs as ones where he didn't make a sufficient amount of money. His least favorite job was working at a cement plant because of its combination of unpleasant work and low pay: "The pay was terrible, and the work was just as bad, and for workin', you know, and what they were payin', it was like—not that you were workin' super hard—it was just the fact of, you know, the pay level." He had similar problems with the mill, where he had worked for a short time and felt that the money wasn't equal to what he made as a logger.

Although he does not have a girlfriend, Sam does in fact have a son whom he's never met. "I know it's a boy and he's 4 years old, and that's all I can tell you," he explained. He was vague with details of the breakup with his son's mother, the daughter of a former employer. According to his confusing story, her mentally unstable family hid her away from him, and he was unable to track down either her or his child, although he was interested in doing so. Sam blamed the breakup on her parents, yet he gave no indication that the woman had any interest in seeing him again. When asked why her parents disliked him, he was again ambiguous but mentioned their suspicions that he used drugs and that they had gone so far as to demand that he take a drug test, which he refused. In response to my first question about whether he hoped to get married and have a functioning family someday, he replied noncommittally, "Yeah, I think so. I don't know." Further questions about the type of woman he'd like to marry or the type of life he envisioned were met with even less straightforward answers; he responded that he just knew he wanted to stay in Golden Valley and that it was a good place to raise children. For Sam, it seemed that marriage and family were not a reality that were attainable, and thus he did not think about them much, although when pressed further he admitted that he would like to have a family someday. He did not seem to think it was particularly likely to happen though:

> Kids are cool. I would like, like I say, I wish I could have some contact with my son, but . . . Yeah, it's something that I like. Yeah, I think I would be ready for that. But I wasn't ready for it before, by no means. And I just haven't, haven't found the person, or maybe, I don't know. . . . Maybe I'll be too old by the time, who knows?

Sam is aware of having basically missed his chance at marriage and family. His story illustrates again two of the main problems that young men have in becoming husbands and fathers: drug use and unemployment, one of which was cited by women as their primary reason for not staying in relationships and the other which makes it difficult for the man to be the sole provider. Sam believes as strongly as Randy that a woman should be at home taking care of the family while the man should be providing for it. His stepfather has always been a strong role model for him, and Sam admires his work ethic. He has a more complicated relationship with his mother, whom he resented as a teenager after her separation from his stepfather, when she "got to where she didn't cook or clean, where if you wanted something to eat you had to cook it yourself." Sam desires a life modeled on the family of his early youth. But without any ability to play the breadwinner role that his stepfather played, he feels that he has no real prospects for achieving this scenario and has a difficult time even articulating his dreams for the future. The most he can be sure of is that he wants to work again someday and to raise his hypothetical children in Golden Valley.

The stories of Greg, Randy, and Sam present three very different scenarios with regard to work and family. But they have in common that all three men are rigid when it comes to maintaining what they believe to be a traditional family structure and a breadwinner/head-of-household identity within the family. Their stories demonstrate the pitfalls of this rigid identity within the context of Golden Valley's current economic conditions. Like most men there who insist on maintaining old gender norms and identities, they struggle for control and power within their families as well as with low self-esteem and substance abuse. These were the same issues that women found the most problematic in their relationships and the ones that were most likely to cause them to end relationships. As their stories illustrate, for men who cling rigidly to traditional ideas of masculinity but are unable to achieve them, the result is often personal difficulty and internal and external conflict, and family units are often unstable, if they form at all.

Flexible Masculinity and Active Fathers

You have to teach your kids good values, work ethics. You have to be involved with your kids, I think. If you spend time with 'em and you're a good role model, I think that's just gonna rub off on the kids. If you don't spend time with 'em, and they see negative things, then you know, that's what they're gonna get used to seein', that's probably how they're gonna turn out. (Keith Bartlett, 32-year-old married, unemployed former logger and construction worker)

I don't know really what kind of father I am. I just try and just love 'em and try and spend time with 'em, and make the time I do spend with 'em fun. Playing games and doin' things and takin' 'em out—takin' 'em out to the creek is really fun for me. I like doin' that, even though it's a little bit more work. (Brian Goodman, 26-year-old hardware store employee and married father of two)

Not all the men in my sample struggle so intensely with their self-images and their relationships with masculinity. As Ray found among male domestic servants in Calcutta,[44] and Waller found among poor urban males in the United States,[45] I discovered in Golden Valley that many men who cannot achieve a traditional form of masculinity are reconstructing the masculine ideal to make it more attainable for themselves. According to Nonn, the development of versatile masculinities can allow even the most downtrodden of men to resist a sense of failure and build self-worth.[46]

About two-thirds of male respondents (eighteen out of thirty)[47] had somewhat more flexible understandings of the masculine ideal and acceptable gender norms within the family, which, although drawing heavily from Golden Valley's dominant gender discourse, nonetheless prioritize different aspects of male identity. Instead of focusing on breadwinning, they associate masculinity with other dominant moral concepts, such as hard work and family values. While these "flexible" men may still have some difficulties reconciling their parents' values with those of their current households and families, they have for the most part allowed themselves to let go of those ideals that are unattainable to them now. Most commonly, their flexibility takes the form of rewriting the expectations of fatherhood in a way that allows them to focus on their strengths and abilities. Since men in Golden Valley now often have large amounts of free time but only limited amounts of money to contribute to the family, their strength lies in being "family men." They thus play active roles in their children's lives, imparting to them masculine skills, values, and work ethics. Most of the "flexible" male respondents focused on involved parenting as the most important part of a father's job and downplayed the importance of financial support. They discussed how they enjoyed it when their fathers had spent time with them or how they felt deprived because their fathers had not been involved with their lives. Thus, by their own standards they are good fathers because they help with homework, attend sports matches, and teach their children to hunt, fish, camp, and understand the value of hard work.

This remaking of the masculine ideal was something I encountered among men of all ages in Golden Valley. Like the "rigid" men, they were men who often were working to some degree but frequently struggled to find or keep jobs and were not always happy with the work they did. Several of the older men had taken early retirement to remain in Golden Valley after the mill left, while a number of the younger men were seasonally unemployed. For the most part they openly acknowledged that their families could not survive without their wives' paychecks and health benefits and showed little shame in admitting this. They also tended to claim that the household work was divided equally, although the women's testimonies and my own observations suggested that housework still tended to be divided along the inside/outside line, with women doing the bulk of daily chores.[48] More than half of these men grew up with mothers who worked, in contrast to the "rigid" men, who mostly had stay-at-home mothers. This difference suggests that those whose backgrounds include more fluidity with regard to gender roles may end up being more flexible themselves as adults.

Ideologically, at least, the "flexible" men did not focus on being the head of household in either economic or power terms. Instead, they found self-esteem through masculine parenting and through being what they considered to be "good fathers." Among this group, good fathering was

almost always conceived of in noneconomic terms. The following comments, typical of Golden Valley's "flexible" men, all were expressed in
answer to the question, *"What is most important about being a good father?"*

> Support. I just have to say support. You know, just making sure you set
> a good example, support everything they want to do. If he wants to go
> play football, then I want to make sure I get him there. Whether it's to
> play a real game or whether it's just to come down and play with some
> of the kids—just supporting them in everything they do, you know?
> A pat on the back and a "Hey, you're doing great." You know? "I like
> the way you do that." (Andy Richards, 40-year-old small-scale mill
> worker and married father of two)

> Being real active with the [girls] personally. Getting to watch them grow
> and really enjoy watching them grow, not just dealing them with a heavy
> finger. And then the ball playing with 'em. . . . If we weren't doing that,
> we were hunting or fishing or they were dating. (Eric McCloud, 48-
> year-old town government employee and married father of two)

> For me it would be to give your kids lots of love. Give them love more
> than anything. Because to me there's no greater thing in the world than
> love. I instill it by being able to spend more time with them, and I
> know that if I were in the city, they'd be alone. I'd be working more,
> and being in that rat race you're not able to spend that quality time
> with them.
>   It's neat to raise the boys to where they're becoming responsible
> enough to set goals and [buy things for themselves]. I would love to
> buy them for them, but I can't. So I say, "If you want it, you have to
> buy it yourselves." And that's just the way it is. (Bill Prader, 45-year-
> old sporadically employed carpenter and married father of two)

These quotes illustrate the men's focus on supportive, involved parenting rather than economic support. Although few grew up with fathers
like themselves to serve as role models, they have adopted paternal
involvement and concern as a masculine ideal. For many, this understanding is directly tied to their sense of themselves as family focused
and the moral imperative to be good parents.

For many of the families who have successfully survived the mill's
closing, this focus on family togetherness and involvement allows men
to feel fulfilled and proud of their lives. Their morphing of masculine
identity draws heavily on the doctrines of equality and involved fathering that were first introduced by the feminist movement, yet it is strongly
rooted in local cultural images of masculinity, such as hunting, fishing,

and team sports. As Waller contends, this new model of fatherhood has become more mainstream since the feminist movement of the 1970s, which encouraged fathers to make emotional connections with their children and share in the work of caring for them.[49] While neither the men nor their wives appear to be aware of this influence, the ideas that they borrowed from the larger U.S. culture permit them to sustain healthy family lives and stable households despite living in a community in which more traditional notions of breadwinning and fatherhood are still prevalent. While many grew up in households that did not adhere to the dominant ideal, most nonetheless grew up believing that they would be breadwinner fathers and heads of their own households.

Jake Robbins, a 52-year-old married father of two, is an example of a man who adjusted his gender ideals to accommodate his changing circumstances. Jake had not expected to have anything less than a traditional family when he got married. Both his mother and mother-in-law had been full-time homemakers. Jake and his wife, Barbara, met in high school and got married at age 20. He went first to work in the woods like his father and later switched to working in the sawmill, where he made enough money to support the family. Barbara stayed home with their young children, going to work at the local preschool only after both kids were in school. Both Jake and Barbara described her original decision to work as one made out of boredom, not out of financial necessity. She described the job at first as one that was consistent with full child-rearing responsibilities:

> My kids were old enough that I got tired of staring at the wall. And you can only do so much cleaning, so that was a job that [allowed me to] be home when they were. You know, and I had their vacations, and everything worked out great.

For Jake, it was not easy to see his wife go to work: "Well, I didn't want her to work. But then she finally told me, 'I'm bored, I gotta go get a job.'"

As Jake's work life became less stable, however, he came to appreciate having a working wife and to recognize the importance of her work to the family's financial survival. When the mill left, Jake moved with it to Adams for several years. Eventually he gave up the well-paid job to return to his wife's side in Golden Valley. It took him nearly a year to find another job, at greatly reduced pay and with no benefits or stability. The money he makes now in a struggling small-diameter sawmill is about equal to what Barbara makes, and they rely on her job's health benefits. He easily acknowledged, "Yeah, I wouldn't have been able to do what I've done had it not been for her." Unlike couples in which the men struggled to hold power over the women, Jake and Barbara both described their current state as a partnership. Jake added jokingly, "It's a partnership? What are you talking about? I get the same allowance now as I ever got!"—in reference to the fact that it is Barbara, not him, who handles their finances.

The current situation does not appear to cause Jake much stress or anxiety, and he described their most difficult times as all in the past. These included their years apart while he worked in Adams and missed being involved with their children's lives, as well as their early years of marriage, during which he drank heavily. Jake eventually gave up drinking regularly: "I realized that I had a really good thing and that I didn't want to lose it. So I tamed it down." Although it had not been easy, the Robbinses had consistently made decisions that prioritized the family and thus ensured its survival. They expressed gratitude for their current lifestyle and their ability to remain in Golden Valley, where they had both grown up and their elderly parents remain. Although their current financial situation is tight, Jake does not regret his decision to return to Golden Valley and maintains that he is much happier now, despite the pay cut. Despite the change in his breadwinning status, Jake believes that he is still a good father to his two children and that the most important thing about being a father is "spending time, yeah—even when they didn't want to."

Brian and Nicole Goodman, whom we met earlier in this chapter, went through a similar change in gender expectations to keep their family afloat. This young, devoutly Christian couple have both always wanted to create the traditional breadwinner/homemaker family that neither of them actually grew up in. When I asked Nicole what her goals in life had been, she replied, "Kids were my goal. My biggest thing I always wanted to do was be a housewife." Both Brian and Nicole maintain that breadwinning is his responsibility and his source of self-esteem, while for her it is a secondary duty:

> BRIAN: That's my job. I feel like it's my job to go work for so many hours a day, as long as I can. That's what makes me feel good, anyway, is going to work. I'd go crazy if I had to be in the house all the time. It can get really hard on guys that are like that up here.

Yet despite their desire to be a more "traditional" family, they both accept that for now there is no way he can earn enough to support their
family of four on his own, and her workforce participation is necessary.
For Brian and Nicole, the moral capital and financial comfort that
come from her added income trumps gender norms and ideals. It allows
them to survive without the shame of relying on welfare, as Brian's parents had:

> BRIAN: I've always just kind of wanted to be better than that, and bet-
> ter than my mom and dad, just kind of scraping by. 'Cause that's
> pretty much what they did when I was growing up. I mean, I can
> think of a lot of Saturdays that I spent in the welfare office in
> Miner's Gulch, and oh, it was just horrible. And so I want to be
> better than that, and do better than that for my boys. So I've really
> tried to keep a better job and, if something happened to my job,
> I'm not sure what we'd do.

Thus for now, the answer is sending Nicole to work and being flexible
with regard to gender norms within their family. While Nicole has had
to bend her expectations to enter the workforce, Brian has responded
with flexibility in fathering and homemaking as well. Nicole described
his willingness to help with household chores and child rearing:

> He's pretty willing to babysit and stuff, and change diapers and bathe
> them and feed them. You know, he doesn't have one of those "It's
> women's work" attitudes. 'Cause like, even his dad says, like, "Diapers
> is women's work"—that old-school kind of attitude. Brian doesn't
> have that.

By letting go of some of their "old school" gender expectations, Brian
and Nicole are able to maintain a decent standard of living as well as a
strong partnership. While prioritizing Golden Valley's work ethics and
moral concerns, they are nonetheless able to adapt their understandings of gender norms and identities within the family context.

For many of the couples in which gender norms were defined less
rigidly, there had been a slow transition from a more traditional idea of
marriage and family, as well as often the cessation of heavy drinking or
substance abuse on the part of one or both partners. In almost all of
these "flexible" couples the wives were in the workforce, and in many
they were the main breadwinners or significant contributors to the family income. When interviewed together, these were couples who commonly held much less tension between them, whether they were older

couples who had weathered difficult pasts or young couples who had only recently taken on grown-up roles and responsibilities. Most are still haunted by financial struggles, but generally they remain confident that they will survive well enough by relying on both partners' salaries and benefits, as well as whatever help family and community can provide. The wives of these men generally take pride in their jobs and accept their roles as co-supporters of the households, whether or not they had originally aspired to be working versus at home. For those men who are able to let go of the breadwinning-centered ideologies of their youths, there seems to be considerably less internal turmoil and a strong sense of satisfaction with their marriages, their roles as fathers, and themselves as men. Because of their abilities to adapt to Golden Valley's changing circumstances, these men's families appear to have a much better chance of long-term stability than do their more traditional and less flexible counterparts.

What sets this group apart from the "rigid" men? As discussed earlier, the flexibility of their natal households appears to be a factor. Similarly, drug and alcohol use also play roles in distinguishing between the two groups, although in this case it is not clear whether substance abuse results from or contributes to the tensions caused by gender rigidity and family and household stress. What is clear from the testimonies is the role that discourses around fatherhood and family play in allowing the transition to occur and allowing new gender roles to be accepted as a return to family values. The ideologies of "flexible" men do not simply accept their changes as deviant, but rather build upon the fluid family discourses discussed in chapter 3 to help construct the new form as another type of traditional family—one in which fathers are present, as fathers should be. For "flexible" men, active fathering was their largest achievement and their clear sign of moral and personal success. Their stories suggest that for most their discourses were constructed in reaction to the structural changes they faced and that for many they differed substantially from their original ideologies regarding parenting and gender roles. Yet they did not consider themselves feminists, liberals, or in any way forward thinkers; instead, they harked back to morality and family values discourses to help construct changes as returns to tradition. Herein lies yet another power of family-centered discourse: it appears to have the ability to allow major changes in gender roles and dynamics to become quickly accepted as normal, traditional, and even superior.

Conclusion

There are many reasons why keeping a family together is difficult under conditions of unemployment and poverty. The daily stresses of living below the poverty line alone create tensions that can damage relationships with family and loved ones. In Golden Valley this is the case, just as in any other location, despite its history of persistent poverty as well as the importance of the nuclear family ideal. Many of the single mothers and noncustodial fathers I knew during my year there were among the poorest residents and had suffered through many different aspects of hard living, including drug use, alcohol abuse, and physical violence. These are problems that are found to be associated with poverty and job loss throughout diverse types of American communities.[50] Many of the stories from Golden Valley reflect themes found throughout the literature on both urban and rural poverty and unemployment, including the tendency for job loss and poverty to be correlated with physical abuse, substance abuse, depression, and marital and family tensions.[51]

Considering these correlations and the high rates of both poverty and unemployment in Golden Valley, it is not surprising that single-parent families have been on the rise there. Not only have families had to contend with persistently high poverty levels, but the decade since the mill closure has also brought with it rising male unemployment and a dramatic fall in the ability of a man to be the sole breadwinner for his household. The loss of this status, so integral to the definition of fatherhood and manhood for so long in Golden Valley, has had profound effects on family life and marital relations. For those poor and unemployed men who cling to the traditional masculine ideals with which they were raised, their current economic and labor market struggles can create an intense dissonance between their goals and their realities. For those who marry anyway, or whose work and financial problems begin after marriage, it frequently creates tense situations in which they feel the need to compensate for their perceived lack by exerting control over their wives in addition to struggling with long commutes, seasonal work, or severe poverty—all of which take their toll on marriages.

Under these conditions, what is perhaps more surprising than the rise in single-parent families is the degree to which many families have managed to adapt to the changing circumstances. As this chapter has demonstrated, adaptation for women has been relatively easy, as entering the workforce has had its benefits in terms of freedom and equality within the family and for many is still seen as consistent with child-rearing and homemaking responsibilities and traditional feminine identities. Yet the results from Golden Valley suggest that men can be flexible too and find ways to adapt to new structural environments. I found that there is more flexibility possible in rural men's gender norms and ideologies than found by previous rural researchers.[52] Many men have managed to not only accept more household responsibilities while sharing breadwinning status, but also to simultaneously remake masculinity in a way that focuses more heavily on realistic goals, such as active fathering. These men's families seem to be able to navigate employment and economic struggles with fewer tensions and with less need for men to exert control over women. In Golden Valley two-parent families are still the majority, and many of them have successfully refocused masculine identity around engaging with children in such activities as hunting, fishing, and team sports while wives contribute substantially to the family finances. For these families, rewriting of gender scripts occurs through fusing family values and moral discourses with pop culture feminist ideologies. These new gender discourses allow women to accept and embody their new roles and help men to retain self-esteem and masculine identity despite their changing roles and status.

Goldscheider and Waite argue that national changes in family structure, including lower marriage rates and higher divorce rates, are due to more than economic conditions and in particular reflect the working out of the "sex-role revolution" that resulted from women's greater workforce participation.[53] Despite its social isolation, Golden Valley is still connected to the rest of the United States through such avenues as television, movies, and print media. Thus, newer ideas about women's roles, masculinity, and fatherhood, such as those introduced by the feminist movement,[54] have slowly filtered into the larger cultural "tool kit"[55] that residents have at their disposal. As Waller found in the urban setting,[56] in Golden Valley as well selective borrowing of feminist concepts has allowed a new model of fatherhood to emerge as the breadwinning model has rapidly become less attainable. These new concepts are adopted only after they are filtered through the community's unique cultural understandings, and in the end appear to exemplify the same moral and family values that the old form of masculinity once did. Thus flexibility in gender ideologies can allow men and women to navigate economic and structural changes with less personal and interpersonal anxiety, while simultaneously claiming ownership of the moral authority that "rigid" men fear will be lost along with breadwinner status.

It should be noted that in these Golden Valley families, flexibility does not necessarily mean *equality* in gender roles. In most cases, gender ideals and discourses have changed just enough to better fit the structural conditions, particularly the dearth of men's employment and the necessity of women's employment. For instance, many reluctantly working women like Nicole Goodman and Rosemary Taylor construct their incomes as secondary, while their husbands' housework is viewed as helping out. While Brian Goodman's willingness to change diapers suggests a change in gender norms and attitudes from those of his father, nonetheless his child care is referred to as "babysitting," while for Nicole it is her main responsibility, despite the fact that she is also contributing substantially to the household income. Neither Golden Valley's women nor its men aim to be pioneers in a gender revolution. Thus, they adjust their cultural expectations in ways that strike the most comfortable balance between the current realities and past cultural norms. It is neither necessary nor realistic for Golden Valley families to completely remake their gender understandings to approximate those of the middle class or feminists. Just a slight tweaking of the main goals and expectations of fatherhood and motherhood suffices to ease the personal strain of the economic and labor market crisis.

These findings echo results of previous research on the importance of role flexibility to rural families[57] while further exploring the relationship of gender ideologies to family structure and stability. Without flexible ideologies and discourses that allow individuals to make sense of and justify new roles, gender role flexibility is less attainable and less sustainable. This research has also illustrated the pitfalls of rigid gender identities in a context of rapid structural changes. This is particularly the case for men, for whom the new gender roles are largely inconsistent with the old identities, creating an intense disconnect between goals and realities. Furthermore, for men the changes represent a loss of status and power rather than a gain. Without discourses to justify and glorify their changing roles, "flexible" men would likely still suffer the self-doubt and lowered self-esteem that haunts their rigid peers. Thus, reinforcing the changing roles with newly constructed ideologies and discourses allows them to transition more smoothly to their new economic and labor market realities. Because men were more likely than women to resist changing both gender norms and gender identities, it was their reactions and behaviors that often were major contributing factors to tense and unstable relationships.

Gender discourses, like those around work ethics and family life, are important cultural factors that structure daily life in Golden Valley. But unlike with the moral discourses discussed in chapters 2 and 3, at this point there remains a fracture within the community regarding the dominant ideologies around fatherhood, masculinity, and family roles. While the community has reached a reasonable consensus regarding the acceptability of women's work outside the home, it is still struggling to create a single coherent discourse regarding men's roles and masculine identity in the wake of the forest industry collapse. The ambivalence regarding men's gender identities is apparent throughout the stories in this chapter, as is the difficulty that this ambivalence can cause for men trying to navigate a muddy new gender terrain. The rising numbers of single-parent families and the anecdotal evidence of unstable marital relationships illustrate the difficulties they are having in adapting to changing work and family roles.

Yet what is more striking is the number of men and families who have managed to remake their gender norms and identities to approximate the best compromise between the present situation and the past cultural norms. While Golden Valley struggles to maintain its cultural traditions and unique identity, and resists many of the changes that the rest of the state and nation have undergone, it nonetheless has subtly adapted most of its cultural discourses to its changing conditions. To remain "traditional," it has been necessary for Golden Valley to redefine success, family, work ethics, masculinity, and even the meaning of tradition. This chapter has illustrated the impressive capacity of Golden Valley's women and men for adapting to change in order to endure. Despite all the challenges it has faced, Golden Valley is far from disappearing, as its residents feared it might after the spotted owl ruling. Instead it has found ways to use its cohesiveness to its advantage, creating new cultural discourses and definitions that allow it to stabilize itself in the aftermath of economic and social collapse.

Conclusion

Understanding Poverty in Rural America

This book has described in depth the roles of moral discourses in a poor rural American community in decline. It has found that morality is an ever-moving target there, with forms and meanings evolving in reaction to changing circumstances. Moral ideas and discourses can adapt to new structural and cultural conditions and can also enable social and personal adaptation to such changing conditions. In Golden Valley moral discourses and understandings have seeped in to fill the gaps left by previous forms of social distinction, including class distinctions and other types of symbolic capital. Morality has slowly become the force underlying these old divisions and has given Golden Valley residents new justifications for them. It has also provided them with new definitions of success and failure and new avenues to achieving the American dream in the absence of so many of the more common status markers found throughout American society. This book has explored both how and why morality has risen to such power and has investigated the consequences of this rise. It argues that while morality is a powerful force throughout American discourse, its power is even greater in circumstances like Golden Valley's, where access to other forms of social distinction and economic and symbolic capital is nearly nonexistent.

While this story is about Golden Valley, it has larger implications for American politics and policy. After the November 2004 reelection of President George W. Bush, National Public Radio reported, based on exit polls, that his supporters tended to be "cultural conservatives, people who were married, lived in rural America, owned guns, went to church regularly." According to NPR's polls, "about half [of Bush's voters] cited moral values as their top concern."[1] Further analysis a few days later found that rural voters were the deciding factor in Bush's reelection in key states such as Ohio. This report stressed the importance of the rural vote and argued that "rural voters [are] cross-pressured by economic struggles, by security and by strong positions on abortion, gay marriage or gun control." It suggested that Democrats needed to find a way to address both rural economic concerns and "cultural values" more effectively for rural Americans.[2]

The days in which rural Americans were populist Democrats are long over,[3] and few were likely surprised that the rural vote was a largely conservative one. News reports for weeks after the election discussed the growing divide between rural and urban America and the importance of moral values to conservative rural and middle-American voters. Although this information was not new, it nonetheless continues to baffle liberals, who remain naively steadfast in their belief that middle Americans are misguided and unaware of their own interests, even "deranged."[4] That so many rural voters have for decades now been more interested in morality and family values than economic concerns does not appear to convince liberals of the importance of moral values as political issues. Instead, it seems only to fuel the growing concerns over the culture wars in the popular press, further polarizing the two sides. Rural conservative voters are characterized by liberal urban dwellers as backward, uneducated "rednecks," while rural conservatives in turn demonize urban liberals as Volvo-driving, latte-drinking, godless killers of babies.[5] These cartoonish stereotypes point to an enormous gulf in understanding between the two sides.

The failure to understand rural America and its concerns has implications that are far-reaching. The rural vote is becoming an increasingly significant and homogeneous force in U.S. politics. But even in states like California, where conservative white rural voters are not a significant political force, their lives are still affected by policies that may or may not be crafted with them specifically in mind. Failure to understand the causes and intricacies of the growing importance of moral values to the rural poor can limit the country's ability to successfully address many of their concerns that are, in fact, economic in origin. Particularly when it comes to poverty alleviation programs such as Temporary Assistance for Needy Families (TANF), Supplemental Security Income (SSI), and unemployment insurance, a failure to take into account the cultural settings of recipient populations can result in gross miscalculations regarding their usage and effectiveness. This book has provided an in-depth exploration of the different types of moral discourses that dominate a rural American community and their vital roles in shaping social and personal life there. But it also lays the groundwork for understanding why many well-meaning policies fail to help the poor—and particularly the rural poor—in anticipated ways. The story of Golden Valley is about more than simply the emergence of moral discourses as powerful influencers. It is also about neglect and ignorance on the part of the United States and indifference to Golden Valley's economic and cultural needs. It is about the failure to understand places like Golden Valley and ineffectiveness in coming to their aid in times of crisis.

In many ways, this is a story about macroeconomics and policy and what happens when the interests of outsiders are able to control a community's destiny. This book began by illustrating the impact of politically and economically motivated policies on Golden Valley's labor market. Neither Republican nor Democrat, environmentalist nor corporate behemoth, was ultimately concerned about sustaining this community or its way of life. Golden Valley's experience is one of political and economic disenfranchisement, leading ultimately to widespread poverty, unemployment, and social and cultural disintegration. It is a tale that is not unique in the United States, and versions of it are to be found in most places where poverty persists, be they rural or urban. I have argued that it is in this setting of political and economic powerlessness that morality is likely to emerge as a stronger force. This book has not only chronicled that emergence, but has also examined its effects within this community. It has maintained that moral discourses are based in preexisting cultural value systems, but that they nonetheless can facilitate transitions to new social and cultural practices. This adaptive quality, along with its ties to such important cultural mythologies as the American dream, underlies the ability of morality to become a powerful creator of social boundaries and a tradable form of symbolic capital. It is also what ultimately makes it relevant to policy in ways that are at times unanticipated.

Morality, Culture, and Social Change

Although economic and social disenfranchisement may contribute to the greater importance of morality in shaping social life, this does not mean that morality is absent from American life in other circumstances. As this book has argued, morality is extremely important to structuring life in the United States, exerting its power throughout the social, economic, and political realms.[6] Lakoff argues that both ends of the American political spectrum have in common that their views and ideologies are predominantly shaped by morality, and in particular moral understandings of the family. He explains that each side conceptualizes the nation through the model of the family, with the government in the role of the parent.[7] What separates them is not that one cares about moral issues and the other does not, but rather that they rely on opposing models of the family, which "give rise to different moral systems and different discourse forms."[8] Thus, it is the underlying family model that shapes the larger political agenda of each side. Yet while morality and the family are central to both of these ideologies, Lakoff explains,

> where conservatives are relatively aware of how their politics relate to their views of family life and morality, liberals are less aware of the implicit view of morality and the family that organizes their own political beliefs. This lack of conscious awareness of their own political worldview has been devastating to the liberal cause.[9]

I argue that a failure to recognize morality and cultural values as fundamental forces that shape decisions, behaviors, and political agendas is not only politically damaging, but it also undermines policymakers' abilities to craft policies that will benefit their target populations.

Nonetheless, the liberal agenda has generally tried to sidestep morality as a policy issue, while the conservatives continually exploit moral issues to gain popularity and power, which they then use to quietly enact economic measures that ultimately favor corporate interests and the wealthy.[10] With regard to such issues as abortion, gay marriage, and the separation of church and state, liberals have generally assumed a pragmatic stance that focuses on individuals' rights to make their own moral

decisions rather than having them set by politicians. Meanwhile, conservatives campaign heavily on promises to legislate morality, yet their
promises seldom materialize as law. I do not argue that either side
should be mandating morality per se, and I do not believe that this is
the lesson from Golden Valley. Rather, Golden Valley provides an important case study for understanding the ways in which moral and cultural
climates interact with and have an impact on political and economic
decisions and policies. Without recognizing the power and importance
of morality to American culture, particularly on the margins, Americans will not be able to create policies that work in the intended ways
even when sincere in their efforts.

To begin with, I told the story of the spotted owl and economic restructuring in Golden Valley. At the time these events took place, the
general consensus was that the changes would, in fact, be devastating
for towns like Golden Valley. It was assumed that the residents of these
communities would have to relocate to areas with better labor market
prospects. This type of mobility is often taken for granted as a necessary
part of American life, and community ties are generally viewed as transient and replaceable. While there was little intervention on the part
of the public sector to facilitate mobility for residents of the Pacific
Northwest's logging country, the private sector did in fact attempt it.
Northwest Timber, at the time that it closed its Golden Valley sawmill,
offered many of its employees jobs at its mills elsewhere in the state.
Many Golden Valley employees took these jobs, but the majority did
not last long in their new locations. They hated the unfamiliar places,
they couldn't afford to buy houses in more competitive markets, and
they missed their families back home. In response, as illustrated, they
returned to Golden Valley, often facing severe reductions in their family incomes and the loss of essential benefits.

Thus, the first way in which policy failed to recognize the importance of culture was through ignoring the importance of place and community ties for rural residents. Unlike the majority of (middle class) urban
and suburban Americans, rural Americans tend more frequently to have
the sorts of deep connections to place and community that were explored
in chapter 1. For them, mobility is not always economically feasible
and is generally not culturally or personally acceptable. Towns like
Golden Valley will not simply disappear, and their populations will not
happily relocate to where the jobs are. The assumption that they will

ultimately contributes to the suffering of the residents that remain. This point applies to the poor more broadly as well. Although in many cities jobs have been migrating to the suburbs, the poor have not been able to do so. They are barred not only by housing costs, discriminatory housing practices, and transportation problems, but also by their own social networks. Scholars from Stack[11] to Newman[12] have argued that the extensive social ties that help the urban poor to survive can often act as disincentives to geographic mobility; the poor rightfully fear life without a social safety net and are thus less likely to change locations than are the relatively financially and socially independent middle class. Thus, often even when the economy is growing, the poor are unable to access newly created jobs. Yet both sides of the political fence continue to support policies such as welfare reform (otherwise known as the Personal Responsibility and Work Opportunity Reconciliation Act of 1996, or PRWORA, which includes time limits and work requirements) that assume the poor turn to welfare because of poor work ethics rather than poor job prospects.

As chapter 2 illustrated, a lack of work ethics is not common to all of the poor in Golden Valley, just as work ethics are also not lacking for many urban poor families.[13] The chapter argued that even in a labor market that provides few living-wage jobs for men, the mainstream American work ethic remains a strong cultural force and tie to understandings of moral worth. It illustrated the tendency of the poor in Golden Valley to assign blame to individuals for their inability to find work even in this setting and their intense struggle to demonstrate strong work ethics even when they were not participating in the formal labor market. So important was this demonstration of morality and work ethic that it evolved into a form of tradable symbolic capital, which became imperative to the ultimate survival of the poor. "Moral capital," as evidenced by one's work ethic and tie to work activities in either the formal or informal sector, could be traded for economic capital in various forms. A lack of it meant one had little access to any forms of capital in the community, including both social and economic capital.

While the existence of moral capital may be a new concept, that the poor adhere to mainstream American cultural norms should not be. Yet despite the numerous works cited in chapter 2 that provide ample evidence of this cultural stance among the urban and rural poor, the myth remains throughout much of American society that the poor lack work ethics and are lazy, deviant, oppositional, and dependent. As a number of scholars have shown, often the poor themselves will describe the "other" (i.e., undeserving) poor this way.[14] This belief in the lack of work ethic and mainstream values among the poor is popular both in the mainstream media and in conservative political rhetoric. Despite abundant evidence that this stereotype describes the exception rather than the norm, U.S. policies crafted by both Democrats and Republicans nonetheless focus almost exclusively on how to force the poor out of dependency and into work—to save them from their lack of morality by coercing them, through an incomprehensible system of carrots and sticks, to enter the labor market that will somehow be their salvation.[15]

In Golden Valley not only does the labor market offer no salvation, but welfare use has long carried a high social cost and stigma. In the absence of either a healthy labor market or a legitimate culture of welfare dependency, welfare time limits have been largely ineffective at alleviating poverty there. Furthermore, these "reforms" ignore the larger implications of local conceptions of morality with regard to public aid. While welfare policies focus consistently on their lack of work ethics, the substantial work ethics of the rural poor have in fact led them to prefer public aid in the form of SSI and unemployment insurance, which both carry higher moral value through their connection to previous work and their interpretation as earned and deserved. In places like Golden Valley, it may be that one form of government assistance has been traded for another and that neither provides sufficient income or social support to sustain the nuclear family that Americans—both poor and nonpoor—value so highly. Their failure to recognize the importance of cultural and moral norms has blinded policymakers to the real needs of the rural poor and impeded their ability to understand the political preferences of the rural poor, as well as to create policies that might succeed in helping them to pull themselves out of poverty.

Chapter 2 did not endeavor simply to illustrate policy failures, but also to create the basis for understanding the larger role of morality in the lives of the rural poor. This book has argued throughout that moral discourses heavily influence the economic, social, cultural, behavioral, and political choices of Golden Valley residents. Chapter 2 focused mostly on economic and work-related concerns. Chapter 3 argued that the importance of morality is not limited to the economic realm, however. The chapter looked in depth at one of the great cultural and political mysteries of the United States: the preoccupation of the poor, particularly in rural and middle America, with moral and family values and "tradition." As argued in this conclusion, no political stance is truly indifferent to these moral issues and concerns, although the liberal agenda tends not to directly acknowledge them. In Golden Valley moral values are at the forefront of political and cultural thought. Chapter 3 questioned why these discourses have such an important place in this community and explored the ways in which they have come to dictate behavioral norms as well as justify choices already made. In this setting, I argued that the belief in the righteousness of the family is one of the main axes along which social boundaries are constructed. The lack of other routes to American ideas of success means that self-esteem and self-worth are mostly crafted with relation to the family and related moral understandings.

As chapter 3 illustrated, moral discourses around family values and tradition may evolve in response to social and economic struggles but can be both responsive and normative with regard to multiple aspects of social life. Such discourses do more than simply provide Golden Valley residents with a political set of preferences. They also bolster personal self-esteem and social status. In a community in which economic collapse has truncated class diversity in the economic sense, conceptions of morality and family values provide a new axis along which the community can hierarchically divide itself. Thus, family values couple with work ethics and moral capital to distinguish the deserving from the undeserving poor in Golden Valley. This distinction in turn helps to create and enforce new behavioral norms, which, although based in preexisting moral understandings, nonetheless present new interpretations of morality specific to the community's present needs. Behaviors that were morally acceptable when jobs were abundant are forbidden by the new conception of family values. In many ways these changes in understanding are adaptive, responding to changing structural conditions.

Chapter 3 demonstrated several ways in which family values and tradition create social boundaries and structure social and personal life in Golden Valley. It argued that the ideal typical nuclear family, which is "traditional" perhaps in name only, provides a sense of safety and stability for individuals who grew up without either. But it also provides these individuals, many of whom grew up in poor, "nontraditional" families, with a sense of their own moral success despite their past and current poverty. This moral stance becomes an important factor both in defining themselves as successful as well as influencing their family and behavioral choices. However, often for the very poor creating the nuclear family alone does not provide sufficient evidence of their success. Thus, the need to prove family values and moral worth contributes to the tradition of creating extended families that include nonbiological children. Despite the economic strain that these extra children create, for many poor families caring for the children of more needy and less upstanding adults provides them with a sense of moral superiority that again helps deemphasize their economic and labor market failures. In these ways family values are reinforced as vital boundaries within Golden Valley's social structure. Just as proving moral worth through work ethics was necessary to maintaining one's place in the labor market, proving family values and traditionality becomes key to maintaining one's social position and sense of self-worth.

But family values do more than create differences between individuals and families. Their power also makes them normative and allows them to police behaviors and influence choices. Thus, chapter 3 also illustrated the ways in which family values have been redefined in response to the changing structural conditions and the implications of these definitional changes. The new understandings of family values exclude behaviors that were once considered to be normal and expected aspects of a male breadwinner's lifestyle. However, now that breadwinning has become difficult for most Golden Valley men, the definition of their role as good husbands and fathers has changed. Their moral worth now comes more from avoiding abusive behaviors than from breadwinning. Meanwhile, these definitions have also adapted in response to women's changing roles within the household economy. Family values now dictate a woman's freedom from abuse as being "traditional" rather than recognizing outside influences such as feminism. Thus, morality in the form of family values rhetoric has come to define behavioral norms that are more appropriate to Golden Valley's current labor market and economic situation. It has also allowed Golden Valley to absorb and integrate ideologies from more liberal spheres of American society without acknowledging any sort of liberal or progressive rhetoric as their sources.

Finally, chapter 3 also argued that discourses around morality, family, and tradition further help to justify and rationalize the choice of Golden Valley as home. While middle-class urban Americans generally neither understand nor approve of the binding ties to place that keep people in economically ravaged rural communities, Golden Valley has created its own discourse to explain, justify, and glorify these ties. They focus on the community's moral superiority and its safety from urban ills, using moral language that masks deeply imbedded racism and fear of racial, ethnic, and class differences. This discourse, like other discourses around family values and tradition, also creates a sense of self-esteem and personal success for Golden Valley's residents. While they may not have achieved the American dream in the raw economic sense, they have, in their own minds, succeeded in capturing some part of its essence.

Thus, overall, these family values discourses are critically important in Golden Valley. Without understanding the many ways in which moral discourses around the family provide self-worth and community standing there, one cannot hope to understand why they resonate so strongly in the political realm for residents of Golden Valley and similarly disadvantaged rural communities. These discourses are not immune to economic factors, but rather are crafted in response to structural and economic conditions. In the face of macroeconomic forces that individuals cannot imagine being able to influence or change, morality allows them to adapt and focus on the positive aspects of their lives.

These responses are both reactive and proactive, as illustrated in chapter 4. The chapter began by exploring the link between single parenting and poverty, which both academic literature and Golden Valley residents themselves often ascribe to the stresses of male unemployment. It argued that many of the problems of male joblessness are common to both rural and urban America, including the stress caused by men's inability to achieve the breadwinner status that is so crucial to American masculine identity. What has occurred in Golden Valley amounts to a crisis in masculinity: men are by and large unable to achieve the culturally accepted masculine ideal. For many men this crisis can result in negative responses that include self-doubt, substance abuse, and controlling behaviors within the family. Yet Golden Valley shows that these male reactions are not inevitable under conditions of unemployment and economic stress. It is here that the moral discourses around the family and its gender norms truly show their power. They enable a redefinition of family values that bridges the old and new structural conditions and cultural norms in ways that allow the family, however defined, to persevere.

The lesson from chapter 4 should not be misinterpreted: it does not argue that a two-parent family is inherently right or correct. However, it does argue that flexibility with regard to gender ideologies can help families adjust to their new economic and labor market realities in ways that increase their chances of enduring happily over time. To illustrate this point, the chapter explored the changing conceptions of femininity, masculinity, and family roles in Golden Valley. While previous research has argued that poor women prefer single parenting and welfare to marriage with unemployed men, chapter 4 illustrated that Golden Valley women exhibited little hesitation toward marrying men without jobs, and most were willing to take on significant income-generating responsibilities to keep households afloat. Most valued two-parent married families highly and were dedicated to their creation and maintenance. However, within this new context of increased female income and financial responsibility within the household, they were unwilling to accept the substance abuse and physical violence that chapter 3 showed has come to be labeled as anti-family. Thus, women were flexible in taking on new roles and responsibilities within the family, yet continued to conceive of and define themselves through discourses that focused on their dedication to their families and "traditional" values. For women this was not a difficult task, at least in part because it was in step with larger U.S. cultural trends and because it represented a net gain in power and status for them. Their moral and gender discourses both reflected and encouraged their transitions.

What was more difficult for women was remaining "traditional" stay-at-home mothers when their husbands could not find enough work. For these women, tensions were more likely to run high, since these arrangements often resulted in material hardships as well as power struggles within their families. In these cases discourse did not save women from oppressive men, and the situations were exacerbated by the fact that both partners were well aware of the men's failures to live up to the norms they exalted. For these families, discourses that were inflexible were unsuccessful in creating positive home environments, and it was here that women were likely to judge and blame their husbands for failing to live up to the breadwinner ideal. Caught between old and new conceptions of gender roles and family responsibilities, these women were unsure of whether they were truly succeeding at creating the "traditional" families that they had idealized and imagined. Their testimonies voiced confusion, frustration, and discontent with their marriages.

The impact of this type of disconnect between old discourses and new realities was even more apparent with regard to the men. For men, the labor market and economic changes have been much more difficult than for women. While women were generally able to spin their new work responsibilities as consistent with their domestic roles, it was not easy for men to create the same continuity to the breadwinner identity when they had little to no paying work. Nonetheless, many tried rather than take on family or gender roles they had long identified as feminine. A number of men were threatened by the loss of power that might accompany changing gender roles within the household and thus steadfastly tried to maintain some semblance of the breadwinner/homemaker divide. It was for these "rigid" men that self-esteem was at its lowest, that substance abuse was most likely, and that marital dissatisfaction was most rampant. Chapter 4 argued that for these men, rigidity with regard to family and gender ideologies created and exacerbated an internal dissonance that tore apart both the individuals themselves and the families they formed. It explored the ways in which these men clung desperately to their previous notions of fatherhood and masculinity, often creating myths and power plays to maintain their positions of control or simply opting out of marriage and fatherhood when they knew they could not adequately approximate their own ideals.

Thankfully, this disheartening scenario described fewer than half of the men in the sample, and as chapter 4 finally showed, many of Golden Valley's men used the same moral discourses around family values and the various meanings of tradition to create new models of masculinity and fatherhood that fit their radically altered circumstances. Several of them describe fatherhood and masculinity in new terms that focus on more attainable goals such as active fathering. While these new gender norms are at odds with previous understandings of both family responsibilities and masculinity, they are strengthened by their connection to the family values discourses that underlie so much of Golden Valley's current social and cultural life. Ideals such as active fathering are very much consistent with the moral discourses around family, which allows men to conceive of themselves as successful fathers and husbands even when they are not the sole or even main breadwinners. Their increased access to self-esteem and social standing, as well as their flexible ideologies, also allows them to be more open to changing gender norms for their wives. Thus, the flexible men were often the same men who encouraged their wives to work and openly acknowledged their financial contributions. The greater freedom and respect that their wives received appeared to further contribute to a satisfactory home environment, in which partnership and family togetherness were stressed over power differentials and separate spheres. Without the connection to these moral discourses around family values, it is likely that these flexible men would encounter more resistance from their peers and find it harder to achieve a sense of success as fathers and family men.

Policy Implications

The evidence from Golden Valley clearly indicates that morality is a powerful force in structuring social, individual, and family life there. But what does one do with this information? I began by arguing that the answer is not to legislate morality, but rather to stop ignoring its influence over the lives and decisions of the rural poor. Morality itself is not what needs to be controlled, but rather its influence should be controlled when policies are created that specifically address the problems of the poor. As a number of scholars have argued, many of our policy decisions regarding poverty alleviation already contain implicit assumptions about the moral failures of the poor and often use punitive measures to correct what we see as their moral deficiencies.[16] Thus, the first and most obvious lesson from Golden Valley is that the rural poor are not morally deficient and their poverty is not caused by a lack of work ethics or other individual attributes. This simple statement has a number of far-reaching implications, particularly regarding welfare reform, which has focused so intensely on forcing people who are assumed to be lazy and dependent to change their attitudes and enter the workforce. Although this characterization is more frequently targeted at the urban poor than the rural poor, welfare and poverty policies do not distinguish between these populations.

In the case of Golden Valley there is no workforce to enter and the poor are not looking for handouts. The many voices represented in this book illustrate time and again the strong work ethics and desire for work among Golden Valley's poorest residents. It also has shown that welfare itself is so highly stigmatized that it is often pursued only in times of the greatest, most desperate need, and the very act of receiving it creates such a sense of failure for the recipients that it often produces, or at least deepens, a cycle of depression, social isolation, and lowered self-esteem. For many the result is eventually substance abuse and removal from social networks, as well as the disintegration of social, family, and romantic ties. Researchers have for decades shown that welfare does not afford recipients even the most basic economic survival.[17] In Golden Valley it also undermines mental health and social standing, as well as eroding future job prospects. Clearly, this is a program that is not adequately helping the rural poor to either survive or get back on their feet. Punitive measures that attempt to force them into a nonexistent labor market and coerce them to marry other poor and possibly abusive individuals are unlikely to improve anyone's quality of life or chances of economic or personal success.

This book has shown that a number of the assumptions and motivating factors behind welfare reform are misguided, particularly with regard to isolated rural communities like Golden Valley. The main focus, to push welfare recipients into the workforce, is pointless in a place where so few jobs exist and even low-paying positions are hard to find. Welfare reform has done nothing to address the larger societal problems of industrial restructuring and labor market collapse. It is, of course, these issues that are responsible for most of Golden Valley's poverty, not poor work ethics or a culture of dependency. Thus, one clear policy implication is the need to focus on economic development in rural poor areas as well as on education and training opportunities. Golden Valley still has very low educational attainment compared to many areas of California, at least in part because it is so difficult to pursue higher education while living there. Much of the money that is being spent on an increasingly punitive and bureaucratic welfare system would be better spent—at least in rural communities like Golden Valley—on creating job training and job opportunities for the poor there, as well as social supports for working families such as subsidized child care.

In Golden Valley, attempts have been made at job creation, but they have been largely unsuccessful and most have created only a handful of new, often insecure jobs. The legacy of the spotted owl ruling has yet to be reversed, and thus despite the efforts of several forward-thinking organizations to find ways to sustainably harvest and make use of the limited types and amount of timber that can still be cut, little large-scale job creation or economic reversal has occurred in the local timber industry. Golden Valley requires additional federal and state support for making sustainable yet profitable use of its natural resources. Its economy also desperately needs more diverse types of development to recover from its overreliance on the forest sector. Rural communities facing economic challenges like Golden Valley's require policies that "focus on community-based approaches to development, not only the needs of individual workers, firms, and industries." Examples of these community-based approaches include "investing in effective social services, basic municipal infrastructure, strong leadership, and proactive local foundations," as well as providing education and training, encouraging the growth of industry and local entrepreneurship, and increasing access to capital.[18] Services that are lacking in Golden Valley—such as higher education, health care, and affordable, safe child care—are other areas that should be targeted for investment and growth. Only when there are available jobs for both skilled and less skilled workers can Golden Valley's population be expected to transition fully away from income-support programs.

Another of the most troubling assumptions behind welfare reform is that the poor are somehow deviant with regard to marriage and family and thus must be coerced into marriage and two-parent families. Among the stated goals of welfare reform are reducing out-of-wedlock pregnancies, promoting marriage as an alternative to welfare, and ensuring that children are cared for in the home.[19] However, the measures to promote such families consist mostly of abstinence education, prevention and prosecution of statutory rape, and the controversial "family cap," which excludes children of welfare-dependent mothers from welfare receipt.[20] This blatant attempt to control poor women's fertility encourages marriage only through increasing the economic vulnerability of welfare-reliant women who have more children, leaving them few choices other than reliance on the (often poor) men in their lives. While such coercive measures may, in fact, help to increase marriage rates among some populations, they do not necessarily improve the economic situations of poor mothers or their families. Furthermore, pushing poor single mothers into marriage may in fact have harmful effects on them, as it may result in them marrying abusive or addicted men whom they otherwise might have chosen to leave. Rather than promoting healthy two-parent families, the pro-marriage "incentives" of welfare reform act more as punishments for having children while poor.

Even if one agrees that two-parent families are superior to other family forms, Golden Valley provides little evidence that the rural poor are uninterested in marriage and nuclear families. Thus, there is no need there for policies that promote and enforce marriage as "the foundation of a successful society."[21] Although it is true that single-parent families are on the rise in Golden Valley, as they are in poor communities throughout the United States, this book has made it abundantly clear that marriage and family are as highly valued among the rural poor as they are among the middle class. Single-parent families in Golden Valley are not generally created due to a lack of interest in marriage, nor to women's preference for welfare "independence" over marriage. Single-parent families are instead often caused by the multiple personal and interpersonal stresses that arise among individuals who are unable to achieve economic security and, more important, a sense of self-worth and success as parents and spouses. Making marriage the only option for poor women will do nothing to eradicate these issues; it will only force women who might otherwise be safe from abusive men to accept them and the slight financial buffer they may provide as preferable to starvation and homelessness.

This book has shown that despite their circumstances, the rural poor demonstrate surprising resilience and abilities to adjust to changing conditions in ways that support family life and marriage. Nonetheless, America cannot expect moral discourses to be enough to change the economic fortunes of the very poor. It is necessary for U.S. policies to work with, not against, the local cultural norms and community strengths to support both adaptation to poverty and eventually an escape from it. The answer is not simply to replace the women at home on welfare with men at home on SSI or unemployment insurance. Both types of households are poor, and both are unable to fully access their visions of the American dream. This book has shown that even the most "traditional" of Americans are willing and able to rewrite their gender and family scripts in ways that help them adapt to new circumstances. This flexibility is reason for hope. Nonetheless, it does not reduce the imperative to focus on their real needs: jobs that pay a living wage, health care, child care, and the ability to make their own choices regarding family structures and gender roles.

The startling ability of Golden Valley's men and their families to rewrite gender scripts in ways that support their community and family life should be interpreted as a sign of the vitality and richness of similar rural communities. As I have argued, such communities are unwilling to be erased from the map. The strong ties that bind residents to their place, environment, community, and lifestyle cannot be replaced or easily rebuilt in new, unfamiliar locations. As the stories of Golden Valley residents illustrated, those who remain consider themselves lucky to live there regardless of their prospects for employment and income, and they are willing to forgo economic security in exchange for what they see as a superior quality of life. They truly consider themselves to be "wealthier with half the income." Nonetheless, half the income is not enough to allow them to survive over the long term and seriously strains their basic survival and abilities to create and sustain healthy lives and families.

Thus, another lesson that should be learned from Golden Valley is the necessity to take into account the individuals who are casualties of policies focused on seemingly unrelated issues. The environmental issues and concerns that led to the spotted owl ruling were not about loggers and were not meant to target them or punish them for their choice of lifestyle or career. Similarly, corporate interests such as the logging and woods-products industries operate with the bottom line as their highest concern, not the lives of their employees. Their policies were also not crafted with the intention of sustaining communities like Golden Valley over the long term. The last twenty years have seen similar patterns throughout the United States, as corporate industries have closed plants and moved production overseas to increase profits, impoverishing blue-collar communities throughout the nation in the process. The voices from Golden Valley beg Americans to examine their priorities as a nation. Will the country continue to put macro-level concerns before the needs of individuals? Will its people continue to see environmental issues as opposed to the needs of rural dwellers, or can they begin to think more holistically and realistically about the interdependence of the two? Will corporations be allowed to continue to make the rules and decide the fate of communities, or will policymakers find ways to ensure jobs and living wages to all Americans who want to work? These are the questions this book cannot answer. But it can argue that the people of Golden Valley do matter, both as political entities and as contributing citizens who need protection. They vote in elections, their children fight in the military, and they receive federal social services that they hope will allow them to survive. The rural poor will not disappear simply through being ignored. Despite the tendency of both scholarly and policy work on poverty to focus on the urban poor, the rural poor have not ceased to exist. They have ceased to be understood, however, at some cost to both themselves and the nation as a whole. Recognition of their separate concerns, unique cultures, and specific adaptations to stress and change is the first step toward ultimately being able to change their fortunes for the better. America's charge is to not forget the people of Golden Valley and the struggles they endure to achieve their unique vision of the American dream. Instead, the nation must recognize that their poverty is not of their own making and thus cannot be alleviated by punishing them for it, assuming they will leave in search of better prospects, or simply ignoring them and leaving them without the education, skills, or resources to improve their economy on their own. In learning to better serve the people of forgotten places like Golden Valley, Americans will perhaps also come to better serve themselves as a whole.

The introduction to this book argued that morality, although important throughout American cultural life, rises to an unequal power in the absence of other forms of symbolic and real capital and other ways of creating social distinction. I have connected the rise of morality to trends in rural dwellers' politic preferences, which include strong rural support for Republican congressional candidates (60 percent in 2002), for pro-life candidates (37 percent versus 34 percent of urban voters), and for the National Rifle Association (42 percent versus 27 percent of urban voters).[22] That the rural poor prioritize moral values as voting concerns is not a given, but rather a situation created by the lack of other relevant issues upon which to focus their interests. As I have argued earlier, they understand that neither political side truly has their economic concerns in mind, and neither side is likely to significantly improve their quality of life or labor market prospects. But should an agenda arise that does affect them, they are likely to prioritize it over moral concerns.

Thus it was that two years after the 2004 elections, with regard to the midterm elections of 2006, National Public Radio again reported on the leanings of rural voters. However, this time its poll found that rural voters were shifting to the Democratic side. Their reasons did not include moral agendas, but rather concerns about the sagging economy and the Iraq war,[23] which included a disproportionate number of rural and poor soldiers, particularly from places like Golden Valley.[24] In 2004, when I left Golden Valley, the parents of many of these soldiers were still optimistic and proud of their fighting sons and daughters, even as some of them began to return home with serious and irreversible injuries and disabilities. By 2006, it seems that rural individuals had grown disillusioned, and the desire to protect their children from the ravages of war trumped moral concerns as key voting issues. Thus, the final policy lesson from Golden Valley is to neither underestimate nor give up on its residents. While the importance of moral concerns to these voters should be taken into account and understood, addressing their more concrete needs will still be the most effective way to win their support.

Appendix

General Interview Protocol for
Male Respondents

All interviews for male respondents were based on the following script; the script for female respondents was essentially identical, with the exception of personal pronouns. The interviews were semistructured, meaning that the questions were not always asked in the order or manner presented here. The exact form of each interview depended on the respondent's answers and interests. Respondents (R) were generally allowed to follow their own narratives as much as possible, but during the course of each interview all of the questions were covered in some form. Before the interviews began, respondents were informed of their right to refuse to answer any question. Occasionally some did exercise this right.

History in Community

1. Ask about how long R has lived in Golden Valley, why came if came from somewhere else. What kinds of ties does R have in community? Is R happy here? What does R like about living in Golden Valley?
2. Has the community changed over R's lifetime? In what ways? Is life here better now than it was in past?

Family History

1. Ask R about what parents did while growing up, how work was allocated within family, what roles each parent played in household and with regard to children. Which parent was R closer to?
2. Ask R to describe father and relationship with him. Was he a role model or someone R wanted to be like?
3. Ask R if he expected his own life to be like that of his parents. What were his expectations of himself with regard to work and family life as an adult?
4. Have R's expectations changed? Is life better or worse than what he envisioned for himself as a child?

Work History and Leisure

1. Ask R about current job or struggle to find work. Is R happy with current work situation?
2. What kinds of work has R done in past? Which were the best jobs? Has work life been affected by the mill closure?
3. If R has struggled to find work, talk about the process. How does he feel about himself when he can't find work? How does he deal with this emotion? Ask R to talk about specific instances when he lost jobs and how this affected him.
4. What does he do for money when he can't find work? Has he made sacrifices in order to stay in community? Why does he stay if he has trouble finding work?
5. What other kinds of activities does R do with free time? What does he enjoy most? Try to find out about hunting/fishing/outdoors activities as well as socializing, drinking, etc.

Marriage and Family

1. Is R married or has ever been? For how long and/or how many times? Is happier married or single? What kind of relationship is he currently in?
2. Does R have children? How many? Who do they live with? How were custody arrangements decided?
3. Talk about relationship with children. What kind of role does R play as father? What are some of the things that he most enjoys doing

with his kids? Does he feel he has been a good father to his children? What does this mean to him? What are some of the happiest moments as a father? What were some of the biggest challenges or disappointments?

4. Is R much like his own father? In what ways is he similar or different? Would he prefer to be more or less like him? What kinds of things make a good father?

5. If R has no children, does he want them? Why? Does he have any relationships with children in his life? If so, describe his role.

6. If R has never been married, does he want to be? What kinds of relationships has he had—cohabitation, etc.? What kinds of qualities is R looking for in a partner? Is he single by choice?

7. What have been some of the biggest challenges or problems in his relationships with partners? Go into depth on causes if possible. How has he dealt with these problems? If multiple relationships, what were some of the causes of the breakups? How does he feel about exes?

8. Have there been ways in which job-related stress (or stress from lack thereof) has affected his relationships? Describe if possible.

Notes

Introduction

1. All identifying details in this book, including the names of people and places, have been changed to preserve the anonymity of subjects.

2. This local colloquialism refers to a combination of drinking and drug use, generally with regard to teenagers but sometimes to adults as well. It was used with reference to weekend binges as well as more serious alcoholism and drug use.

3. Lamont and Fournier 1992.

4. Bourdieu 1984.

5. Stein 2001, 8.

6. Montagne and Williams 2004.

7. Frank 2004.

8. Bellah et al. 1996.

9. McGirr 2001.

10. O'Hare and Bishop 2006.

11. Sayer 2005, 167.

12. Bourdieu 1986.

13. See Duneier 1999 and Gowan 2003.

14. Lamont 1992.

15. Purser 2007.

16. Swidler 1986.

17. Bellah et al. 1996; Gowan 2003.

18. Labao 2006, 268.

19. Coontz 1992.
20. Frank 2004; Stacey 1996.
21. Lamont similarly finds that American morality is not tied strongly to religion. She explains, "With some exceptions . . . interviewees rarely made reference to religion in their discussions of moral purity, apparently dissociating moral character from religious attitudes" (1992, 57). Instead, she finds that morality tends to be defined "in terms of work ethics, humility, conspicuous honesty, and straightforwardness" (1992, 61).
22. Burawoy 1998, 17.
23. Ibid., 5.
24. Anderson and Jack 1991.
25. U.S. Census Summary Files 2000.
26. See Appendix for instrument upon which interviews were based.
27. Gluck and Patai 1991.

1. The Place I Found

1. California State Association of Counties 2006.
2. A friend who moved to Golden Valley as an adult once recounted to me this exchange, which epitomized the community's attitude toward garbage disposal. During a parents' meeting at the grade school, she complained that the coffee cups were made of Styrofoam, which doesn't break down in landfills. Another mother, who was born and raised in Golden Valley, responded to her, "Duh! That's why you *burn* them!" (Field Notes 5/5/04).
3. Duncan 1999; Fitchen 1991; Knapp 1995.
4. Duncan 1999; Elder, Robertson, and Ardelt 1994; Elder, Robertson, and Foster 1994; Fitchen 1991; Norem and Blundall 1988.
5. Duncan 1999; England and Brown 2003.
6. Binkley 2000; Mederer 1999; Smith et al. 2003.
7. Daniels et al. 2000; Danks 2000; Kusel and Fortmann 1991.
8. Nelson and Smith 1999.
9. Bokemeier and Garkovich 1991; Dehan and Deal 2001; Tickamyer and Henderson 2003.
10. Daniels and Brehm 2003.
11. U.S. Census Summary Files, 2000.
12. "Public assistance income includes general assistance and Temporary Assistance to Needy Families (TANF). Separate payments received for hospital or other medical care (vendor payments) are excluded. This does not include Supplemental Security Income (SSI)" (U.S. Census Summary Files 2000).
13. U.S. Census Summary Files 1990, 2000.
14. Ibid. Women's employment population ratio rose from 31.5 percent in 1990 to 35 percent in 2000. In 1990, 36 percent of women were in the labor force, rising to 41 percent by 2000. For men the opposite pattern held and was more drastic: their employment population ratio dropped from 50 percent to 36

percent over the decade and their labor force participation rate dropped from 56 percent to 48 percent.

15. Ibid.

16. U.S. Census Summary Files 2000.

17. Ibid.

18. U.S. Census Bureau 2006.

19. U.S. Census Summary Files 2000. Rural California as a whole resembles the state average for most of these measures. This is reflective of the great diversity of rural places across California, including many wealthier areas, particularly on the coast and in the Sierra foothills. However, Golden Valley is not unique in the northern forested part of the state, which includes many communities with similar economic and labor market concerns.

20. U.S. Census Summary Files 2000.

21. U.S. Census Summary Files 1980.

22. U.S. Census Summary Files 2000.

23. Conger and Elder 1994; Mederer 1999; Norem and Blundall 1988; Smith et al. 2003.

24. Mitchell 1993.

25. Mitchell (1993, 38) reported that timber jobs in the Pacific Northwest declined by 14 percent over the decade of the 1980s due to "increased exports of raw logs, increased automation, and a decline in lumber industry investment in the Pacific Northwest since 1978." Thus, according to this account, environmentally motivated timber harvest reductions were simply "aggravating an already serious situation" (39). However, the timber industry disputed such claims in the 1980s, arguing that it was "the largest manufacturing employer in the Northwest" and that it was "maintaining a stable workforce" (Northwest Forest Resource Council 1989, 3).

26. Carroll 1995; Durbin 1996. Carroll et al. (2005) described the spotted owl controversy as vitriolic and fought mainly through the media, in which "the industry was often portrayed as a logger, thereby conflating the roles of decision makers and workers" (167).

27. Carroll 1995; Mitchell 1993.

28. Carroll 1995.

29. Mitchell 1993.

30. Dietrich 1992; Durbin 1996; Thomas et al. 1990.

31. Dietrich 1992.

32. Yaffee 1994.

33. Bart and Forsman 1992.

34. Durbin 1996.

35. Thomas et al. 1990.

36. Dietrich 1992, 54.

37. Northwest Forest Resource Council 1989.

38. Dietrich 1992; Yaffee 1994.

39. Yaffee 1994.

40. Dietrich 1992.
41. Durbin 1996.
42. Lujan et al. 1992.
43. Yaffee 1994.
44. Dietrich 1992; Mitchell 1993.
45. Durbin 1996.
46. Carroll 1995, 129.
47. Yaffee 1994.
48. Daniels and Brehm 2003; Durbin 1996.
49. Pryne 1994.
50. Gordon 2005; Milstein 2004.
51. Milstein 2004.
52. U.S. Census Summary Files 2000.
53. Fitchen 1991.
54. Bederman 1995; Kimmel 2005.
55. Interestingly, despite Golden Valley residents' beliefs to the contrary, this system of neighbors and friends watching out for each other's children has been documented in poor urban neighborhoods as well. Newman (1999) found the same type of social control pattern in Harlem, and her respondents made almost identical comments. For example, one Harlem mother is quoted as saying of her neighbors: "We all know each other. . . . If my kids [do something bad], I know it before they know it!" (222).
56. My own observations in the community confirmed that in-migration of the poor looking to stretch their public aid dollars further in a low cost-of-living environment does occur. However, it did not appear to be anywhere near as prevalent as was commonly believed by almost everyone in the community. Fitchen (1992, 197) found a similar perception in rural New York, where "long term residents often state that the new people moving into the village apartments have come from a neighboring county 'to take advantage of our easy-going welfare department,' or from out of state 'to take advantage of New York's higher welfare benefits.'"
57. Gibbs 2005.

2. Workers and Welfare

1. Fitchen 1991.
2. U.S. Census Bureau 2006.
3. The importance of the outward appearance of homes, and the implications of their appearances in terms of the perceived moral character of their occupants, has been noted by urban ethnographers as well. Kefalas (2003), in her study of a white working-class Chicago community, and Patillo-McCoy (1999), in her study of an African American middle-class Chicago community, both find similar types of stigma and judgment aimed toward community members who fail to keep up their houses properly. Kefalas argues that the state of housing creates symbolic distances and moral boundaries between "'good and

bad neighbors'" (100). She observes, "Home-ownership also serves as a clear social marker that separates hardworking, contributing members of the community from the more transient and shiftless ones.... The fastidious upkeep of lawns and houses is inextricably linked to homeowners' ongoing efforts to establish, and also insulate, their social status" (99).

4. Sassen 1998; 1991, 284.

5. Dohan 2003, 13.

6. Ibid.

7. Edin and Lein 1997; Ehrenreich 2001; Jensen and Eggebeen 1994; Nelson and Smith 1998, 1999; Newman 1999; Stack 1974; Tickamyer and Wood 1998; Venkatesh 2000.

8. Wilson (1996, 69) contrasts "mainstream norms and ideas of acceptability" with "ghetto-related" behaviors, which include "existing without a steady job or pursuing illegitimate means of income" (71). Mainstream values, according to Wilson, focus on work and morally sanctioned behaviors and contribute to the creation of social capital.

9. Anderson 1989, 1990; Bourgois 1995; Venkatesh 2000.

10. Dohan 2003; Purser 2007.

11. Dohan 2003; Wilson 1996.

12. Lamont 2000.

13. Edin and Lein 1997, 146.

14. Newman 1999.

15. Gowan 2003.

16. Duneier 1999.

17. Wilson 1996.

18. Larson 1978; Snyder and McLaughlin 2004.

19. Fischer (1975) argues that in the urban setting, sheer numbers and the competition between people create variation and allow for greater subcultural variety, intensity, and diffusion, as well as generally higher rates of "unconventionality" than is found in most rural settings.

20. Davis 2000; Fitchen 1991; Nelson and Smith 1998; Norem and Blundall 1988.

21. Jensen, McLaughlin, and Slack 2003; Nelson and Smith 1998, 1999; Tickamyer and Wood 1998.

22. England and Brown 2003; Moore 2001.

23. Fitchen 1991; Struthers and Bokemeier 2000.

24. Jensen and Eggebeen 1994; Lichter, Roscigno, and Condron 2003.

25. Bokemeier and Garkovich 1991; Duncan 1999; Struthers and Bokemeier 2000.

26. McGranahan 2003.

27. Sayer 2004; Wilson 1996.

28. Wilson 1996.

29. Duncan 1999, Lamont 2000.

30. Lamont 2000.

31. Sayer 2000, 2004.

32. Bourdieu 1991.
33. Coleman 1988; Putnam 2000.
34. Wilson 1996, 70.
35. Sayer 2004, 10.
36. Fischer 1975.
37. Stack 1974; Newman 1999.
38. Erkulwater 2006, 5.
39. U.S. Census Summary Files 2000.
40. U.S. Census Summary Files 1990, 2000.
41. This social stigma against welfare receipt has been found in small rural communities throughout the United States. According to Bokemeier and Garkovich (1991, 119–20), "strong cultural traditions prevent many rural families from using public assistance and the intimate nature of social interaction in rural communities makes others aware of individual or family decisions to access public assistance. As a result, rural people are less likely to express a need for social services or to utilize them if they are available."
42. Fraser 1989, 153.
43. According to Hays (2003), these negative associations between welfare and immorality are common across the United States. She argues, "The mere mention of welfare, for many people, brings to mind not just poverty, but a whole series of daunting social problems: teenage pregnancy, unwed parenting, divorce, abortion, drug abuse, unsafe streets, volatile race relations. . . . The image of [welfare recipients] as deviant and dangerous people, suffering from forms of immorality that seem almost contagious, is so ubiquitous that it tends to seep into one's consciousness almost unnoticed" (121).
44. Field Notes 11/8/02.
45. While this was the trend in 2003–2004, in the following years Golden Valley and Jefferson County experienced an increase in both large- and small-scale marijuana growing, due in part to the loosening of restrictions on the growth and use of medical marijuana in both the state of California and the county itself.
46. Anderson 1989, 1990; Bourgois 1995; Venkatesh 2000.
47. According to many subjects, this type of common-law marriage is common in Golden Valley and has been for generations. In general they are treated as identical to legal marriages. A number of unmarried, cohabiting subjects referred to their partners as husbands or wives, despite the lack of official legal status.
48. Edin and Lein 1997; Ehrenreich 2001; Newman 1999.
49. Rubin 1976; McLanahan, Garfinkel, and Mincy 2001; Elder, Robertson, and Ardelt 1994; Davis 1993.
50. Widom and Hiller-Sturmhöfel 2001.
51. Lamont 2000.
52. Bourdieu 1986.
53. Burt 1992.
54. Harrington 1962.

55. Frank 2004; Stacey 1996.

56. See, for example, Frank 2004. Frank uses the term "middle American" to refer to average-income, conservative voters, mostly from midwestern "red states." He describes them as "regular, down-home working stiff[s]" (23). They are exemplified by the anti-liberal backlash in Kansas.

3. Family Life

1. Hays (2003, 130) argues that the prioritization of family and its elevation above career as a source of self-esteem are class-based phenomena. She explains that "working class and poor people, relative to their wealthier counterparts, are more likely to value their family over their paid work, following largely from the fact that raising children can offer a great deal more satisfaction, fulfillment, and social status than a job in fast foods, cleaning bedpans, or manufacturing widgets."

2. The third childless woman, in her late 20s, did not mention having fertility problems. However, her husband said in a separate interview that he suspected that they may have fertility issues, as they had been trying unsuccessfully to conceive.

3. Stacey 1996, 2.

4. Ibid., 4.

5. Frank 2004.

6. Ibid.

7. Rubin 1994, xiv.

8. Bourdieu 1984, 172.

9. Newman 1988, 175.

10. They did tend to be mostly heterosexual couples, however. During my year in Golden Valley, I did not meet, nor was I made aware of, any same-sex couples residing in the community. The only such couple that anyone seemed to remember had moved away several years earlier and did not have children. This, of course, does not mean that there were no homosexual individuals or couples in Golden Valley, but rather that if they were there, they were not publicly open about their sexuality.

11. Coontz 1992, 28.

12. Stacey 1991.

13. Ibid., 252.

14. Lamont 2000.

15. Stack 1974.

16. Hansen 2005; Roberts 2002; Stack 1974.

17. Collins 1994; Hansen 2005; Nelson 2000; Stack 1974; Stack and Burton 1994.

18. General Educational Development, a credential equivalent to a high-school diploma.

19. Based on the 2003 federal poverty guidelines.

20. Collins 1994; Hansen 2005; Stack 1974; Stack and Burton 1994.

21. Hansen 2005.
22. Nelson 2000.
23. Stack 1974.
24. Hansen 2005.
25. Collins (2000, 122) notes that the rise of crack cocaine in poor urban neighborhoods has led to a similar phenomenon in which neighborhood "other-mothers" take in children whose parents are deemed incompetent due to their drug use. However, this type of care has not been documented to the extent that kin care has in this setting.
26. Rosenfeld and Wise 2000, xxv.
27. Warner 2005, 33.
28. Lareau 2002, 748.
29. Connell 1995; Kimmel and Ferber 2006; Marsiglio 1995; Rubin 1976.
30. This finding contrasts with those from urban areas. For example, Edin and Kefalas's (2005) study of poor urban women found that while physical and substance abuse were among the reasons women gave for not marrying, these issues were accompanied by many other concerns, including male infidelity, unemployment, and incarceration. Among women in my Golden Valley sample, unemployment was a much less important concern, and there was no mention of either infidelity or incarceration as factors motivating either relationship breakup or nonmarriage.
31. Hochschild 1989.
32. Cottle 2001; Davis 1993; Elder, Robertson, and Ardelt 1994; McLanahan, Garfinkel, and Mincy 2001; Rubin 1976.
33. California Department of Justice 2001.
34. Rosenfeld and Wise 2000; Warner 2005.
35. Lareau 2002, 773.
36. Bourdieu 1984, 124.

4. Remaking Masculinity

1. Schafft (2006) documents a similar pattern in rural upstate New York. He found high levels of residential mobility in poor communities, "not driven by economic opportunity but rather by chronic economic insecurity coupled with inadequate access to safe and affordable housing" (228). The poor, highly mobile families whom he sampled also tended to be mostly single-parent or non-parent families (222).
2. U.S. Census Bureau Summary Files 1990, 2000.
3. Bane 1986; Cancian and Reed 2000; Eggebeen and Lichter 1991; Lichter and McLaughlin 1995; McLanahan et al. 2001; McLaughlin et al. 1999; Testa et al. 1989; Wilson 1987.
4. Albrecht et al. 2000; Edin 2000; Goldscheider and Waite 1991; Lichter and McLaughlin 1995; McLaughlin et al. 1999; Snyder and McLaughlin 2004; Waller 2002, 5.

5. Edin 2000; McLanahan et al. 2001; Testa et al. 1989; Wilson 1987.

6. Albrecht et al. 2000; Lichter and McLaughlin 1995; McLaughlin et al. 1999; Snyder and McLaughlin 2004.

7. Edin and Kefalas 2005.

8. Connell (1995, 111) defines protest masculinities as exaggerated forms of masculine conventions and claims to gendered power positions, which arise in response to men's lack or loss of power.

9. Anderson 1990.

10. Edin 2000; Furstenberg 2001; Wilson 1996.

11. Jarrett et al. 2002; Stier and Tienda 1993; Sullivan 1993.

12. Larson, Wilson, and Beley 1994; Liem and Liem 1990.

13. Cottle 2001, 2–5.

14. Newman 1988, 135.

15. Marsiglio 1995.

16. Segal 1990, 97.

17. Campbell 2006.

18. Bartlett 2006, 57.

19. Conger, Ge, and Lorenz 1994; Davis 1993.

20. Davis 1993.

21. Connell 1995, 111.

22. Davis 2000, 349; 1993, 473.

23. Davis 1993; Knapp 1995.

24. Norem and Blundall 1988, 25.

25. Nelson and Smith 1998, 80.

26. Hochschild 1989; Nelson and Smith 1998; Skaptadóttir 2000.

27. Hochschild 1989, 12–13.

28. Binkley 2000; Gringeri 1994; Nelson and Smith 1998.

29. Mederer 1999, 223.

30. Hochschild 1989.

31. In my year in Golden Valley, women complained of many past and potential problems with men, but fears of or experiences with infidelity were seldom, if ever, voiced. This stands in stark contrast to many urban-based studies, in which men's infidelity is found to be a major deterrent to marriage and contributing factor to breakups (Anderson 1990; Edin and Kefalas 2005; Kurz 1995). Interestingly, in my interviews and fieldwork, men tended to complain of women's infidelity far more frequently than the other way around. This does not mean, of course, that men's infidelity does not occur in Golden Valley, but rather that it may be less common than in other settings.

32. Edin 2000; Furstenberg 2001; Jarrett et al. 2002; Wilson 1987.

33. Davis 1993, 2000; Gringeri 1994; Hochschild 1989; Nelson and Smith 1998, 1999.

34. West and Zimmerman 1987.

35. Gringeri 1994; Hochschild 1989; Nelson and Smith 1998.

36. Deutsch 1999.

37. Goldscheider and Waite 1991; Hochschild 1989.
38. Kurz 1995, 74.
39. Kimmel and Ferber 2006, 132. See also Marsiglio 1995.
40. Kurz 1995; Rubin 1976. Kurz (1995, 21) argues that "as wages decline, and as good jobs become more scarce . . . men may increasingly resent the loss of family privilege."
41. Campbell 2006.
42. According to Connell (1995, 77), "hegemonic masculinity can be defined as the configuration of gender practice which embodies the currently accepted answer to the problem of the legitimacy of patriarchy, which guarantees (or is taken to guarantee) the dominant position of men and the subordinate position of women." He further explains, "Hegemonic masculinity is not a fixed character type, always and everywhere the same. It is, rather, the masculinity that occupies the hegemonic position in a given pattern of gender relations, a position always contestable" (76).
43. Similar dichotomous ideal-types have been created to express divergent gender identities in other rural settings as well. For example, Peter et al. (2006) construct ideal-types of masculinity that express similar differences with regard to male farmer's conceptions of masculinity as it relates to the environment. Their definition of "monologic masculinity" looks similar to "rigid" masculinity: "a single-voiced, conventional masculinity with rigid expectations and strictly negotiated performances that clearly differentiate between men's and women's work." This is contrasted with "dialogic masculinity," similar to "flexible," which "presents a broader, more open, multivoiced understanding of what it is to be a man" (28). Because their categories relate specifically to relationships with farming and the environment, rather than within marriage or the family, they have not been adopted here.
44. Ray 2000.
45. Waller 2002.
46. Nonn 2004.
47. Two of the thirty men in the interview sample were not classified as either rigid or flexible, because their interviews did not yield enough information about their family lives and gender ideologies to make them classifiable.
48. Greenstein 1996; Hochschild 1989; Nelson and Smith 1998. This contrasts with previous studies, which have found that men who rely more on their wives for economic support tend to do less housework (Arrighi and Maume 2000; Brines 1994; Greenstein 2000; Hochschild 1989).
49. Waller 2002, 40.
50. Cottle 2001; Davis 1993; Elder, Robertson, and Ardelt 1994; McLanahan et al. 2001; Rubin 1976.
51. Conger and Elder 1994; Cottle 2001; Faludi 1999; Larson et al. 1994; Liem and Liem 1990; Robertson et al. 1991; Segal 1990.
52. See, for example, Nelson and Smith 1998.
53. Goldscheider and Waite 1991.

54. Hochschild 1989; Waller 2002.
55. Swidler 1986.
56. Waller 2002.
57. Mederer 1999; Norem and Blundall 1988.

Conclusion

1. Montagne and Williams 2004.
2. Berkes 2004.
3. Frank 2004.
4. Ibid., 5.
5. Ibid.
6. Lamont 1992; Kane 2001.
7. Lakoff 2002.
8. Ibid., 12.
9. Ibid., 31.
10. Frank 2004.
11. Stack 1974.
12. Newman 1999.
13. Edin and Lein 1997; Hays 2003; Newman 1999.
14. Hays 2003; Newman 1999.
15. This despite abundant evidence that the majority of welfare-reliant women have strong and active ties to the labor market (Edin and Lein 1997; Harris 1993; Hays 2003).
16. Hays 2003.
17. Edin and Lein 1997.
18. Glasmeier and Salant 2006, 6.
19. Hays 2003, 64.
20. Ibid., 67–68.
21. U.S. Congress 1996.
22. W. K. Kellogg Foundation 2002.
23. Berkes 2006a, 2006b.
24. O'Hare and Bishop 2006.

Bibliography

Albrecht, Don E., and Carol Mulford Albrecht. 2004. "Metro/Nonmetro Residence, Nonmarital Conception, and Conception Outcomes." *Rural Sociology* 69 (3): 430–52.

Albrecht, Don E., Carol Mulford Albrecht, and Stan L. Albrecht. 2000. "Poverty in Nonmetropolitan America: Impacts of Industrial, Employment, and Family Structure Variables." *Rural Sociology* 65 (1): 87–103.

Anderson, Elijah. 1989. "Sex Codes and Family Life among Poor Inner-City Youths." *Annals of the American Academy of Political and Social Science* 501: 59–78.

———. 1990. *Streetwise: Race, Class, and Change in an Urban Community.* Chicago: University of Chicago Press.

Anderson, Kathryn, and Dana C. Jack. 1991. "Learning to Listen: Interview Techniques and Analyses." In *Women's Words: The Feminist Practice of Oral History*, ed. Sherna Berger Gluck and Daphne Patai. New York: Routledge.

Arrighi, Barbara A., and David J. Maume. 2000. "Workplace Subordination and Men's Avoidance of Housework." *Journal of Family Issues* 21 (4): 464–87.

Bane, Mary Jo. 1986. "Household Composition and Poverty." In *Fighting Poverty: What Works and What Doesn't*, ed. Sheldon Danziger and Daniel H. Weinberg. Cambridge, Mass.: Harvard University Press.

Bart, Jonathan, and Eric D. Forsman. 1992. "Dependence of Northern Spotted Owls *Strix occidentalis caurina* on Old-Growth Forests in the Western USA." *Biological Conservation* 62 (2): 95–100.

Bartlett, Peggy. 2006. "Three Visions of Masculine Success on American Farms." In *Country Boys: Masculinity and Rural Life*, ed. Hugh Campbell, Michael

Mayerfeld Bell, and Margaret Finney, 47–65. University Park: Pennsylvania State University Press.

Bederman, Gail. 1995. *Manliness and Civilization: A Cultural History of Gender and Race in the United States, 1880–1917.* Chicago: University of Chicago Press.

Beisel, Nicola. 1992. "Constructing a Shifting Moral Boundary." In *Cultivating Differences: Symbolic Boundaries and the Making of Inequality,* ed. Michèle Lamont and Marcel Fournier, 104–28. Chicago: University of Chicago Press.

Bellah, Robert N., Richard Madsen, William M. Sullivan, Ann Swidler, and Steven M. Tipton. 1996. *Habits of the Heart: Individualism and Commitment in American Life.* Berkeley: University of California Press.

Berkes, Howard. 2004. "The Emerging Importance of the Rural Vote." *National Public Radio Morning Edition,* November 10, 2004.

———. 2006a. "Rural Voters Helped Put Democrats in Charge." *National Public Radio Morning Edition,* November 10, 2006.

———. 2006b. "Poll Shows Rural Voters Shifting to Democrats." *National Public Radio Morning Edition,* October 27, 2006.

Bianchi, Suzanne. 1995. "The Changing Economic Roles of Women and Men." In *State of the Union,* ed. Reynolds Farley, 107–54. New York: Russell Sage Foundation.

Binkley, Marian. 2000. "'Getting By' in Tough Times: Coping with the Fisheries Crisis." *Women Studies International Forum* 23 (3): 323–32.

Blau, Francine D., Lawrence M. Kahn, and Jane Waldfogel. 1999. "Understanding Young Women's Marriage Decisions: The Role of Labor and Marriage Market Conditions." Russell Sage Foundation Working Paper. http://www.russellsage.org/publications/.

Bokemeier, Janet L. 1997. "Rediscovering Families and Households: Restructuring Rural Society and Rural Sociology." *Rural Sociology* 62 (1): 1–20.

Bokemeier, Janet L., and Lorraine E. Garkovich. 1991. "Meeting Rural Family Needs." In *Rural Policies for the 1990s,* ed. Cornelia B. Flora and James A. Christenson, 114–27. Boulder, Colo.: Westview Press.

Bourdieu, Pierre. 1977. *Outline of a Theory of Practice.* Cambridge: Cambridge University Press.

———. 1984. *Distinction: A Social Critique of the Judgement of Taste.* Cambridge, Mass.: Harvard University Press.

———. 1986. "The Forms of Capital." In *Handbook of Theory and Research for the Sociology of Education,* ed. J. G. Richardson, 241–58. New York: Greenwood Press.

———. 1991. *Language and Symbolic Power.* Cambridge, Mass.: Harvard University Press.

Bourgois, Philippe. 1995. *In Search of Respect: Selling Crack in El Barrio.* Cambridge: Cambridge University Press.

Brines, Julie. 1994. "Economic Dependency, Gender, and the Division of Labor at Home." *American Journal of Sociology* 100 (3): 652–88.

Brown, Beverly A. 1995. *In Timber Country: Working People's Stories of Environmental Conflict and Urban Flight.* Philadelphia, Pa.: Temple University Press.

Brown, David L., and Louis E. Swanson, eds. 2003. *Challenges for Rural America in the Twenty-First Century.* University Park: Pennsylvania State University Press.

Bumpass, Larry, and Sara McLanahan. 1989. "Unmarried Motherhood: Recent Trends, Composition, and Black-White Differences." *Demography* 26 (2): 279–86.

Burawoy, Michael. 1998. "The Extended Case Method." *Sociological Theory* 16 (1): 4–33.

Bureau of Labor Statistics, data provided through the Government Information Sharing Project, Oregon State University. http://govinfo.kerr.orst.edu/.

Burt, Ronald S. 1992. *Structural Holes: The Social Structure of Competition.* Cambridge, Mass.: Harvard University Press.

California Department of Justice. 2001. "Criminal Justice Statistics Center." Office of the Attorney General. http://caag.state.ca.us/cjsc/.

California State Association of Counties. 2006. "CA County Population." http://www.csac.counties.org/.

California State Rural Health Association. 2006. "Rural California Fact Sheet." http://www.csrha.org/.

Campbell, Hugh. 2006. "Real Men, Real Locals, and Real Workers: Realizing Masculinity in Small-Town New Zealand." In *Country Boys: Masculinity and Rural Life,* ed. Hugh Campbell, Michael Mayerfeld Bell, and Margaret Finney, 87–103. University Park: Pennsylvania State University Press.

Campbell, Hugh, and Michael Mayerfeld Bell. 2000. "The Question of Rural Masculinities." *Rural Sociology* 65 (4): 542–46.

Campbell, Hugh, Michael Mayerfeld Bell, and Margaret Finney. 2006. "Masculinity and Rural Life: An Introduction." In *Country Boys: Masculinity and Rural Life,* ed. Hugh Campbell, Michael Mayerfeld Bell, and Margaret Finney, 1–22. University Park: Pennsylvania State University Press.

Cancian, Maria, and Deborah Reed. 2000. "Changes in Family Structure: Implications for Poverty and Related Policy." In "Understanding Poverty: IRP Conference May 2000." University of Wisconsin–Madison Institute for Research on Poverty. *Focus* 21 (2): 1–7.

Carlson, Marcia J., and Sara S. McLanahan. 2002. "Fragile Families, Father Involvement, and Public Policy." In *Handbook of Father Involvement,* ed. Catherine S. Tamis-LeMonda and Natasha Cabrera, 461–88. Mahwah, N.J.: Lawrence Erlbaum Associates.

Carroll, Matthew S. 1995. *Community and the Northwestern Logger: Continuities and Changes in the Era of the Spotted Owl.* Boulder, Colo.: Westview Press.

Carroll, Matthew S., Robert G. Lee, and Rebecca J. McLain. 2005. "Occupational Community and Forest Work: Three Cases from the Pacific Northwest." In *Communities and Forests: Where People Meet the Land,* ed. Robert G. Lee and Donald R. Field, 159–75. Corvallis: Oregon State University Press.

Casper, Lynne M., Sara S. McLanahan, and Irwin Garfinkel. 1994. "The Gender-Poverty Gap: What We Can Learn from Other Countries." *American Sociological Review* 59 (4): 594–605.

Castle, Emery N., ed. 1995. *The Changing American Countryside*. Lawrence: University Press of Kansas.

Clarkberg, Marin. 1999. "The Price of Partnering: The Role of Economic Well-Being in Young Adults' First Union Experiences." *Social Forces* 77: 945–68.

Cohen, Theodore. 1993. "What Do Fathers Provide? Reconsidering the Economic and Nurturant Dimensions of Men as Parents." In *Men, Work, and Family*, ed. Jane C. Hood, 1–22. Newbury Park, Calif.: Sage Publications.

Coleman, James S. 1988. "Social Capital in the Creation of Human Capital." In Supplement "Organization and Institutions: Sociological and Economic Approaches to the Analysis of Social Structure," *American Journal of Sociology* 94: S95–S120.

Collins, Patricia Hill. 1994. "Shifting the Center: Race, Class, and Feminist Theorizing about Motherhood." In *Mothering: Ideology, Experience, and Agency*, ed. Evelyn Nakano Glenn, Grace Chang, and Linda Rennie Forcey, 45–65. New York: Routledge.

———. 2000. *Black Feminist Thought: Knowledge, Consciousness, and the Politics of Empowerment*. New York: Routledge.

Conger, Rand D., and Glen H. Elder Jr., eds. 1994. *Families in Troubled Times: Adapting to Change in Rural America*. New York: Aldine de Gruyter.

Conger, Rand D., Xiao-Jia Ge, and Frederick O. Lorenz. 1994. "Economic Stress and Marital Relations." In *Families in Troubled Times: Adapting to Change in Rural America*, ed. Rand D. Conger and Glen H. Elder Jr., 187–203. New York: Aldine de Gruyter.

Conger, Rand D., Glen H. Elder Jr., Frederick O. Lorenz, Katherine J. Conter, Ronald L. Simons, Les B. Whitbeck, Shirley Huck, and Janet N. Melby. 1990. "Linking Economic Hardship to Marital Quality and Instability." *Journal of Marriage and the Family* 52 (3): 643–56.

Connell, R. W. 1987. *Gender and Power*. Cambridge, UK: Polity Press.

———. 1995. *Masculinities*. Berkeley: University of California Press.

Coontz, Stephanie. 1992. *The Way We Never Were: American Families and the Nostalgia Trap*. New York: Basic Books.

Corcoran, Mary. 2000. "Mobility, Persistence, and the Intergenerational Determinants of Children's Success." In "Understanding Poverty: IRP Conference May 2000." University of Wisconsin–Madison Institute for Research on Poverty. *Focus* 21 (2): 1–74.

Cottle, Thomas J. 2001. *Hardest Times: The Trauma of Long Term Unemployment*. Westport, Conn.: Praeger.

Daniels, Steven E., and Joan M. Brehm. 2003. "Fur, Fins, and Feathers: Whose Home Is It Anyway?" In *Challenges for Rural America in the Twenty-First Century*, ed. David Brown and Louis E. Swanson, 329–39. University Park: Pennsylvania State University Press.

Daniels, Steven E., Corrine L. Gobeli, and Angela J. Findley. 2000. "Reemployment Programs for Dislocated Timber Workers: Lessons from Oregon." *Society and Natural Resources* 13 (2): 135–50.

Danks, Cecilia. 2000. "Community Forestry Initiatives for the Creation of Sustainable Rural Livelihoods: A Case from North America." *Unasylva* 202 (3).

Davis, Dona L. 1993. "When Men Become 'Women': Gender Antagonism and the Changing Sexual Geography of Work in Newfoundland." *Sex Roles* 29 (7/8): 457–75.

———. 2000. "Gendered Cultures of Conflict and Discontent: Living 'The Crisis' in a Newfoundland Community." *Women Studies International Forum* 23 (3): 343–53.

Dehan, Laura, and James Deal. 2001. "Effects of Economic Hardship on Rural Children and Adolescents." In *The Hidden America: Social Problems in Rural America for the Twenty-First Century*, ed. Robert M. Moore III. Cranbury, N.J.: Associated University Presses.

Deutsch, Francine M. 1999. *Halving It All: How Equally Shared Parenting Works*. Cambridge, Mass.: Harvard University Press.

Dietrich, William. 1992. *The Final Forest: The Battle for the Last Great Trees of the Pacific Northwest*. New York: Simon and Schuster.

Dill, Bonnie Thornton, and Bruce B. Williams. 1992. "Race, Gender, and Poverty in the Rural South: African American Single Mothers." In *Rural Poverty in America*, ed. Cynthia M. Duncan. New York: Auburn House.

Dohan, Daniel. 2003. *The Price of Poverty: Money, Work, and Culture in the Mexican American Barrio*. Berkeley: University of California Press.

Dudley, Kathryn Marie. 1994. *The End of the Line: Lost Jobs, New Lives in Postindustrial America*. Chicago: University of Chicago Press.

Duncan, Cynthia M. 1999. *Worlds Apart: Why Poverty Persists in Rural America*. New Haven, Conn.: Yale University Press.

———, ed. 1992. *Rural Poverty in America*. New York: Auburn House.

Duncan, Greg J. 1984. *Years of Poverty, Years of Plenty*. Ann Arbor: University of Michigan Institute for Social Research.

Duncan, Stephan F., Robert J. Volk, and Robert A. Lewis. 1988. "The Influence of Financial Stressors upon Farm Husbands and Wives' Well-Being and Family Life Satisfaction." In *Families in Rural America: Stress, Adaptation, and Revitalization*, ed. Ramona Marotz-Baden, Charles B. Hennon, and Timothy H. Brubaker, 32–39. St. Paul, Minn.: National Council of Family Relations.

Duneier, Mitchell. 1999. *Sidewalk*. New York: Farrar, Straus, and Giroux.

Durbin, Kathie. 1996. *Tree Huggers: Victory, Defeat, and Renewal in the Northwest Ancient Forest Campaign*. Seattle, Wash.: The Mountaineers.

Edin, Kathryn. 2000. "What Do Low-Income Single Mothers Say about Marriage?" *Social Problems* 47 (1): 112–33.

Edin, Kathryn, and Laura Lein. 1997. *Making Ends Meet: How Single Mothers Survive Welfare and Low-Wage Work*. New York: Russell Sage Foundation.

Edin, Kathryn, and Maria Kefalas. 2005. *Promises I Can Keep: Why Poor Women Put Motherhood before Marriage*. Berkeley: University of California Press.

Edin, Kathryn, and Timothy J. Nelson. 2001. "Working Steady: Race, Low-Wage Work, and Family Involvement among Noncustodial Fathers in Philadelphia." In *Problem of the Century: Racial Stratification in the United States*, ed. Elijah Anderson and Douglas S. Massey, 375–404. New York: Russell Sage Foundation.

Eggebeen, David J., and Lichter, Daniel T. 1991. "Race, Family Structure, and Changing Poverty among American Children." *American Sociological Review* 56 (6): 801–17.

Ehrenreich, Barbara. 2001. *Nickel and Dimed: On (Not) Getting By in America*. New York: Metropolitan Books.

Elder, Glen H. Jr., Elizabeth B. Robertson, and Monika Ardelt. 1994. "Families under Economic Pressure." In *Families in Troubled Times: Adapting to Change in Rural America*, ed. Rand D. Conger and Glen H. Elder Jr., 79–103. New York: Aldine de Gruyter.

Elder, Glen H. Jr., Elizabeth B. Robertson, and E. Michael Foster. 1994. "Survival, Loss, and Adaptation: A Perspective on Farm Families." In *Families in Troubled Times: Adapting to Change in Rural America*, ed. Rand D. Conger and Glen H. Elder Jr., 105–26. New York: Aldine de Gruyter.

England, Lynn, and Ralph B. Brown. 2003. "Community and Resource Extraction in Rural America." In *Challenges for Rural America in the Twenty-First Century*, ed. David Brown and Louis E. Swanson, 317–28. University Park: Pennsylvania State University Press.

Epstein, Cynthia Fuchs. 1992. "Tinkerbells and Pinups: The Construction and Reconstruction of Gender Boundaries at Work." In *Cultivating Differences: Symbolic Boundaries and the Making of Inequality*, ed. Michèle Lamont and Marcel Fournier, 232–56. Chicago: University of Chicago Press.

Erkulwater, Jennifer L. 2006. *Disability Rights and the American Social Safety Net*. Ithaca, N.Y.: Cornell University Press.

Faludi, Susan. 1999. *Stiffed: The Betrayal of the American Male*. New York: William Morrow and Company.

Ferree, Myra Marx. 1990. "Beyond Separate Spheres: Feminism and Family Research." *Journal of Marriage and the Family* 52 (4): 866–84.

Fischer, Claude S. 1975. "Toward a Subcultural Theory of Urbanism." *American Journal of Sociology* 80 (6): 1319–41.

Fitchen, Janet. 1991. *Endangered Spaces, Enduring Places: Change, Identity, and Survival in Rural America*. Boulder, Colo.: Westview Press.

———. 1992. "Rural Poverty in the Northeast: The Case of Upstate New York." In *Rural Poverty in America*, ed. Cynthia M. Duncan, 177–200. New York: Auburn House.

Flora, Cornelia Butler and Jan L. Flora with Susan Fey. 2004. *Rural Communities: Legacy and Change*. Boulder, Colo.: Westview Press.

Frank, Thomas. 2004. *What's the Matter with Kansas? How Conservatives Won the Heart of America*. New York: Metropolitan Books.

Fraser, Nancy. 1989. *Unruly Practices: Power, Discourse, and Gender in Contemporary Social Theory*. Minneapolis: University of Minnesota Press.

Fraser, Nancy, and Linda Gordon. 1994. "A Genealogy of 'Dependency': Tracing a Keyword of the U.S. Welfare State." *Signs* 19 (2): 309–36.

Fuguitt, Glenn V. 1995. "Population Change in Nonmetropolitan America." In *The Changing American Countryside*, ed. Emery N. Castle, 77–100. Lawrence: University Press of Kansas.

Furstenberg, Frank F. Jr. 2001. "The Fading Dream: Prospects for Marriage in the Inner City." In *Problem of the Century: Racial Stratification in the United States*, ed. Elijah Anderson and Douglas S. Massey, 224–46. New York: Russell Sage Foundation.

Gibbs, Robert. 2005. "Education as a Rural Development Strategy." *Amber Waves* 3 (5): 20–25.

Glasmeier, Amy, and Priscilla Salant. 2006. "Low-Skill Workers in Rural America Face Permanent Job Loss." Carsey Institute Policy Brief No. 2. http://carseyinstitute.unh.edu/publications/.

Gluck, Sherna Berger, and Daphne Patai, eds. 1991. *Women's Words: The Feminist Practice of Oral History*. New York: Routledge.

Goldscheider, Frances K., and Linda J. Waite. 1991. *New Families, No Families? The Transformation of the American Home*. Berkeley: University of California Press.

Gordon, Susan. 2005. "Recovery Plan for Rare Owl in Works." *Tacoma (Wash.) News Tribune*, August 14, A-12.

Gowan, Teresa R. 2003. Sin, Sickness, and the System: Discursive Constructions of Male Homelessness in San Francisco and St. Louis. Ph.D. dissertation, University of California, Berkeley.

Greenstein, Theodore N. 1996. "Husbands' Participation in Domestic Labor: Interactive Effects of Wives' and Husbands' Gender Ideologies." *Journal of Marriage and the Family* 58 (3): 585–95.

———. 2000. "Economic Dependence, Gender, and the Division of Labor in the Home: A Replication and Extension." *Journal of Marriage and the Family* 62 (2): 322–35.

Gringeri, Christina. 1994. *Getting By: Women Homeworkers and Rural Economic Development*. Lawrence: University Press of Kansas.

Gumbel, Andrew. 1998. "Fear among the Redwoods." *American Times Scotia, California*. November 4, 1998.

Halle, David. 1984. *America's Working Man: Work, Home, and Politics among Blue-Collar Property Owners*. Chicago: University of Chicago Press.

Hannan, Michael T., Nancy Brandon Tuma, and Lyle P. Groeneveld. 1978. "Income and Independence Effects on Marital Dissolution: Results from the Seattle and Denver Income-Maintenance Experiments." *American Journal of Sociology* 84 (3): 611–33.

Hansen, Karen. 2005. *Not-So-Nuclear Families: Class, Gender, and Networks of Care*. Piscataway, N.J.: Rutgers University Press.

Harrington, Michael. 1962. *The Other America: Poverty in the United States*. New York: Penguin Books.

Harris, Kathleen Mullan. 1993. "Work and Welfare among Single Mothers in Poverty." *American Journal of Sociology* 92 (2): 317–52.

Hays, Sharon. 2003. *Flat Broke with Children: Women in the Age of Welfare Reform*. Oxford: Oxford University Press.

Historylink.org. 2006. "U.S. District Court Judge William Dwyer blocks timber sales to protect the northern spotted owl on March 7, 1991." http://www .historylink.org/.

Hochschild, Arlie, with Anne Machung. 1989. *The Second Shift*. New York: Avon Books.

Hoffmann, Sandra A., and Louise Fortmann. 1996. "Poverty in Forested Counties: An Analysis Based on Aid to Families with Dependent Children." *Sierra Nevada Ecosystem Project: Final Report to Congress, vol. II, Assessments and Scientific Basis for Management Options*. Davis: University of California, Centers for Water and Wildland Resources.

Jarrett, Robin L., Kevin M. Roy, and Linda M. Burton. 2002. "Fathers in the 'Hood': Insights from Qualitative Research on Low-Income African-American Men." In *Handbook of Father Involvement*, ed. Catherine S. Tamis-LeMonda and Natasha Cabrera, 211–48. Mahwah, N.J.: Lawrence Erlbaum Associates.

Jensen, Leif, and Yoshimi Chitose. 1997. "Will Workfare Work? Job Availability for Welfare Recipients in Rural and Urban America." *Population Research and Policy Review* 16: 383–95.

Jensen, Leif, and David Eggebeen. 1994. "Nonmetropolitan Poor Children and Reliance on Public Assistance." *Rural Sociology* 59 (1): 45–65.

Jensen, Leif, Diane K. McLaughlin, and Tim Slack. 2003. "Rural Poverty: The Persisting Challenge." In *Challenges for Rural America in the Twenty-First Century*, ed. David Brown and Louis E. Swanson, 118–31. University Park: Pennsylvania State University Press.

Kane, John. 2001. *The Politics of Moral Capital*. Cambridge: Cambridge University Press.

Kefalas, Maria. 2003. *Working-Class Heroes: Protecting Home, Community, and Nation in a Chicago Neighborhood*. Berkeley: University of California Press.

Kilbourne, Barbara, Paula England, George Farkas, Kurt Beron, and Dorothea Weir. 1994. "Returns to Skill, Compensating Differentials, and Gender Bias." *American Journal of Sociology* 100 (2): 689–719.

Kimmel, Michael S. 2005. *The History of Men: Essays in the History of American and British Masculinities*. Albany: State University of New York Press.

Kimmel, Michael, and Abby L. Ferber. 2006. "White Men Are This Nation: Right-Wing Militias and the Restoration of Rural American Masculinity." In *Country Boys: Masculinity and Rural Life*, ed. Hugh Campbell, Michael Mayerfeld Bell, and Margaret Finney, 122–37. University Park: Pennsylvania State University Press.

Knapp, Tim. 1995. "Rust in the Wheatbelt: The Social Impacts of Industrial Decline in a Rural Kansas Community." *Sociological Inquiry* 65 (1): 47–66.

Kurz, Demie. 1995. *For Richer, for Poorer: Mothers Confront Divorce*. New York: Routledge.

Kusel, Jonathan, and Louise Fortmann. 1991. "Well Being in Forest-Dependent

Communities." Forest and Rangeland Resources Assessment Program, California Department of Forestry and Fire Protection. Volume 1.

Kusel, Jonathan, Susan Kocher, Jonathan London, Lita Buttolph, and Ervin Schuster. 2000. "Effects of Displacement and Outsourcing on Woods Workers and Their Families." *Society and Natural Resources* 13 (2): 115–34.

Labao, Linda. 2006. "Gendered Places and Place-Based Gender Identities: Reflections and Refractions." In *Country Boys: Masculinity and Rural Life*, ed. Hugh Campbell, Michael Mayerfeld Bell, and Margaret Finney, 267–75. University Park: Pennsylvania State University Press.

Lakoff, George. 2002. *Moral Politics: How Liberals and Conservatives Think*, Second Edition. Chicago: University of Chicago Press.

Lamont, Michèle. 1992. *Money, Morals, and Manners: The Culture of the French and American Upper-Middle Class*. Chicago: University of Chicago Press.

———. 2000. *The Dignity of Working Men: Morality and the Boundaries of Race, Class, and Immigration*. New York: Russell Sage Foundation.

Lamont, Michèle, and Marcel Fournier (eds). 1992. *Cultivating Differences: Symbolic Boundaries and the Making of Inequality*. Chicago: University of Chicago Press.

Lancaster, Roger N. 1992. *Life Is Hard: Machismo, Danger, and the Intimacy of Power in Nicaragua*. Berkeley: University of California Press.

Lareau, Annette. 2002. "Invisible Inequality: Social Class and Childrearing in Black Families and White Families." *American Sociological Review* 67 (5): 747–76.

Larson, Jeffrey H., Stephan M. Wilson, and Rochelle Beley. 1994. "The Impact of Job Insecurity on Marital and Family Relationships." *Family Relations* 43 (2): 138–43.

Larson, O. 1978. "Values and Beliefs of Rural People." In *Rural U.S.A.: Persistence and Change*, ed. T. R. Ford, 91–112. Ames: Iowa State Press.

Lerman, Robert I. 1993a. "A National Profile of Young Unwed Fathers." In *Young Unwed Fathers: Changing Roles and Emerging Policies*, ed. Robert I. Lerman and Theodora J. Ooms, 27–51. Philadelphia, Pa.: Temple University Press.

———. 1993b. "Employment Patterns of Unwed Fathers and Public Policy." In *Young Unwed Fathers: Changing Roles and Emerging Policies*, ed. Robert I. Lerman and Theodora J. Ooms, 316–34. Philadelphia, Pa.: Temple University Press.

Lerman, Robert I., Signe-Mary McKernan, and Nancy Pindus. 2001. "Welfare Reforms and Employment of Single Mothers: Are Rural Areas Keeping Pace?" *Rural America* 16 (3): 22–27.

Lewis, Oscar. 1959. *Five Families: Mexican Case Studies in the Culture of Poverty*. New York: Basic Books.

Lichter, Daniel T., and Leif Jensen. 2001. "Poverty and Welfare among Rural Female-Headed Families before and after PRWORA." *Rural America* 16 (3): 28–35.

Lichter, Daniel T., and Diane K. McLaughlin. 1995. "Changing Economic Opportunities, Family Structure, and Poverty in Rural Areas," *Rural Sociology* 60 (4): 688–706.

Lichter, Daniel T., Deborah Roempke Graefe, and J. Brian Brown. 2003. "Is Marriage a Panacea? Union Formation among Economically Disadvantaged Unwed Mothers." *Social Problems* 50 (1): 60–86.

Lichter, Daniel T., Diane K. McLaughlin, and David C. Ribar. 2000. "Economic Restructuring and the Retreat from Marriage." Russell Sage Foundation Working Paper. http://www.russellsage.org/publications.

Lichter, Daniel T., Vincent J. Roscigno, and Dennis J. Condron. 2003. "Rural Children and Youth at Risk." In *Challenges for Rural America in the Twenty-First Century*, ed. David Brown and Louis E. Swanson, 97–108. University Park: Pennsylvania State University Press.

Lichter, Daniel T., Diane K. McLaughlin, George Kephart, and David J. Landry. 1992. "Race and the Retreat from Marriage: A Shortage of Marriageable Men?" *American Sociological Review* 57 (5): 781–99.

Liem, Joan Huser, and G. Ramsay Liem. 1990. "Understanding the Individual and Family Effects of Unemployment." In *Stress between Work and Family*, ed. John Eckenrode and Susan Gore, 175–204. New York: Plenum Press.

Little, Jo, and Owain Jones. 2000. "Masculinity, Gender, and Rural Policy." *Rural Sociology* 65 (4): 621–39.

Lorenz, Frederick O., Rand D. Conger, and Ruth Montague. 1994. "Doing Worse and Feeling Worse: Psychological Consequences of Economic Hardship." In *Families in Troubled Times: Adapting to Change in Rural America*, ed. Rand D. Conger and Glen H. Elder Jr., 167–86. New York: Aldine de Gruyter.

Lourdes, Benería, and Shelley Feldman, eds. 1992. *Unequal Burden: Economic Crises, Persistent Poverty, and Women's Work*. Boulder, Colo.: Westview Press.

Lujan, Manuel Jr., Donald R. Knowles, John Turner, and Marvin Plenert. 1992. "Summary of the Draft Recovery Plan for the Northern Spotted Owl." Portland, Ore.: U.S. Fish and Wildlife Service.

MacTavish, Katherine, and Sonya Salamon. 2003. "What Do Rural Families Look Like Today?" In *Challenges for Rural America in the Twenty-First Century*, ed. David Brown and Louis E. Swanson, 73–85. University Park: Pennsylvania State University Press.

Marotz-Baden, Ramona, and Peggy Lester Colvin. 1986. "Coping Strategies: A Rural-Urban Comparison." *Family Relations* 35 (2): 281–88.

Marotz-Baden, Ramona, Charles B. Hennon, and Timothy H. Brubaker, eds. 1988. *Families in Rural America: Stress, Adaptation and Revitalization*. St. Paul, Minn.: National Council of Family Relations.

Marsiglio, William, ed. 1995. *Fatherhood: Contemporary Theory, Research, and Social Policy*. Thousand Oaks, Calif.: Sage Publications.

McDowell, D. R., and J. E. Allen-Smith. 1995. "Poverty among Southern Workers: Metro and Nonmetro Differentials." *American Journal of Agricultural Economics* 77 (3): 796–802.

McGirr, Lisa. 2001. *Suburban Warriors: The Origins of the New American Right*. Princeton, N.J.: Princeton University Press.

McGranahan, David A. 2003. "How People Make a Living in Rural America." In *Challenges for Rural America in the Twenty-First Century*, ed. David Brown and Louis E. Swanson, 135–51. University Park: Pennsylvania State University Press.

McLanahan, Sara, and Irwin Garfinkel. 1989. "Single Mothers, the Underclass, and Social Policy." *Annals of the American Academy of Political and Social Science* 501: 92–104.

McLanahan, Sara, Irwin Garfinkel, and Ronald B. Mincy. 2001. "Fragile Families, Welfare Reform, and Marriage." *Welfare Reform and Beyond*, Policy Brief No. 10. Washington, D.C.: Brookings Institution.

McLaughlin, Diane K., and Daniel T. Lichter. 1997. "Poverty and the Marital Behavior of Young Women." *Journal of Marriage and the Family* 59 (3): 582–94.

McLaughlin, Diane K., Erica L. Gardner, and Daniel T. Lichter. 1999. "Economic Restructuring and Changing Prevalence of Female-Headed Families in America." *Rural Sociology* 64 (3): 394–416.

MDRC: Building Knowledge to Improve Social Policy. http://www.mdrc.org/.

Mederer, Helen J. 1999. "Surviving the Demise of a Way of Life: Stress and Resilience in Northeastern Commercial Fishing Families." In *The Dynamics of Resilient Families*, ed. Hamilton I. McCubbin, Elizabeth A. Thompson, Anne I. Thompson, and Jo A. Futrell, 203–35. Thousand Oaks, Calif.: Sage Publications.

Michel, Sonya. 1998. "Childcare and Welfare (In)Justice." *Feminist Studies* 24 (1): 44–54.

Milstein, Michael. 2004. "Decade-Old Forest Plan Hurts As It Helps." *Sunday Oregonian*, April 11, A15.

Mink, Gwendolyn. 1998. "The Lady and the Tramp (II): Feminist Welfare Politics, Poor Single Mothers, and the Challenge of Welfare Justice." *Feminist Studies* 24 (1): 55–64.

Mitchell, Jonathan. 1993. "Rural Timber-Dependent Communities of the Pacific Northwest and the Spotted Owl Controversy: A Case Study." In *Case Studies in Rural Development Policy*. Princeton University: Center of Domestic and Comparative Policy Studies, Woodrow Wilson School of Public and International Studies.

Montagne, Renee, and Juan Williams. 2004. "Voters' Reactions in Exit Polling." *National Public Radio, Morning Edition*, November 3, 2004.

Moore, Robert M. III. 2001. *The Hidden America: Social Problems in Rural America for the Twenty-First Century*. Cranbury, N.J.: Associated University Presses.

Murray, Charles. 1984. *Losing Ground*. New York: Basic Books.

Nelson, Margaret K. 2000. "Single Mothers and Social Support: The Commitment to, and Retreat from, Reciprocity." *Qualitative Sociology* 23 (3): 291–317.

Nelson, Margaret K., and Joan Smith. 1998. "Economic Restructuring, Household Strategies, and Gender: A Case Study of a Rural Community." *Feminist Studies* 24 (1): 79–114.

————. 1999. *Working Hard and Making Do: Surviving in Small Town America.* Berkeley: University of California Press.

Nelson, Timothy J., Susan Clampet-Lundquist, and Kathryn Edin. 2002. "Sustaining Fragile Fatherhood: Father Involvement among Low-Income, Noncustodial African-American Fathers in Philadelphia." In *Handbook of Father Involvement*, ed. Catherine S. Tamis-LeMonda and Natasha Cabrera. Mahwah, N.J.: Lawrence Erlbaum Associates.

Newman, Katherine S. 1999. *No Shame in My Game: The Working Poor in the Inner City.* New York: Vintage Books.

————. 1988. *Falling from Grace: The Experience of Downward Mobility in the American Middle Class.* New York: Free Press.

Nonn, Timothy. 2004. "Hitting Bottom: Homelessness, Poverty, and Masculinity." In *Men's Lives*, ed. Michael S. Kimmel and Michael A. Messner, 258–67. Boston, Mass.: Pearson.

Norem, Rosalie Huisinga, and Joan Blundall. 1988. "Farm Families and Marital Disruption during a Time of Crisis." In *Families in Rural America: Stress, Adaptation, and Revitalization*, ed. Ramona Marotz-Baden, Charles B. Hennon, and Timothy H. Brubaker, 21–31. St. Paul, Minn.: National Council of Family Relations.

Northwest Forest Resource Council. 1989. "Spotted Owls, Old Growth, and the Economy of the Northwest." Portland, Ore.: Northwest Forest Resource Council.

O'Hare, William, and Bill Bishop. 2006. "U.S. Rural Soldiers Account for a Disproportionately High Share of Casualties in Iraq and Afghanistan." Carsey Institute Fact Sheet No. 2. http://www.carseyinstitute.unh.edu/.

Orloff, Ann. 1996. "Gender in the Welfare State." *Annual Review of Sociology* 22: 51–78.

Pattillo-McCoy, Mary. 1999. *Black Picket Fences: Privilege and Peril among the Black Middle Class.* Chicago: University of Chicago Press.

Peter, Gregory, and Donna Bauer. 2000. "Coming Back across the Fence: Masculinity and the Transition to Sustainable Agriculture." *Rural Sociology* 65 (2): 215–33.

Peter, Gregory, Michael Mayerfeld Bell, Susan Jarnagin, and Donna Bauer. 2006. "Cultivating Dialogue: Sustainable Agriculture and Masculinities." In *Country Boys: Masculinity and Rural Life*, ed. Hugh Campbell, Michael Mayerfeld Bell, and Margaret Finney, 27–45. University Park: Pennsylvania State University Press.

Polakow, Valerie. 1999. "Savage Distributions." In *A New Introduction to Poverty: The Role of Race, Power, and Politics*, ed. Louis Kushnick and James Jennings. New York: New York University Press.

Pryne, Eric. 1994. "Clinton Forest Plan Upheld." *Seattle Times*, December 21, 1994, A-1.

Purser, Gretchen. 2009. "The Dignity of Job-Seeking Men: Boundary Work among Immigrant Day Laborers." *Journal of Contemporary Ethnography* 38 (1): 117–39.

Putnam, Robert D. 2000. *Bowling Alone: The Collapse and Revival of American Community*. New York: Simon and Schuster.

Ray, Raka. 2000. "Masculinity, Femininity, and Servitude: Domestic Workers in Calcutta in the Late Twentieth Century." *Feminist Studies* 26: 691–718.

Roberts, Dorothy. 2002. *Shattered Bonds: The Color of Child Welfare*. New York: Basic Books.

Robertson, Elizabeth B., Glen H. Elder Jr., and Martie L. Skinner. 1991. "The Costs and Benefits of Social Support in Families." *Journal of Marriage and the Family* 53: 403–16.

Roos, Patricia A. 1990. "From Hot-Metal to Electronic Composition: Gender, Technology, and Social Change." In *Job Queues, Gender Queues*, ed. Barbara F. Reskin and Patricia A. Roos, 275–98. Philadephia, Pa.: Temple University Press.

Rosenfeld, Alvin, M.D., and Nicole Wise. 2000. *Hyper-Parenting: Are You Hurting Your Child by Trying Too Hard?* New York: St. Martin's Press.

Rubin, Lillian Breslow. 1976. *Worlds of Pain: Life in the Working-Class Family*. New York: Basic Books.

———. 1994. *Families on the Fault Line: America's Working Class Speaks about the Family, the Economy, Race, and Ethnicity*. New York: HarperCollins.

Rural Sociological Society Task Force on Persistent Rural Poverty. 1993. *Persistent Poverty in Rural America*. Boulder, Colo.: Westview Press.

Sapiro, Virginia. 1990. "The Gender Basis of American Social Policy." In *Women, the State, and Welfare*, ed. Linda Gordon. Madison: University of Wisconsin Press.

Sassen, Saskia. 1991. *The Global City: New York, London, Tokyo*. Princeton, N.J.: Princeton University Press.

———. 1998. *Globalization and Its Discontents*. New York: New Press.

Sayer, Andrew. 2000. "Equality and Moral Economy." Department of Sociology, Lancaster University, Lancaster, UK. http://www.comp.lancs.ac.uk/sociology/papers/.

———. 2004. "Moral Economy." Department of Sociology, Lancaster University, Lancaster, UK. http://www.comp.lancs.ac.uk/sociology/papers/.

———. 2005. *The Moral Significance of Class*. Cambridge: Cambridge University Press.

Schafft, Kai. 2006. "Poverty, Residential Mobility, and Student Transiency within a Rural New York School District." *Rural Sociology* 71 (2): 212–31.

Segal, Lynne. 1990. *Slow Motion: Changing Masculinities, Changing Men*. London: Virago Press.

Skaptadóttir, Unnur Dís. 2000. "Women Coping with Change in an Icelandic Fishing Community: A Case Study." *Women Studies International Forum* 23 (3): 311–21.

Smith, Suzanna, Steve Jacob, Michael Jepson, and Glenn Israel. 2003. "After the Florida Net Ban: The Impacts on Commercial Fishing Families." *Society and Natural Resources* 16 (1): 39–59.

Snyder, Anastasia R., and Diane K. McLaughlin. 2004. "Female-Headed Families and Poverty in Rural America." *Rural Sociology* 69 (1): 127–49.

Snyder, Anastasia R., Susan L. Brown, and Erin P. Condo. 2004. "Residential Differences in Family Formation: The Significance of Cohabitation." *Rural Sociology* 69 (2): 235–60.

South, Scott. 1993. "Racial and Ethnic Differences in the Desire to Marry." *Journal of Marriage and Family* 55 (2): 357–70.

Stacey, Judith. 1991. *Brave New Families: Stories of Domestic Upheaval in Late Twentieth Century America.* New York: Basic Books.

———. 1996. *In the Name of the Family: Rethinking Family Values in the Postmodern Age.* Boston, Mass.: Beacon Press.

Stack, Carol B. 1974. *All Our Kin: Strategies for Survival in a Black Community.* New York: Harper and Row.

Stack, Carol, and Linda M. Burton. 1994. "Kinscripts: Reflections on Family, Generation, and Culture." In *Mothering: Ideology, Experience, and Agency,* ed. Evelyn Nakano Glenn, Grace Change, and Linda Rennie Forcey, 33–44. New York: Routledge.

Stein, Arlene. 2001. *The Stranger Next Door: The Story of a Small Community's Battle over Sex, Faith, and Civil Rights.* Boston, Mass.: Beacon Press.

Stier, Haya, and Marta Tienda. 1993. "Are Men Marginal to the Family?" In *Men, Work, and Family,* ed. Jane C. Hood, 23–44. Newbury Park, Calif.: Sage Publications.

Struthers, C. B., and J. L. Bokemeier. 2000. "Myths and Realities of Raising Children and Creating Family Life in a Rural Community." *Journal of Family Issues* 21 (1): 17–46.

Sullivan, Mercer L. 1993. "Young Father and Parenting in Two Inner-City Neighborhoods." In *Young Unwed Fathers: Changing Roles and Emerging Policies,* ed. Robert I. Lerman and Theodora J. Ooms, 52–73. Philadelphia, Pa.: Temple University Press.

Summers, Gene F. 1995. "Persistent Rural Poverty." In *The Changing American Countryside: Rural People and Places,* ed. Emery N. Castle, 213–28. Lawrence: University Press of Kansas.

Swidler, Ann. 1986. "Culture in Action: Symbols and Strategies." *American Sociological Review* 51 (2): 273–86.

Testa, Mark, Nan Marie Astone, Marilyn Krogh, and Kathryn Neckerman. 1989. "Employment and Marriage among Inner-City Fathers." *Annals of the American Academy of Political and Social Science* 501: 79–91.

Thomas, Jack Ward, Eric D. Forsman, Joseph B. Lint, E. Charles Meslow, Barry R. Noon, and Jared Verner. 1990. "A Conservation Strategy for the Northern Spotted Owl." Portland, Ore.: U.S. Forest Service, U.S. Bureau of Land Management, U.S. Fish and Wildlife Service, and U.S. National Park Service.

Thornton Dill, Bonnie, Maxine Baca Zinn, and Sandra Patton. 1999. "Race, Family Values, and Welfare Reform." In *A New Introduction to Poverty: The Role of Race, Power, and Politics,* ed. Louis Kushnick and James Jennings. New York: New York University Press.

Tickamyer, Ann R., and Debra A. Henderson. 2003. "Rural Women: New Roles for the New Century?" In *Challenges for Rural America in the Twenty-First Century*, ed. David Brown and Louis E. Swanson, 109–117. University Park: Pennsylvania State University Press.

Tickamyer, Ann R., and Teresa A. Wood. 1998. "Identifying Participation in the Informal Economy Using Survey Research Methods." *Rural Sociology* 63 (2): 323–39.

U.S. Census Bureau. 2006. "Poverty: Poverty Thresholds." http://www.census.gov/.

U.S. Census Summary Files, 1970, 1980 and 1990, 2000.

U.S. Congress. 1996. *Personal Responsibility and Work Opportunity Reconciliation Act of 1996.* Public Law 104–193, HR 3734, Title I, Section 101.

Venkatesh, Sudhir Alladi. 2000. *American Project: The Rise and Fall of a Modern Ghetto.* Cambridge, Mass.: Harvard University Press.

Waller, Maureen R. 2002. *My Baby's Father: Unmarried Parents and Paternal Responsibility.* Ithaca, N.Y.: Cornell University Press.

Warner, Judith. 2005. *Perfect Madness: Motherhood in the Age of Anxiety.* New York: Riverhead Books.

Weber, Bruce A., Greg J. Duncan, and Leslie A. Whitener, eds. 2002. *Rural Dimensions of Welfare Reform.* Kalamazoo, Mich.: W. E. Upjohn Institute for Employment Research.

———. 2001. "Welfare Reform in Rural America: What Have We Learned?" *American Journal of Agricultural Economics* 83 (5): 1282–92.

Western, Bruce, Jeffrey Kling, and David F. Weiman. 2001. "The Labor Market Consequences of Incarceration." Working Paper, no. 450, Princeton University, Industrial Relations Section, January 2001.

Widom, Cathy Spatz, and Susanne Hiller-Sturmhöfel. 2001. "Alcohol Abuse as a Risk Factor for and Consequence of Child Abuse." *Alcohol Research and Health* 25 (1): 52–57.

Wilson, William Julius. 1987. *The Truly Disadvantaged.* Chicago: University of Chicago Press.

———. 1996. *When Work Disappears: The World of the New Urban Poor.* New York: Knopf.

W. K. Kellogg Foundation. 2002. "News Release: Cultural Issues in Rural America Gave Republicans a Wide Margin of Success in Recent Election." http://www.wkkf.org.

Yaffee, Steven Lewis. 1994. *The Wisdom of the Spotted Owl.* Washington, D.C.: Island Press.

Index

Jennifer Sherman is assistant professor of sociology at Washington State University.